The
Educational
MINISTRY
Of A Church

REVISED & EXPANDED

Charles A. Tidwell

The Educational MINISTRY Of A Church

A Comprehensive Model for Students and Ministers

BROADMAN
& HOLMAN
PUBLISHERS

Nashville, Tennessee

© 1996
by Broadman & Holman
All rights reserved
Printed in the United States of America

4210–63
0-8054-1063-5
Dewey Decimal Classification: 268
Subject Heading: Religious Education
Library of Congress Card Catalog Number: 92–38095

Unless otherwise stated, all Scripture citations are from the Revised English Bible. Copyright © Oxford University Press and Cambridge University Press, 1989. Reprinted by permission.

Typography by TF Designs

Library of Congress Cataloging-in-Publication Data
Tidwell, Charles A.
The Educational ministry of a church/ Charles A. Tidwell—Revised and Expanded
  p. cm.
  Rev. ed. of: Educational ministry of a church, 1982.
  Includes bibliographical references.
    ISBN 0-8054-1063-5
    1. Christian education.   2. Church and education.   I. Tidwell, Charles A.
    Educational ministry of a church. II. Title.
  BV1471.2.T53 1996
  268'.86132—dc20   92–38095
                                                    CIP

1 2 3 4 5 6 01 00 99 98 97 96

To the churches
in whose fellowship it has been my joy
to belong and to serve

Emmanuel Baptist Church, Montgomery, Alabama
Seventh and James Baptist Church, Waco, Texas
Bruceville Baptist Church, Bruceville, Texas
Clayton Street Baptist Church, Montgomery, Alabama
(now Heritage Baptist Church)
Gentilly Baptist Church, New Orleans, Louisiana
Durant Chapel Baptist Church, Bay Minette, Alabama
First Baptist Church, Newnan, Georgia
First Baptist Church, Canton, Mississippi
Daniel Memorial Baptist Church, Jackson, Mississippi
Clinton Baptist Church, Clinton, Mississippi
Brook Hollow Baptist Church, Nashville, Tennessee
Columbia Baptist Church, Falls Church, Virginia
Faith Baptist Church, Kaiserslautern, West Germany
Neckar Valley Baptist Church, Stutgart, West Germany
(now International Baptist Church)
University Baptist Church, Fort Worth, Texas

and many others
whose fellowship I did not join
but who allowed me to render some ministry
and to be blessed by them

Contents

Appendix Two

Appendix Three

Appendix Four

Preface

Changepace! That's a new word this author has created for the ever-increasing pace of change. And there seems to be no end to it. There must not be an end to it as long as most of the changes represent genuine progress—residual gain, with positive residue after the smoke of action clears.

The educational ministries of churches change. Thank goodness for the improvements! The reader must judge the extent and the value (positive or negative) of changes such as these:

- more focus on the learner in the teacher–learner setting
- less training for learning leaders-teachers in actual teaching skills
- more support-group types of short-term learning experiences
- more special events and "happening" scheduling
- more undated curriculum materials
- more flexible and temporary organizations for education
- more difficulties for continuing, cyclical curriculum
- more focus on ministries, less on "programs"
- more problems maintaining continuing organizations
- more worker enlistment for short terms
- less per capita financial support for ministries as a percentage of total buying power of income
- less knowledge of basic Christian doctrines
- more confrontational, mutually excluding behaviors
- more efforts to lead by leadership teams
- more new leadership terms and organizational names

Are these enough changes to require revising this textbook on administering the educational ministry of a church? I think so! Does this revision offer solutions to all the implications of the above list? I doubt it! And there are many other indicators of change not yet mentioned. I address several of the areas of significant changes in this revised edition. I hope that the suggestions will portend improvement for all who attempt to apply them in the various ministries of education in churches. This textbook is also designed to meet the needs of colleges and extension programs. Further, I also want to help church leaders—pastors, ministers of education, other church staff personnel, and lay leaders—understand this vital area of a church's ministry. Indications from the previous edition encourage me to believe that my hopes have been realized. Hence comes this revised edition.

There are some limits intentionally placed on this volume. No attempt is made to present a complete philosophic rationale for the educational ministry of a church. Our approach is intentionally more general. In part 1, "Necessity," the focus is on biblical examples and commands that a church educate; the historical affirmation of the place and value of education in the church; the needs of persons for religious education; the imperative—growing out of its nature and mission—that a church educate; and the conditions and trends of our world which demand that a church educate.

Part 2, "Basic Components," presents several components of educational ministry that almost all churches assume to be basic: Bible teaching and learning; discipleship training; mission education and action; music education and performance; and ministries of enrichment and support.

I hope that this presentation will be taken as a model, though not an exclusive design within which the author conceives that all valid educational ministries must operate. The bias is explained simply: the author has been a Southern Baptist from childhood, and has been educated and has had experience in the practice and teaching offered by Southern Baptist churches and schools. Even so, not all these churches and schools follow the model exactly.

Part 3, "Leadership Personnel," identifies the roles of educational leaders in a church: the pastor, the minister of education, other staff leaders, and volunteer leaders in the educational ministry of a church. Leadership through group processes is advocated as vocational ministers and others work together to lead a church in its educational ministry. Definitions of various leadership theories are intentionally not extensive, but are left to further study by the reader.

Part 4, "How Leaders Lead," has a functional, practical emphasis. The major concerns are planning and organizing to meet needs; discovering, recruiting, and training workers; providing resources; and implementing and evaluating. For some, these processes are the sum of administration.

One of the secondary hopes is that persons will come to see that, as vital as the how-to processes are to administration, they are necessarily associated with "what-to," "why-to," and "who-to." ("When-to" and "where-to" would complete the scope of administrative concerns, but even these items must be left for other times and places.)

Educational administration is far more than doing what some individual or group predetermines. Vital to both the educational and the administrative aspects of the term is participation with genuine meaning in all levels of leadership activity by all who need to be included. Such an approach to leadership in the church's educational ministry is part of the ministry itself.

Grateful appreciation is due to many persons for encouragement, counsel, patience, and other help during the preparation of this book: to Raymond Rigdon; to Broadman & Holman personnel; to my teaching colleagues at Southwestern Baptist Theological Seminary. Special gratitude goes to my faithful and efficient secretary, Suzanne Woosley Gray, who typed the manuscript for the original edition; and to Jo Brackney, Billie Cate, Misty LaFavor, Clare Woods, and several others who helped me with the revision of the current manuscript. Carol Causey gave valuable help in revising the chapter on the ministry of missions education and action.

My dear family—my wife, Jean, our son, Al, and our daughter, Evelyn—deserve my eternal gratitude for their patience and, most of all, for their love that helped sustain me during this time of labor. And beyond them, I have sensed a great cloud of witnesses who remain unnamed; they have touched my life and helped form many of the concepts here reflected. For all of these I give thanks to God.

Finally, I feel compelled to say to one and all that whatever help might be found within these pages, plus whatever supplementary knowledge and skills one might acquire from other sources and experiences, are but a "sounding brass or a tinkling cymbal" without a generous and authentic measure of the 1 Corinthians 13 concept of love. This is "the main thing" without which any and all other "main things" are empty. May all of God's children both experience and transmit this love!

Charles A. Tidwell
Fort Worth, Texas

PART ONE

NECESSITY

The educational ministry of a church is necessary. It belongs to the very nature or essence of a church. Indeed, the educational ministry is so necessary that its removal would jeopardize the church itself.

How can we justify referring to the educational ministry as being essential to a church? The remainder of this book is based on this premise. A beginning perspective is important at this point. No more than a beginning is possible, for there are many volumes on each dimension herein introduced: *education, ministry, church.*

What is education? What is ministry? What is church? These are old words. They represent basic ideas whose inherent characters might not have changed, but whose forms and methods have changed, and the descriptions of which have changed even more frequently. What do these words mean? What do we mean when we use them?

Education is the act or process of developing and cultivating mentally or morally. It is preparing one for a calling by systematic instruction. It is teaching, training, disciplining, or forming. It is the disciplining of mind or character. It is a science dealing with the principles and practices of teaching and learning. Some trace it to the Latin infinitive *educare,* to bring up (a child), to train, to nourish. Some relate it to the Latin infinitive *ducere,* to lead, which when accompanied by the prefix *e,* means "to lead out." There are elements of both origins in our use of the word. In the context of the educational ministry of a church, education is not mental or moral, but mental *and* moral; it is not mind or character, but mind *and* character. It is bringing up, training, nourishing, and leading out. It includes knowledge of facts—cognitive learning. It includes attitudes, how we feel about things—affective learning. Somewhere beyond the cognitive and the affective there is wisdom—that capacity to assess facts and feelings, and to respond in the best way for the long term. The response of wisdom might appear unrelated to the facts or feelings apparent to others.

One can be considered educated only when measured by an accepted standard. Most standards are finite. The only infinite standard is God himself. The inference we draw from this concept regarding education is that it is partial and incomplete, short of measuring up to God. In the context of the educational ministry of a church, we must see education as a lifelong enterprise, completed only when we attain "the measure of the stature of the fullness of Christ" (Eph. 4:13).

Education occurs by way of experiences, some direct and some indirect with regard to the involvement of the sensory systems. Some educational experiences can be accounted for only as revelations (see Gal. 1:12 and Matt. 16:17). Education that is Christian might occur in any of these ways. Typically, education occurs through what one sees, hears, touches, smells, and/or tastes. Such experiences might be either planned or unplanned (even accidental!). In speaking of an educational ministry of a church, we usually have in mind the experiences we intend or plan to occur. These intended or planned experiences we call the *curriculum.* In truth, a great deal of education occurs through experiences that are neither intended nor planned to be primarily educational. This education occurs as we live, strive, and love together. A church would do well to make the most of the laboratory of life to bring about more desirable educational experiences.

Ministry is the act of doing things needful or helpful. From a Christian perspective, ministry has a connotation of service rendered, labor or duty performed for the benefit of another. In biblical times the services rendered were often associated with labor or duty done by a person of servant or even slave status. Jesus did many lowly acts of service, as though he were a servant. Christian ministry, however, is not limited to that which is menial. There are things to be done that are needful or helpful and that are not lowly. There are some very demanding and complex tasks that some must perform. Ministry is ministry because of the helpfulness of that which is done, without regard for who does it or for where the task ranks in terms of status. It comes out of love.

In the context of the educational ministry of a church, ministry is that which is done to advance the educational intentions of those who comprise a church. This leads us to look briefly at the definition of a "church."

A church is a body of persons who have become children of God by receiving Jesus Christ, by believing in his name, and who have voluntarily joined themselves together to share the fellowship of his love and carry out his will in the world. Loving obedience to him as we live our lives together is a primary focus of a church.

Essential to the life of this body, a church, are the functions of worship, proclamation and witness, nurture and education, and ministry. These are the natural, essential, and characteristic actions of a church. These are vital to the life of a church. To whatever extent a church fails to perform these characteristic actions, to that extent the vitality of a church is threatened. Conversely, a church that faithfully and obediently performs these functions is reflecting the life—his life—which is in the body.

We make no great distinction in this book between "religious education" and "Christian education." The religious education fostered by a Christian church certainly could benefit by presenting fairly the basic beliefs of other religions. None should fear to engage in a comparative study of religions. However, it is our view that a Christian church should advocate and promote education in the Christian faith, and that religious education in such a church should be understood to be Christian education.

Why a church must educate is the concern of part 1. Our objective is to help persons gain increased understanding of the necessity of the educational ministry of a church. We shall review the biblical example and command that a church educate, survey the historical affirmation of the place and value of education in the church, consider the needs of persons for religious education, reflect on the nature and mission of a church that require that it educate, and describe conditions and trends of our world that demand that a church educate.

CHAPTER 1

Biblical Precedent

The Bible is the basic book for the educational ministry of a church. Biblical truth in all its rightful expressions in text and in life has been the content of religious education from the earliest days of the faith. This was true in the time of the lawgiver Moses. It continued to be true through the centuries of the Old Testament era and the New Testament period.

Church leaders in education of any time must know something of the powerful precedent the Bible reveals regarding the necessity of teaching and learning. Those who accept the authority of the Bible as the guide for faith and practice cannot justify ambiguity; education is a primary function of a church.

Christian educators must avoid the inclination to think of their ministry as educational rather than biblical and theological. Good methodology is vital, but it cannot make up for shallowness or for inaccuracies in dealing with the truths of the gospel. Christian educators must know good methodology and good biblical theology and find ways to bring these together effectively in the lives of learners.

Pastors must not fall prey to the misconception that they can fulfill the responsibilities of ministry without emphasizing education—teaching and learning. Even those who have other ministers or laypersons responsible for giving specialized leadership to the educational ministry of a church must not relinquish their responsibility of being pastor to the educational ministry. With or without others to help carry the load of leadership in education, the pastor must be the primary educator in a church. Fortunate is the pastor who can count on others to share the leadership; unwise and incomplete is the ministry of any pastor who forfeits this leadership responsibility.

James D. Smart aptly characterizes the all-too-frequent plight and response of the pastor:

> Under heavy pressure, if any duty has to be dropped or left with scant attention, it is the educational one. When asked why they do not have classes for the training of teachers, ministers invariably answer that there is no time for them. They would not excuse themselves from preaching or . . . from any of the other essential functions of their ministry with a plea of "no time." Yet here they do so without any qualms, for to them the educational function is not essential to their ministry. Many theological seminaries in their curriculums mirror this defective conception of the ministry. They are organized for the training of a ministry that will be almost exclusively homiletic and pastoral and in which education is not expected to have much place.[1]

The following sketch of the biblical precedent does not claim to be complete. This overview, however, will show that the educational ministry of a church is essential.

EDUCATION IN OLD TESTAMENT TIMES

The Bible is its own strongest advocate of education in the faith and life of God's people. In the earliest section of the Bible, the Law steadily repeats God's command that Israel teach the Law. The Law was considered to be God's voice to men. One passage, Deuteronomy 6:4–9 (called the "Shema"), "has embedded itself in Jewish consciousness more deeply, perhaps, than any Constitution or similar document has ever been woven into the mind of any Gentile people."[2]

> Hear, O Israel: The Lord our God is one Lord; and you shall love the Lord your God with all your heart, and with all your soul, and with all your might. And these words which I command you this day shall be upon your heart; and you shall teach them diligently to your children, and shall talk of them when you sit in your house, and when you walk by the way, and when you lie down, and when you rise. And you shall bind them as a sign upon your hand, and they shall be as frontlets between your eyes. And you shall write them on the doorposts of your house and on your gates (Deut. 6:4–9, RSV).

The *Law* and *history* were the main subject matter of Hebrew education. The Law was the foundation of the written Torah. Together with the Prophets (which included history books as well as the prophets) and with the Hagiographa, or Holy Writings (which included such books as Psalms, Proverbs, and Job), the Hebrew Scriptures were complete. In addition to the written Torah was the body of oral interpretations of the legal portions, especially of the Pentateuch, which was called the "Mishnah." The importance of Torah and its teaching came to be equated with life (Prov. 13:14).

History, along with law, was essential in the teachings of Israel. History showed how God works among men. "The Hebrew was profoundly convinced of God's leading in the past. One of his gravest fears was that a generation might forget God's hand in the past, and thus become incapable of seeing that same hand in one's own day."[3] (See Deut. 4:9–10 and Exod. 10:2.) Historical events were told and retold to the point that brief references in a discourse could enable a listener to recall whole sets of facts and events.

Education in the Old Testament developed along with the life experiences of the nation of Israel. It is helpful to examine the education of this era in the periods before and after the Babylonian Exile, which followed the destruction of Jerusalem in 586 B.C.

THE PRE-EXILIC PERIOD

Before the Exile, "Education took place in the midst of living. The family was the chief educational institution. The teachers of first importance were parents, prophets, priests, sages, and poets."[4] Education was not lifted out or segregated from the other major sectors of life. It was so intricately interwoven with life that to fail in teaching and learning was to fail in life itself.

Parents. Parents had the major responsibility. In the context of the family, they were directed to be the principal teachers. "Fathers and mothers were enjoined in the most impressive manner to teach the history, the precepts, and the ordinances of the Law to their children."[5] This teaching in the life of the family was implemented in three ways: through informal participation by family members in the everyday activities and in the special events (such as feasts and fasts); through the parental control of children's conduct; and through oral tradition passed along in the family.[6]

The mother began this informal education of the children by the way she performed household duties. Her preparation of the sabbath meal, the lighting of the sabbath lamp, the setting apart of a portion of the dough from the bread of the household, prayers, and various domestic rites were part of the child's development.

Fathers were expected to assume the initiative for teaching their children. The faithful ones considered this responsibility to be an honor. A father taught his child a birthday text at a very early age. This text was associated with the child's name, such as a verse beginning with, ending with, or containing the letters of the name.

The father served as drill master for his children as they recited portions of Scripture. The ability to repeat accurately the Law was considered as knowing the law. Much attention was given to memorizing and to reciting. To forget what had been memorized was considered as bad as not knowing in the first place.

The father worked patiently and earnestly to impart knowledge, and to keep before his children the purpose of the learning. His teaching focused on the repulsiveness of sin; on industry, honesty, sobriety, and obedience as virtues; and fear of the Lord as the beginning of wisdom. That the faithful father felt most seriously the responsibility for teaching his children, especially his sons, is illustrated by the fact that when a son reached the age of personal accountability under the Law (bar mitzvah—son of the law), the father would stand in a public place, look into heaven, and beat his own breast and thank God that no longer was he himself responsible for the actions of the son. Until that time the father was responsible.

Not incidental in the family educational setting was the observance of the commands of the "Shema." The frequent telling by either parent of stories of patriarchs, prophets, poets, patriots, and national heroes contributed significantly to education in the home. Further, the regular observances of the rituals related to the feasts and fasts, often including dramatic enactments of events, served to stimulate learning not only for children in the family, but also for parents. The latter constituted an indirect way of educating adults, as parents retold and interpreted, doubtless with new insights of their own, the facts related to these occasions. Nowhere in the Bible has parental responsibility been rescinded regarding the teaching of children.

Prophets. Prophets were significant as unique educators in the time before the Exile. They proclaimed knowledge of the will of God drawn from events in daily affairs and from inner experiences. Predominantly they were forthtellers, those who spoke forth for God; less frequently they were foretellers, those who predicted what was to come. Often they were esteemed as towering individuals who served as God's voice, bringing his revelation to people.

Prophets interpreted the meanings of events. They sounded ethical notes and declared spiritual insights that found meaning among the disinherited, the victims of injustice, the sincere official, or the laborer.[7] "It was especially their role to speak forth for God in times of degeneracy, or in times of national danger. Even more significant, the prophet could speak of unfulfilled possibilities in one man or in a race. He could stir popular thought, making it reach out beyond the limitations of the sacrificial system. He could teach richer conceptions of the nature of God. And he could expand the understanding of human duty until men saw it was never set forth in any mere letter of the law."[8]

The great Samuel, who served his nation as it became a kingdom, had established schools of prophets at his official posts in Ramah, Shiloh, Gilgal, and Mizpeh. "In this way promising young men were brought together to live and study under the direction of a prophet or teacher. Presumably they studied the law of Moses, sacred music and poetry. Under able and experienced teachers they would learn much that would enable them to go back to their respective communities as the harbingers of better days. Undoubtedly these schools were largely responsible for the improved conditions that were to come in the political, moral and religious life of the people of Israel."9

Some might claim that the prophets belong to the exhortative train, focusing only on their public preaching to describe their place in the life of Israel. Such could scarcely be the case. According to James D. Smart:

> The prophet himself seems to have been both preacher and teacher. It is impossible to conceive of an Isaiah or a Jeremiah contenting himself with saying no more concerning God and his purpose with Israel than what could be expressed in those public utterances to the nation as a whole which are preserved in the collections of their prophecies. We have in their books only fragments of all that they had to say in their lifetime. From a prophet of such stature as Nathan we have only a single dramatic incident, preserved because of its importance in the history of David. But here and there we find hints that groups of disciples gathered about the great prophets. Only once are they mentioned by Isaiah (8:16). Jeremiah had his disciple and scribe, Baruch, and may well have had others who were not satisfied to hear him only on public occasions. Second Isaiah, with his warm personal message of encouragement to faith, drew about him a circle of believers. They appeared at a number of points in his writings. He distinguished them sharply from the unbelievers (50:10, ll; 57:1–3), and addressed them as "ye that tremble at his [God's] word" (66:5). In circles of disciples such as this, the prophets exercised a teaching function. We see it quite distinctly with John the Baptist, who preached to the crowds but taught his disciples. Thus, even in the prophet, alongside the work of preaching stands the work of teaching, both of them services required of the prophet by the word of God which he served.[10]

Prophets were teachers of adults. They taught and preached that God's purpose and reign extended beyond Israel and that his love embraced even those who had never bowed before his altars.

Priests. The priests reflected their understanding of God's will through ritual, altar, and sacrifice. Their stance that those who were participating with them in the priest-led practices of worship were the people of God created some stimulating tensions between priest and prophet in the minds of Hebrew adults. Their contrasting ways set in motion conflicting thought processes that are seen as constructive in the educational life of the Hebrews. The tensions seemed to be felt by parents, even as they taught their children in the homes. As a father repeatedly reflected on truths of God as conveyed by prophet and by priest, he often had a learning experience himself that he would not have otherwise had. "From the angle of education one would say that the most daring imagination could hardly have devised so stimulating a way for causing adults to learn."[11]

The priest was responsible for teaching the details of the temple service and for teaching the Law itself. Deuteronomy 31:9–13 declares that Moses wrote the Law, gave it to the priests, the sons of Levi, and commanded that they read it to all Israel, to include men, women, children, and sojourners, so that they might hear the law and learn to fear the Lord. In effect, priests were the public teachers for Israel.

Sages. Wise teachers were mostly unidentified figures, but they had an impact upon Hebrew education. Their work began before the Exile but climaxed in the post-exilic period.[12]

In the East, where there was great emphasis given to meditative thought, it was not unusual for a sage who had observed life keenly to condense his wisdom into a pithy saying—a proverb which summed up a view about some facet of life. Such sayings were especially suited to people who were accustomed to much learning by hearing. Proverbs became part of the legacy of each succeeding generation.

Eventually, much of the wisdom of the sages was written down and became a rich body of material to guide people, especially the young, in morals and conduct. That these truths were designed for teaching and remembering is evident in that often they are presented in ways to make them easier to teach and to remember. For example, many of the sayings are in a kind of free verse, in poetic form, in which the second line of the two-line saying is either antithetical to the first line, or progressive, or comparative. The Book of Proverbs has illustrations of this poetic form.

Poets. The poets of Israel, particularly the psalmists and the writers of certain proverbs, surely instructed by way of their writings. The reading of poetry, sometimes by various groups, sometimes in unison and sometimes antiphonally, must have been strikingly impressive. Many were sung, others were chanted. "Among the Christians . . . no part of the Old Testament has been taken more deeply into living than the Psalms. If the singers of Israel have taught Christians so well, surely they must also have left their mark upon their own people."[13] "No other poems are so cherished and so continuously studied and appreciated as the works of the singers of Israel. Many scholars hold that the poetry of the Old Testament is the most significant contribution of the Hebrew people to the literature of the world."[14]

Festivals. Feasts were celebrations of great events in the nation's history. The feast of the Passover recalled the deliverance of Israel from Egypt. Fasts were solemn days of commemoration, generally to recall defeat, loss, or some other calamity. Both feasts and fasts had an educational function. This can be seen in connection with the institution of the Feast of the Passover: "You shall observe this rite as an ordinance for you and for your sons forever. And when you come to the land which the Lord will give you, as he has promised, you shall keep his service. And when your children say to you, 'What do you mean by this service?' you shall say, 'It is the sacrifice of the Lord's passover, for he passed over the houses of the people of Israel in Egypt, when he slew the Egyptians but spared our houses.' And the people bowed their heads and worshiped" (Exod. 12:24–27).

The festival cycle included the Feast of Purim, the Feast of Tabernacles, the Feast of the New Year, and the Day of Atonement. On these public occasions, the priests instructed in an official capacity. Parts of the festivals were observed in the homes, where the parents were the teachers.

Government. Government support of religious instruction was a clearly expected dimension of pre-exilic education. Any king God chose to give to Israel was to heed this admonition: "And when he sits on the throne of his kingdom, he shall write for himself in a book a copy of this law, from that which is in charge of the Levitical priests; and it shall be with him, and he shall read in it all the days of his life, that he may learn to fear the Lord his God, by keeping all the words of this law and these statutes, and doing them" (Deut. 17:18–19).

Good kings, such as Jehoshaphat (2 Chron. 17), Hezekiah (2 Chron. 30:22), and Josiah (2 Chron. 35:2–3), were faithful in their commitment to religious instruction. Sherrill credits Sanday with the idea that the publication of the document (believed to have been the main body of the Book of Deuteronomy) discovered and read to all the people under Josiah's reign is perhaps the greatest landmark in the history of Israel in that it marked Israel's religion's beginning as a religion of a book![15]

THE POST-EXILIC PERIOD

The Temple at Jerusalem was destroyed and Judah went into exile in 586 B.C. The Hebrews who were not taken captive to Babylonia were scattered. Biblical accounts focus mainly upon those who were taken to Babylonia. The captivity itself was a time of great learning and of change.

The minority that chose to return to Jerusalem and to rebuild the Temple had learned valuable lessons and instituted significant changes. They were thoroughly cured of idolatry. They began to use smaller houses for worship and instruction because they no longer had a Temple. These synagogues also served as social centers. The Jews collected much of their literature during the Exile. Their religion became more spiritual and personal. The Law of Moses took on such new significance for them that it is said that Judaism was born in this period. The Jews became genuinely united in ideals and purpose. They came to a new understanding and appreciation of their destiny as a nation. They became a people with a mission.[16] It seems as though what relative prosperity and opportunity had failed to teach them in previous centuries, adversity taught them in about seventy years!

Religious education received unprecedented emphasis. The most important change to result from the Babylonian Exile was the new emphasis on religious education.[17] Those who chose to return to Jerusalem and rebuild the Temple and restore their national identity were from the most religiously devout segment of the captives.

Family responsibility remained foremost. After the Exile, the Jewish education system had three major dimensions: the home, the synagogue, and the school system (part of which related integrally to the synagogue). The Hebrews continued to emphasize the family as the foundational setting for religious instruction. Among the faithful, this emphasis on family responsibility has not diminished through the succeeding centuries. When through oppression, calamity, and suffering the formal schools and the synagogues have had to be abandoned, the family has been the sustaining link that has strengthened and continued the faith.

Schools emerged, especially synagogue schools. The school system developed to include elementary and secondary education and, eventually, academies for use in advanced studies by scholars and for the higher education of the rabbis. Most formal education was limited to boys, though girls were instructed in the home and in synagogue services through worship and ritual. At times there was also instruction for proselytes to Judaism as part of the systematic plan.

The synagogue became the main public institution in Judaism. The Temple had its place, but the synagogue became the center around which Jewish corporate life revolved. It had three major roles to serve in Jewish life: it was a worship center, a center for teaching and learning, and a social center.

The principal purpose of the synagogues was teaching and learning. This was so evident by the time of the "New Testament [that the words] "synagogue" and "teaching" are constantly used in the same breath, as if everyone understood that a synagogue was a place where teaching is carried on."[18] The teaching was centered in the Scriptures.

The worship in the synagogue changed the emphasis from sacrifice to teaching. Teaching was seen as an act of worship. Sherrill stated the impact of this fact: "The synagogue represents, as it were, a marriage between worship and education, so close that thereafter genuinely religious education, whether in its Jewish or its Christian stream, cannot be entirely divorced from worship and still remain whole."[19] Sherrill indicated that the influence of the synagogue worship service on Christian worship was strong, and that in early days of Christian worship, "preaching was teaching . . . until the costly mistake of separating the two was made in modern times, with extreme peril to both."[20]

The rabbi was the synagogue teacher. The rabbi became the most important leader in the school system in the synagogue. In some instances, the rabbi was also a scribe. He taught the Law, delivered addresses in the synagogue, and had custody of the Scriptures. Rabbi means "my teacher" or "my master." One rabbi was allowed to have up to twenty-five pupils. If the number grew to forty, an assistant was engaged. At fifty, a second rabbi was appointed.

The rabbi was generally held in highest esteem. Benson explains:

> The honor shown to a teacher bordered on that given to God. To dispute with a rabbi, or to murmur against him, was as sinful as to murmur against God. The Jew gave preference to his teacher over his father; the one gave him temporal life, the other eternal life. The highest and most honored profession to which a Jew could attain was to be a rabbi or teacher. Wealthy merchants with marriageable daughters were accustomed to visit the schools to discover some bright student whose tuition they would gladly defray that they might be honored in having a rabbi for a son-in-law.[21]

Children began attending the elementary school of the synagogue at age five, six, or seven. Apparently the age of first admission moved up from the earlier age of five as the new system was improved and refined. The Book of Leviticus—a book of laws—was the first subject of instruction. There were sessions in the morning, in the afternoon, and sometimes at night to accustom a child to learn at any hour. Vacations were granted only on the afternoon before the sabbath or a holiday, and on the holiday itself.

On the sabbath the students could review lessons, but they were not to learn anything new. The rabbi could look to see if a pupil were reading from the right location on the sabbath, during the review, but could not himself read the Scriptures during that time.

Pupils were to learn at least one verse or short section of Scripture each day. It was to be committed to memory. Also, pupils were taught to ask questions of the rabbi, whose responses often came as counter questions or parables. This interlocutory method kept participation at a high level. The rabbi might pose a question to the students, hear their several answers, and then conclude by declaring which answer was most appropriate. Reflecting on this approach to teaching and learning, one can easily see the naturalness of the experience of Jesus and the teachers in the Temple when he was there at the age of twelve. The extraordinary aspects of this experience were the wise questions and answers he offered (Luke 2:46–47).

EDUCATION IN NEW TESTAMENT TIMES

Many of the primary aspects of education operating in the Old Testament continued into New Testament times. With the notable exception of John the Baptist, there is almost no notice of the work of prophets in New Testament times. There is even less evidence of contemporary sages. Nevertheless, even their wisdom, as well as the great literature of the poets, and the rest of the Scriptures that comprised the Old Testament, served as the literary base for education in the New Testament.

The basic streams that made up the education of the Old Testament continued into the New Testament: the family, the system of schools, and the synagogue. This section highlights the place of education—teaching and learning—in the life and ministry of Jesus and of Paul.

EDUCATION IN THE MINISTRY OF JESUS

Jesus demonstrated by every essential indicator that he was the master teacher. He had the most important concepts of life and eternity as his subject matter. He excluded no one from the concern of his teachings. And he was the master of the skills of teaching.

He sometimes preached, always with great and unmatched power and skill. He sometimes healed, and the impact of these occasions uniquely underscored and magnified the power of God. More rarely, he raised individuals from the dead, but these extensions of physical life were not his main mission. Almost always, in the biblical record, he taught. Preaching, teaching, raising from the dead, and healing were important enough for him to take up his time doing them. Although contemporary Christians do not have power to restore physical life to the physically dead, there are contemporary ministries of preaching, teaching, and healing that Christians share with him in the redemptive enterprise.

It serves nothing to exhalt one of the ministry methods of Jesus above others. He belongs to no function or method of the church to the exclusion of any other. The preacher cannot identify his role with the role Jesus filled and fills as head of the church. Those in healing ministries (and here we refer to ministries such as Christian medical care) cannot assume authority over others because they identify with Jesus as a healer. Neither can those who teach set themselves over others, even though the evidence of the biblical record shows Jesus preponderantly used the teaching approach in his ministry.

We point out some of the evidence that Jesus made extensive use of education in his ministry in order to encourage others to see its great potential for extending the gospel. This potential has only begun to be acknowledged and used to share the gospel with the world (that portion of society that does not order its life around Jesus and his way). Each dimension of Christian ministry has its rightful place as a way of functioning in the work of the church, and all are to be subordinated to Christ, the head of the body, and used harmoniously and with mutual respect in the redemptive enterprise.

Jesus considered himself a teacher. Most of his recorded contacts were with individuals or small groups whom he was teaching. Only occasionally did he address crowds, as in the Sermon on the Mount. (Notice in Matt. 5:1 that even here "he sat down"; and in 5:2, "he opened his mouth and taught them"; and in 7:28–29, "the crowds were astonished at his teaching, for he taught them as one who had authority, and not as their scribes.") Jesus forthrightly acknowledged that he was a teacher when he said to his disciples (his pupils), "You call me Teacher and Lord; and you are right, for so I am" (John 13:13).

Friends, followers, and foes considered Jesus a teacher. They addressed him as teacher, and he permitted them to do so. He seemed to welcome the title. "Of the ninety times our Lord was addressed in the Gospel record, sixty times He was called rabbi or teacher. Only rarely did His disciples address their Lord by any other title."[22] His disciples called him teacher (as in Luke 11:1 and Mark 4:38). Nicodemus called him teacher in John 3. So did the rich young ruler in Matthew 19. Even the accusing scribes, Pharisees, and the Herodians addressed him as teacher (Matt. 22:24; Mark 9:17; 12:13–14, 32; Luke 12:13; 19:39).

Jesus taught masterfully. This fact further attests to the emphasis he placed upon teaching. His knowledge of Scriptures, his ability to extend the teachings of Scriptures to their deeper and more significant meanings, his personality for teaching, his ability to relate to his learners, his appropriate use of varied teaching methods, his manner of teaching, his capacity to communicate, his living demonstration of the lofty spiritual and moral concepts he taught, his grasp of essential elements of teaching theory, his effectiveness in the lives of his disciples, all support the claim that he was the master teacher.

Jesus commissioned followers—then and now—to teach. The Great Commission (Matt. 28:18–20) is a commission to make disciples—professed followers who receive instruction—of all nations, to baptize them, and to teach them to observe all Jesus commanded. He bracketed that commission with his assertion that he has all authority and that he will be with his disciples always. That his followers of that time took his commission seriously can be seen in the developments recorded in Acts (see especially Acts 5:17–21, 40–42; 11:19–26). It surely is not incidental that following the year of teaching by Barnabas and Saul at Antioch the disciples were for the first time called Christians. The most effective disciples of all the ages since the New Testament period, including today, have been those who have continued faithfully to carry out this commission. It is at its heart an educational strategy for communicating the gospel.

EDUCATION IN THE MINISTRY OF PAUL

The other prime illustration of the place and importance of education in New Testament times is the apostle Paul. Paul stands second in greatness as a teacher only to Jesus, the master teacher. Of the followers of Jesus, he has been the most influential.

Paul was educationally advantaged from birth. Although Paul did not study directly with Jesus, he was uniquely suited to teach. He was born a Roman citizen, in Tarsus. The scholarly reputation of that city was such that, when Paul was arrested in Jerusalem and the tribune asked him if he knew Greek, he had only to respond, "I am a Jew, from Tarsus in Cilicia, a citizen of no mean city" (Acts 21:39). The soldier then knew he was dealing with a learned person.

Paul had a superior education. Paul declared that he was brought up "at the feet of Gamaliel, educated according to the strict manner of the law of our fathers" (Acts 22:3). Though a Roman citizen, Paul was a Jew—a member of a nation noted for its strong emphasis on education. Moreover, he had studied at the feet of Gamaliel, one of the greatest teachers of the day. Perhaps Paul (then Saul) was the prize pupil of Gamaliel and was in line to succeed the great teacher until the time of Paul's conversion on the road to Damascus. He had received the best education Judaism could offer, and he had been one of its most promising scholars.

Paul was perceived as a teacher. Paul felt some need to assert his claim and to advocate his right to apostleship, apparently because some were not easily convinced of the validity of his apostleship. But none contested his claim that he was a teacher. Even those who clamored for his arrest accused him of teaching (for example, see Acts 21:28).

Paul's teaching was effective. This is apparent early in his ministry from the account in Acts 11:19–26. The church at Jerusalem sent Barnabas to Antioch of Syria to inspect the unprecedented responses of Greeks to the gospel. Barnabas was pleased with the situation he found. He exhorted Christians there to remain faithful to the Lord with steadfast purpose. Later he went to Tarsus, found Saul, and brought him to Antioch. "For a whole year they met with the church, and taught a large company of people; and in Antioch the disciples were for the first time called Christians" (v. 26*b*). They established an educational ministry! Some would even say that Paul was the first minister of education! And the ministry was effective to the extent that they were called Christians, apparently by those outside the church and probably not as a label of commendation.

Paul taught in the synagogues. Paul was received in the educational institution, the synagogue, to teach in the early days of his missionary travels. He would enter a community, go to the synagogue, and attempt by teaching to show the Jewish people how Jesus was the fulfillment of their hopes, their prophecies, and their Scriptures. Acts 13:14–52 and 17:1–3, 10–12 are among the passages that illustrate his approach. Later he changed his strategy to concentrate on carrying the gospel to Gentiles.

Paul taught wherever and whomever he could. Paul taught in various places—homes, marketplaces, courthouses, prisons, and by the riversides. He taught Hebrews, Greeks, Romans, slaves, friends, enemies, strangers, and rulers. Preach he did. But he also introduced and explained the gospel through teaching.

Paul used various methods to teach. He used discourse and discussion (see Acts 13:14–52). Even in his writings he was teaching—to instruct, to correct, to persuade. His Letter to the Romans is a kind of discussion like he might have carried on orally with the Romans had he been with them. "Every one of his epistles was a teaching document, intended for the instruction of his converts."[23]

Paul admonished pastors to teach. Paul explicitly required that anyone who aspired to the office of bishop (comparable to our pastors) "must be . . . an apt teacher" (1 Tim. 3:2). He wrote his pupil in ministry, Timothy, instructing him to follow the pattern of the sound words he had heard from Paul, and to guard the truth (2 Tim. 1:13–14). He wrote, "And what you have heard from me before many witnesses entrust to faithful men who will be able to teach others also" (2 Tim. 2:2). Again, he stated that "All scripture is inspired by God and profitable for teaching, for reproof, for correction, and for training in righteousness, that the man of God may be complete, equipped for every good work" (2 Tim. 3:16–17). "Preach the word, be urgent in season and out of season, convince, rebuke, and exhort, be unfailing in patience and in teaching" (2 Tim. 4:2).

Paul taught faithfully throughout his ministry. Paul was faithful in his practice of what he advocated. In his last reference to Paul's confinement in Rome, Luke wrote: "And he lived there two whole years at his own expense, and welcomed all who came to him, preaching the kingdom of God and teaching about the Lord Jesus Christ quite openly and unhindered" (Acts 28:30–31). Paul believed in education. He advocated it for others. He modeled his convictions!

CONCLUSION

Education is an essential part of the ministry of a church. Church leaders stand on solid biblical precedent when they attempt to maximize the possibilities of extending the gospel and developing persons through good religious education. Any who would slight or avoid responsibility for giving appropriate leadership to the educational ministry of a church are on shaky footing, to the point of being unbiblical.

Those who would heed biblical precedent, and who would look to the ministries of Jesus or of Paul for guidance in ministry, must have in their own ministry a major place for education. A church whose members would likewise learn from these must do the same.

CONCERNS FOR FURTHER STUDY

Consider these questions as you continue to reflect on the meaning of the biblical precedent for education.

1. What are the implications for our time of the biblical responsibility of parents for educating children: (1) to parents, (2) to a church, (3) to ministers, and (4) to others?

2. What could be done to help ministers and church leaders appropriately maximize the potential of education in the work of a church?

3. What importance are you willing to give education in your ministry? How do you justify the importance you are willing to give?

CHAPTER 2

History

History is a systematic account of events. One who would relate most effectively to the present and the future must have some awareness, understanding, and appreciation of events that have gone before.

The history of religious education is like a rugged terrain with lofty peaks and dark valleys with ordinary landscape here and there. Equating religious education with the Bible school, H. Clay Trumbull, in his classic *Yale Lectures on the Sunday School,* noted the parallel between the history of the Christian church and that of the Bible school, and the dependence of the church on the Bible school.

> From the beginning, in short, all the way down the centuries, the history of the Christian Church shows that just in proportion as the church Bible School . . . has been accorded the place our Lord assigned to it in the original plan of his Church, has substantial progress been made in the extending of the membership, and in the upbuilding—the "edifying"—of the body of Christian believers in the knowledge of God's Word and in the practice of its precepts. And just in proportion as the Sunday-school agency, or its practical equivalent under some name or form, has been lacking, or has been ignored, has the Church failed of retaining and continuing the vital power of its membership.[1]

Such strong endorsement of the educational function encouraged historian Clarence H. Benson to state: "The progress and permanency of Christianity has been dependent on a program of education."[2]

Claims like these, and those of many other observers of the history of religious education and of Christianity in general, support the assumption of this chapter that *history affirms the value of education.* We will describe the place of education among the earliest Christians, then review the centuries until the present.

EARLY CHRISTIANS AND EDUCATION

Christianity spread gradually and somewhat mysteriously westward from Jerusalem to Antioch to Athens, Corinth, and Alexandria, and later to Rome and Carthage. Across the centuries, the westward movement reached the western hemisphere. With this westward flow, education was an integral part of the Christian faith.

TEACHING CONTINUED AS A MAJOR RESPONSIBILITY

In early Christian history, during the lifetimes of those who had been with the Lord and others who had been in their company, there was a continuation of education in much the same way as there had been during the earlier New Testament times. Colson and Rigdon explain: "In characterizing the Christian community as it functioned after the great ingathering at Pentecost, Luke wrote that 'they were continually devoting themselves to the instruction given by the apostles, to the fellowship, to the breaking of bread, and to the prayers' (Acts 2:42, author's translation). By this process of sharing, the church assimilated the new converts to its own distinctive way of life and worked to bring them to maturity in Christian character and service."[3]

The church of the New Testament was a teaching–learning fellowship, and that teaching was its very lifeblood.[4]

Every pastor was expected to be "an apt teacher" (1 Tim. 3:2). In addition, there was a special order in the ministry charged with the primary task of teaching. (See Rom. 12:6–8; 1 Cor. 12:4–10, 27–31; Eph. 4:11; 1 Tim. 3:1–13; and Titus 1:7–9.) Furthermore, many other Christians, though not identified as ministers, were active as teachers and as preachers. Citing Acts 8:1, 4, Colson comments, "At the time of persecution that arose in connection with Stephen's martyrdom, the Christians 'were all scattered . . . except the apostles' . . . and 'those who were scattered went about preaching the word.' If the average Christian in those days was a preacher, are we stretching the point to say that doubtless the average Christian was also a teacher?"[5] The involvement of the "average Christian" in teaching has received recurring emphasis throughout the history of religious education since New Testament times.

There is evidence, also, that great importance continued to be placed on parental responsibility for teaching the children. Paul declared, "Fathers, do not provoke your children to anger, but bring them up in the discipline and instruction of the Lord" (Eph. 6:4). Hence, Christians of the New Testament times followed essentially in the directions, if not all the forms, of their Jewish predecessors in teaching and learning about the faith.

Formally and informally, these early Christians taught. For a time they tried to continue to relate through Judaism, with its synagogue schools, the feasts and fasts, and many other features. But the significant differences between the faith of Christians and that of Jews who remained unconverted to Christ eventuated in the separation of Christians from formal Judaism.

NEW CONCERNS EMERGED

The gospel was too potent to stay confined to the "old wineskins." People from various social strata responded to the gospel—poor, rich, slave, soldier, artisan, man, woman, Jew, Gentile, official, peasant, Greek, and Roman. There was an exhilarating sense of equality of believers before God and of unique power through the Spirit. This first flush of the awareness of the implications of the gospel brought with its wondrous excitement some inevitable concerns which this minority called Christians had to face and resolve.

These concerns stemming from the religious commitment of the Christians ranged across vast areas of consideration: ethical, moral, social, legal, civil, familial, administrative, and economic. How should a Christian live and deal appropriately with other Christians, cults, pagans, misguided believers, family, work, property, social rank, slaves, masters, divorce, remarriage, the Torah, the sabbath, the tithe, ritual, feasts, fasts, worship, government, their own governance, children, history, doctrine, eschatology, and precept, to name some major concerns? Sherrill aptly focused on preaching and teaching as the approaches these early Christians used to inform themselves and to deal with the concerns they faced.

> Education in the primitive church, as pictured in the New Testament and other earliest Christian writings, took its form from the issues created when men, liberated into Christian autonomy under God, began to launch out into a growing Christian society, with no precedent to guide them. Teaching is closely related to preaching, yet distinct from it. It is carried on in the Christian meetings and elsewhere, especially in families. The earliest Christian writings, those which we call the New Testament and others as well, are perhaps without exception directly related to primitive Christian education.[6]

Early Christians educated through preaching. The best preaching not only warms the heart: it warms the mind. Early Christian preaching informed the mind about the truths of the gospel, the proofs of the gospel's validity. And it exhorted both heart and mind to repent and believe.

The Christian message was a clear statement of Jesus' life, death, burial, resurrection, appearances, ascension, and return. This was usually a brief statement at the beginning of the sermon, and comprised part one of the message. Part two, the proofs of the truth of the message, had two parts: the use of Scriptures to show that Jesus was the fulfillment of their prophecies, and the testimony of witnesses to the passion and the resurrection. This latter feature, in time, was replaced by the written accounts of the witnesses. Of the third part, the exhortation, Sherrill's description is noteworthy: "The sermon ended with two great imperatives: Repent! Believe!

Repentance, as in the preaching of Jesus, was changing one's mind, turning away from sins and vain things. Its direction was toward God. The outward sign of the inward change was being baptized into Christ. And the faith called for was believing that the report of the witnesses was true, believing that Jesus was the Messiah, and entrusting the whole self to him, in the present and forever."[7] While this preaching was intended to persuade and to exhort those convinced that they must respond to Christ in faith, it was based on informing the hearers about gospel truth and why they should respond. It was a good blend of preaching and teaching.

Early Christians educated through teaching. In the early church teaching was an essential complement to evangelizing. From the time of the apostles, almost always those who preached also taught. Moreover, some received the unique gift of teaching; recipients of this gift were considered divinely appointed teachers. And, as we have seen earlier, ordinary Christians must have taught as they were scattered abroad.

Christian educational efforts included at least five types of teaching:

- Christian interpretation of the Hebrew Scriptures, especially when the gospel was proclaimed to Jews.

- Teaching about the central facts of "our gospel" (2 Thess. 2:15).

- Public confession of faith. This simple, though varied, assertion was a public avowal, at times, of obedience and loyalty to Christ as king, to be ruled by his will, and to seek his mind on the issues of life. It may have been uttered at the moment of one's baptism; at times it was a greeting, such as "Jesus is Lord," from one believer to another.

- Oral transmission of information about the life and sayings of Jesus. Some New Testament books were written to set forth accurate accounts of this information (Luke, for example). These oral teachings continued even after the New Testament was written.

- Ethical instruction dealing with the Two Ways (the Way of Life and the Way of Death). An example is the *Didache* or *Teaching of the Twelve Apostles*, a manual dated about the end of the first century.[8]

One of the principal times for teaching in a professed believer's life was just before baptism. Instruction prior to baptism came to be such a focal time of teaching that distinctive educational jargon developed to identify the elements of the teaching situation. The pupil was a catechumen, and the content was catechesis (later "catechism"). The method of teaching was a system of questions with prescribed answers, which came to be called the catechetical method. This vital instruction, originally devised for adult converts, was intended to discipline the convert's moral life, acquaint him with the Christian tradition, and create in him a profound devotion to the Christian faith and way of life.[9] At one point in the early centuries this period of instruction lasted up to three years, though this length of time was probably not uniformly practiced. Later it was reduced to two years and eventually was shortened or eliminated altogether, at least as a requirement for entry into the church. By the seventh century, in the churches of the West, this instruction almost disappeared and was replaced by brief liturgical acts.

Early Christians educated in their meetings. At least two, possibly three, types of meetings contributed to Christian educational efforts. These meetings were held in a variety of places—homes, riversides, and eventually the catacombs of Rome.

The meeting for the Word was intended to edify.[10] This meeting included prayer; psalms, hymns, and spiritual songs; occasional reading of apostolic letters; a period of teaching; prophecies; and, in the New Testament times, speaking with tongues—of which there appeared no more mention in the New Testament after Paul's instruction.

The common meal was followed by observance of the Lord's Supper. The fellowship during the meal and the time of instruction and examination that comprised the Lord's Supper were very meaningful to Christians.

In addition to the meeting for the Word and the common meal, some believe the early church had a regular business meeting. First Corinthians 5:1ff. and 2 Corinthians 2:5ff. may refer to a church meeting for discipline and forgiveness of certain members. Any who have ever observed a congregation in session for these kinds of purposes can attest to the educational potential in such meetings!

Early Christians educated in the family. Less is known about details of teaching in the home among early Christians than about such teaching in Judaism. But it is a reasonable assumption that Christians valued instruction in the family setting. Some entire households received Christ. Other families were divided in their faith. Christians often met in private homes. It was not until the third century that independent buildings were erected by churches, or set apart for their use. Even then, they were frail. "During the persecution of Diocletian, the famous church of Nicodinea was leveled to the ground by the Praetorian guard in the course of a few hours."[11]

Jewish converts to Christianity probably continued to instruct in their homes much as they had done before their conversion. Use of Scriptures might have been increased in the homes of converts, but the use of ritual probably diminished rapidly among Jewish Christians. Sherrill writes, "It is reasonable to conclude that in the latter part of the first century children of Christian parents were being taught from our Old Testament and from parts or all of at least the first three Gospels. It is not clear whether this was in the household or in Christian meetings. Perhaps both were intended."[12] The instructions of Paul regarding the parental responsibility to teach and guide their children can be supposed to have been obeyed not only by those who first received his letters, but also by those who followed there-after.

Early Christians educated through worship services. By the year 100, the three meetings described earlier were combined into one. This meeting consisted of Scripture reading, instruction (including exhortation), and the Lord's Supper. In the period from A.D. 300 to 600, Christian worship in the East and the West differed at many points, but services in both regions had two major parts: the first, with the catechumens present, and the second for the faithful, with the catechumens dismissed. The first segment of worship was largely given over to instruction; and this instruction was largely for adults.[13] These catechumens were adult converts preparing for church membership.

Early Christians educated in catechetical schools. Relatively few cities in these early centuries had the formal educational institution known as the "Catechetical School." The most notable of these schools were at Alexandria, Antioch, Edessa, and Nisibis. Of these, the school at Alexandria excelled. It was a school of higher education. Traditions identify either Mark or Athenagoras as its founder. Its most famous teachers were Clement, who began teaching there about A.D. 190, and Origen, his pupil and successor. Origen took charge of the school when he was only eighteen years of age and taught there from A.D. 202 to 231. Later he taught at Caesarea until 254. In the fourth century, Jerome was one of the pupils in the school of Alexandria.

Of all the teachers at Alexandria, Origen left the greatest legacy. Rumors suggest that he wrote six thousand books. He was considered a great teacher because his teaching liberated the greatness in his pupils. No subject was considered out of the bounds of his legitimate interest in his classes. Such openness cost him posthumous condemnation at Rome, Alexandria, and Constantinople.[14]

Most of the catechetical schools closed before the year 500. By that time the world into which Christianity had intruded, and in which it eventually flourished, had changed radically for the worse.

EDUCATION ACROSS THE CENTURIES

In the year A.D. 312, Roman emperor Constantine decided "that it would be better to conquer in the sign of the cross than to try to conquer the cross."[15] Until then, Christians had been a minority group. The state had tried to stamp out the church through prohibitions, campaigns, and persecutions. These measures snuffed out the lives of thousands of martyrs, yet the church continued to grow. Morally, Christians outlived the adherents of pagan religions and emperor worship.

In the year 313, Constantine's Edict of Milan proclaimed full religious freedom as a right to every man, recognized the church as a corporate body, and promised reparations to the churches. Persecution of Christians ended, and the church became favored by the state. In 380, Theodosius I established Christianity as the religion of the Empire and authorized the name of Catholic Christians.[16]

THE PERIOD OF DARKNESS

These developments, which established Christianity as the state religion, brought significant changes in the Christian movement and to Christian education. A Christian had to be loyal to the state and to its approved interpretation of the Christian tradition. Infants were declared to be members of the church. The preparation of catechumens (mostly adult converts) for membership waned and soon disappeared. Nothing substantial replaced the teaching about membership in the Christian body. The earlier awareness of the equality of all members before God, in which the church had gloried and had prospered, was replaced by the ascendancy of a spiritual hierarchy that soon fixed itself as a hierarchy of governance for the corporate body, the church.

Eventually there arose a "metropolitan bishop" in each major population center. After some time of tensions regarding who of these should be preeminent, the predictable assumption by the bishop of Rome that he was the Pope prevailed. His determination of the mind of God in spiritual and moral concerns was to be taken as the voice of God himself. Although throughout these centuries various groups of Christians did not comply or conform to the development of a state church, the state church dominated the development of the Christian movement for centuries, and with it the educational activities.

The blend of church and state brought on dramatic reversals that impacted both life and learning. "In the second and third centuries, death was the risk of being a Christian. But by the fourth century, and thereafter, until the conscience of men would bear it no longer, death was the possible price of not being a Christian. Therefore when a man taught the Christian faith he must keep an eye out, discreetly. And when a man heard any Christian teaching it was more natural to ask whether it conformed, than to ask whether it was true."[17]

The Roman Empire began to decline. Hordes of tribal groups pressed in on the Empire, wreaking devastation. Even the city of Rome itself was sacked. Paralysis spread into every aspect of life, resulting in broken trade, disorganized economic life, soaring prices, oppressive taxes, spreading poverty, vanishing personal security, neglected roads, closed schools, common ignorance and illiteracy, and declining literature, arts, and sciences.[18] The world that Christianity knew was plunged into centuries of darkness from which it emerged only after great agony.

Until the time of Martin Luther and the Reformation, the church turned more to liturgy than to education. Priestly acts and penitent responses according to prescribed and approved forms replaced, for many, the internal qualities of the Christian experience. The result was an externalizing of religion, similar in many ways to the religion Christ had come to change. Jesus could have preached and taught again the Sermon on the Mount (Matt. 5–7), easily substituting the forms more recently developed for those he addressed as he contrasted evidences of approved righteousness with the way he came to proclaim.

Conditions for education were deplorable during these dark centuries. Here and there were pockets of people who struggled to preserve the legacy of learning and rational understanding of the faith. Some strong and often strange individuals isolated themselves from society for study and contemplation of the faith. These hermits drew about them others of similar interest, and their isolation developed into little colonies of hermits who ate, prayed, and worked together in monasteries or nunneries. Some copied the Scriptures and other writings, thereby preserving some basis for continuing limited training for clergy and a reservoir of materials for future reference when the lights of learning were rekindled.

Even so, many church leaders were illiterate and ignorant of the great truths of the faith. Many lacked foundational cognitive knowledge that might have served them in their search for these truths. Benson wrote: "When Hooper was bishop of Gloucester, he found that out of 311 of his clergy, 168 were unable to repeat the Ten Commandments. Thirty-one did not know where to find them. Forty could not tell where the Lord's Prayer is to be found and thirty-one did not know the Author."[19] The established church had become a custodian of the religious heritage and of general culture and was no match for the challenge. A few leaders had some access to formal education. Any scholar of conscience who excelled in a search for truth risked failing to conform and was discouraged. Those who proceeded in the face of the risk became the objects of persecution from the very institution, the church itself, which had been their base.

The plight of the masses of Christians can be described simply. They were largely ignorant and illiterate, subject to the institutional church that itself had but a flickering light aglow. Teaching was reduced to rudimentary forms and formulas that were crystallized and authoritative. Teaching "was communicated through drama and sacraments, through architecture, through pictures of mosaic and stained glass, and through the confessional where sacramental developments led believers to seek priestly guidance. Thus in the absence of formal schooling and literate culture, liturgy, drama, and architecture became more important educative instruments."[20]

The Dark Ages produced ignorance and fed on ignorance. World governments were in repeating states of chaos, and the official church could claim to be in no better condition. Leaders and members leaned on the authoritarian church and looked to it for grace to be given or withheld. When given, such grace came through "mysterious rites which no mind could understand, but in which they must trust."[21]

Christianity and its child, the teaching and learning of truth, had reached a point of darkness so that even little glimmers of light here and there stood out in contrast. Numerous antichurchly sects struggled to find and follow the way of Christ. Their stories in history have been documented in many volumes. Eventually they, as well as some searchers for truth within the established church, were to become the instruments of change for the better, again turning on the light of learning. Until these years of Renaissance and Reformation came, the cause of education, even in the authorized church, was grim. "Instead of advocating education, the popes were busy hunting and murdering the Waldensian believers. John Huss and Jerome of Prague were martyred as by barbarians. The monasteries were filled with the timid, the lazy, and the disappointed. The pulpit was largely given up to what was fanatical, ridiculous or political, and in many parts scarcely employed at all. The whole ecclesiastical system was used mainly either for money-getting or the gaining of secular power."[22]

THE REFORMERS AND EDUCATION

Truth will come out. However slowly, persons here and there began to break through the darkness of ignorance.

Copernicus propounded his theories of astronomy, describing that the earth rotates daily on its axis and that the planets revolve in orbits around the sun. The world actually was not flat, as had been supposed! Johann Gutenberg printed the first Bible to be produced with the use of movable type in Mainz, Germany, in 1456. Until that development the literature had been limited to what could be copied by hand.

The city of Constantinople fell in 1453 to a Moslem army, causing the few remaining Greek scholars to flee to northern and western Europe, taking with them the keys to the long-suppressed world of classical thought, literature, and art. Linguists began translating the Bible into the language of the people. Several were martyred for their work, and others were forced to spend their lives as fugitives from religious and civil authorities. John Wycliffe initiated the first complete Bible in English about 1384. He survived as a fugitive, only to have his body exhumed, burned, and scattered after his death!

Nations of Europe became interested in knowing more about the cultures of Greece and Rome. The ways of other peoples of the earth became of interest to Europeans. Their interests developed in the possibilities of interchange with other peoples for commerce and industry. Nationalism developed rapidly, accompanied by colonizing and empire building.

Explorers sought new trade routes. Columbus, on a voyage in search of a new route to the East, came on the Western hemisphere.

The awakened interest in learning, labeled the Renaissance, prepared the way for the awakening of widespread interest in the Christian faith. The growing availability of Bibles in the language of the people set the stage for a growing interest in the contents of the Scriptures.

Eventually, increasing numbers of scholars and persons of the general populace were convinced that the Bible should be taken as the sole authority for Christian faith and life. Luther and his followers held that justification comes by faith alone. Perhaps most disturbing to those in power, these troublesome people were convinced of the priesthood of all believers. They wanted to share these newly discovered truths with others, and to let them impact and reform the established church.

But, in a repetition of history's cycle reminiscent of the situation Jesus faced, the religious power structure, accumulated over numerous centuries of focusing on the external evidences of religion, was incapable of receiving the new wine of biblical truth that the Reformers proffered. The old wineskins burst in a revolution that historians have termed the Reformation.

Some reformers were expelled from the church. Others left before they were expelled. In the spirit of Martin Luther, they could do no other. They continued their search for truth and biblical faith, and they wanted others to study and to learn of it. Several were outstanding in their advocacy of and contribution to teaching and learning.

Erasmus advocated popular Bible study. Erasmus was a Dutch scholar whose life spanned parts of the fifteenth and sixteenth centuries. He translated the New Testament from Greek into Latin, offering scholars improved versions of both. With this, scholars later moved toward giving individuals the Scriptures to read for themselves. Erasmus edited and translated the works of classical authors and the church fathers. He declared that everyone should have opportunity to read the Bible for himself (even herself!). He wrote:

> I totally dissent from those who are unwilling that the sacred Scriptures translated in the vulgar tongue should be read by private individuals, as if Christ had taught such subtle doctrines that they can with difficulty be understood by a very few theologians; or as if the strength of the Christian's religion lay in man's ignorance of it. The histories of kings it were perhaps better to conceal. But Christ wishes His histories to be published as widely as possible. I would wish even all women to read the Gospels and the epistles of Paul. And I wish they were translated into all languages of all people. I wish that the husbandman may sing parts of them at his plow; that the weaver may warble them at his shuttle; that the traveler may, with their narratives, beguile the weariness of the way.[23]

His work made the way more sure for those who later made possible what Erasmus could only advocate. He was a man ahead of his time.

Martin Luther championed education. The bold German whose name is associated most prominently with the Reformation, Martin Luther, was firmly committed to education. He preached and wrote often of the importance of teaching. He strongly admonished parents to teach their children. He challenged the government to support compulsory education. For the preachers he exalted teaching and exhorted them to teach without fail.

Luther called parental responsibility to teach children "the big work of parents, and when they do not attend to it, there is a perversion of nature as when fire does not burn or water moisten."[24] He even said that people should not marry until they were competent to teach their children in religion and bring them up as true Christians.[25]

Luther saw the education of the public as essential for the success of the church, and for the future of the state. He called on the government to compel the people to send their children to school.[26] He thought the state should be the agent of education that advanced the teachings of the church.

Luther highly esteemed the work of teaching school and decried the inclination of young preachers to avoid it. He was not sure which should be preferred, preaching or teaching.[27] He wrote: "I would I knew one chosen for a preacher who had previously been a school teacher. But at the present time our young men want to become preachers at once and to avoid the labor of school keeping. Yet the schoolmaster is as important to a city as a pastor. We can do without mayors, princes and noblemen, but not without schools, for these must rule the world."[28]

Phillip Melanchthon reformed education. Melanchthon influenced the development of the University of Wittenberg, Germany, through forty-two years of working there. The University took on Protestant lines and became a model for many new universities throughout Germany. He was to educational reform what Luther was to religious reform. At age sixteen he prepared a Greek grammar that served as the universal text for German schools. He later produced a popular Latin grammar, along with texts in rhetoric, ethics, and theology. He was considered the preceptor, the master teacher of Germany. Benson wrote of Melanchthon that "At his death there was scarcely a city in the entire country that had not modified its schools according to his program of learning, or that did not number some pupil of his among its teachers."[29] He was clearly the outstanding leader of the Protestant revival in education.

John Calvin urged the church to teach the young. John Calvin in France and elsewhere was a staunch proponent of the use of the interlocutory teaching approach to instruct the young and ignorant. To assist in these times of instruction he prepared catechetical lesson guides in French and in Latin. Some consider these to be his greatest contribution to the cause of religious education. He also stressed the importance of careful parental instruction of children in the home.

Calvin encouraged parents to teach their children to sing church songs in order to encourage their participation in congregational singing. He also insisted on good training in "sound learning and doctrine . . . in manners, good morals, and common sense."[30] He believed that the work of the Reformation required a systematic program of reaching and teaching the young. Both the Heidelberg Catechism prepared by Ursinus and the Westminster Catechism of England were based on Calvin's system of catechetical helps.

John Knox advanced Sunday education. John Knox of Scotland called for a full Sunday of religious activity centered around worship and education. He taught that Sunday should be strictly kept and attendance at worship carefully observed. He instructed ministers that young children should be publicly examined in the afternoon in their catechism, in the audience of the people. He instructed ministers to be diligent to see that the people understood the questions and the answers and the doctrine with which they dealt. According to his *Book of Discipline*, the minister was to instruct the children and youth of the parish in their first rudiments, with special emphasis on the catechism.

Knox also directed that "the principles of the Christian religion"[31] be taught to children, servants, and families in all households. He charged the master of every household either to instruct or cause to be instructed those of his house.

Ulrich Zwingli favored indoctrinating children. Ulrich Zwingli of Switzerland believed that "when the truth entered the consciousness of the people evil practices would fall into decay."[32] He courageously led his people step by step in reform, with faithful dependence on the Scriptures for authority. Zwingli's principal connection with education was *The Christian Education of Youth*, a book he prepared for publication.

The catechisms and related materials that the great reformers wrote or encouraged, used, and directed others to use comprise perhaps their greatest educational contributions. Luther's *Short Catechism* ranks close to the Bible as one of the most widely circulated and translated books ever published.

All in all, these reformers and their followers were the instruments of renewed focus on the value of education in the Christian faith. To them, education was not an option but a necessity if the faith were to be truly received and followed. The reformers were united in their commitment to the necessity of the Christian education of the children. They all advocated the responsibility of the home, the school, and the church in this endeavor.

POST-REFORMATION EDUCATION

The Reformation set in motion many developments that bear on religious education history, some of which are felt even in the present generation. Certain highlights will be indicated here.

The Catholic Church countered with education. Threatened by the virtual capture of entire nations by the sweeping tides of the Reformation, there arose in the established church a movement recorded as the Counter-Reformation. Prominent in this movement was the work led by the Society of Jesus, a brotherhood within Catholicism founded by Ignatius Loyola. Some within the Catholic Church tried to stamp out opposition through the Inquisition, a vast search-and-destroy plan. Meanwhile, the Jesuits moved ahead of the distracted Protestants in two significant fields: missions and education.

In the 1500s these missionary Jesuits entered and made substantive gains in North America, South America, the Orient, and other parts of the world. They established missions and started schools. Francis Xavier, a companion of Loyola, sought to carry salvation to India and Japan, with hopes of moving into China. He died without entering China. "In the two and a half years that Xavier labored in Japan he founded more than two hundred churches and baptized 150,000 persons."[33] He focused especially on teaching little children. He is credited with saying, "Give me the children until they are seven years old and anyone may take them afterward." By the time Protestantism developed a missionary vision in the eighteenth century, Catholic missionaries had preceded them to many parts of the world.

Jesuit educational work was significant. Jesuits established free schools for children and offered quality education in religion and in secular subjects. Their scholars wrote the textbooks. Their teachers received quality training. "Jesuit teachers thus were far superior to any of their contemporaries, and they not only commanded the Catholic universities, but also found their way into such schools as received State support. Not until the rise of the normal school in the nineteenth century did either the State or the Church give such careful attention to the preparation of teachers."[34]

The Counter-Reformation, including work of the Jesuits, stemmed the tide of Protestantism and fixed boundaries between Protestants and Catholics, especially in Europe, that have changed little since 1555. Both Catholic and Protestant historians agree that the Jesuit school system played the major part in this arrest.

Education in North America reflected the Reformation. Most of the settlers of what is now the United States of America came from the countries of Europe that had embraced Protestantism in some form. Those who migrated for predominantly religious motives were committed to the religious education of their children. "From the landing of the Pilgrims in

1620 until the birth of the American Republic in 1787, there was scarcely any difference in secular and religious education."[35]

In colonial America the forms of education were molded by the uniqueness of the settlers of any given area. Virginia and some other Southern colonies were led in settlement by persons of the English upper class. These leaders provided private education for their own children and apprenticeship education in the trades for the poor. The middle colonies had mostly parochial schools related to the various sponsoring faith groups; clergy usually served as teachers. These schools often favored religious instruction to the neglect of other subject matter. Out of the Puritan concepts of New England developed the democratic idea of state support for education for all, and in colonial days, there was no separation of religious education from public education.

The most important volume in colonial education was the *New England Primer*. Next to the Bible, it is regarded by many as the most important literary molder of those who founded the republic. This eighty-eight-page book was in every school and in most homes. It was said that this book taught millions to read, and not one to sin. What did this powerful little book contain? "The contents of the primer included the alphabet, vowels and consonants, capitals and small letters, easy syllables for children, the Lord's Prayer, the Apostles' Creed, the Shorter Catechism, an account of the martyrdom of John Rogers, and a dialogue between Christ, youth and the devil. Eighty-seven percent of the wonderful book was made up of selections from the Bible."[36]

Religious influence on education continued for many years, but American public education gradually became more secularized. Religious, educational, and political debate continued to focus on the appropriate relationships that should prevail. One primary result of the secularization of public education seems clear: churches must generate, sponsor, and support the religious education they desire their constituents and others to experience.

THE MODERN ERA

The extent and effectiveness of religious education varied among the countries of Europe, as did the general education of the populace. It seems fair to conclude that neither the religious nor the general education of the masses reached any admirable level by the eighteenth century. The same was true in America, though it was in America that the most was to be made of religious education.

Historians James E. Reed and Ronnie Prevost join in the opinions of many others in saying that "The Sunday School is the best known institution of Christian education among Evangelicals today. It is so much a part of Christian education that it seems almost normative."[37] The Sunday

School has become a major part of the educational ministries of churches of many denominations.

The Sunday school movement set the pattern. While churches in Europe and America were seeking ways to educate their constituents and others, the masses remained without instruction in religion or in much of anything else. Robert Raikes, of Gloucester, England, was a reformer and philanthropist, a layman who published a weekly newspaper. Through the complaint of a resident about the rowdy behavior of some children in a slum area, Raikes became concerned about the welfare of the children.

There were then no child labor laws to protect the children from having to work from sunup to sundown six days a week in the factories in England in the wake of the Industrial Revolution. Moreover, there was no provision for the education of the masses of children. On their only day off, Sunday, they often roamed the streets in packs. They were dirty, ignorant, and unchristian. Many were unwanted, except for their economic value as laborers.

Raikes believed that if these children could be taught to read, they might read the Bible for themselves and learn the way of salvation. In 1780 he rented a meeting place, employed teachers, and started a school on Sunday for these children to receive secular instruction and knowledge of God and the Bible. Only the teachers had a copy of the Bible, the textbook.

Each child had to stand inspection at the door for admittance. The price of admission was a washed face and combed hair. At the end of each session, as students piled out the door, each received a coin for attending. Friends labeled Raikes's efforts "Bobby Wild Goose and his ragged regiment." The churches thought his efforts were hopeless. Further, they thought such use of the sabbath to be a sacrilege. Many came to feel the Sunday school was in competition with the church. Some ministers preached sermons against this "work of the devil," but Raikes continued and the movement grew.

A problem emerged that had to be solved to release the movement to the populace. The money to support the Sunday school was consumed in the modest wages for the teachers. There was no money for students' Bibles or for other learning materials. After three years of success with the school, Raikes published an account of its work in November 1783. His article was reprinted widely, even beyond Great Britain. As a result, some ladies of fashion volunteered their services as Sunday school teachers. Even the Queen sent for Raikes and had him tell her his story about the Sunday school.

Others helped Sunday schools expand. William Fox, a wealthy Baptist merchant of London, learned of Raikes's Sunday schools. On September 7, 1785, he organized the Sunday School Society for the express purpose of organizing and supporting Sunday schools. The Society furnished

Bibles, Testaments, and spelling books for the schools and money for teachers. Paying the teachers continued to drain the financial resources.

Then, John Wesley aligned himself with the movement. He called for volunteer teachers to replace paid ones. More literature and the free services of teachers contributed significantly to the preservation and extension of the Sunday school movement. By the time of Raikes's death in 1811 there were Sunday schools scattered over England with a combined attendance of 400,000 pupils.[38]

In America, William Elliot began a Sunday school in his Virginia plantation home one evening in 1785. He taught blacks and whites at separate times. In 1801 the school was moved to the Oak Grove Church building, a Methodist church in Accomac County, Virginia. It is considered to be the oldest Sunday school in America. Some consider the Sunday school established in the Broadway Baptist Church of Baltimore, Maryland, in 1804, to be the oldest and first denominational Sunday school in America, as well as the first Raikes-type school in the United States.

Southern Baptists experienced phenomenal educational growth. Many Baptist churches in the South had Sunday school for women and children (and a few men) even before the Southern Baptist Convention was organized in 1845.[39] Southern Baptists had able representation on the editorial board of the Uniform Lesson committee from its beginning in 1872. This committee is an interdenominational effort to bring some pattern to the selection of Scriptures for use in preparing Bible study materials for the Sunday schools. Each participating denomination then may write and publish its own materials for use of these selections of Scriptures by their own churches.

In 1891, after several earlier attempts had failed, Southern Baptists established a publishing house for Sunday school materials. With the addition of materials for several other teaching and training ministry approaches and organizations, the Sunday School Board of the Southern Baptist Convention became the largest publisher of periodical religious materials in the world.

Using the Sunday school as the principal agency for Bible teaching and learning, Baptists also learned to use the Sunday school as the principal method for organized outreach to persons not engaged in active church life or study. Presently it is the largest denomination of Evangelicals in America, and more than 99 percent of Southern Baptist churches have a Sunday school. They consider the Sunday school to be the foundational organization in growing churches.

In addition, Woman's Missionary Union, founded in 1888 by some women of the denomination with deep concern for missions, sponsors an age-graded organization in the churches for missions education, action, and support. In 1907 laymen in the denomination organized a Laymen's

Missionary Movement, known today as Baptist Men or as the Brotherhood. This organization is similar to the Woman's Missionary Union in its design for ministry, with a unique focus on involving men and boys in mission action and in personal ministry.

In 1918 the denomination in Convention session directed the Sunday School Board to foster the work of training Baptist young people in the church. A youth organization already existing in many churches since 1912, the Baptist Young People's Union, then came under the sponsorship of the Sunday School Board. This action made that Board more than a board for Sunday school support. By 1931 this educational organization expanded to become an all-age plan. It has the responsibility for training church members, training church leaders, and for new church member orientation. The current name for this organization, the largest of its kind in Christendom, is Discipleship Training.

Other educational developments have emerged among Southern Baptists. In organized church music ministries they have a vital and fast-growing program of music for worship and a music education structure that serves their churches well. Since the 1960s Southern Baptists have continuously worked on a comprehensive local church model for ministries. The current publication that reflects this model most succinctly is *Being God's People* by Robert A. Orr (Nashville: Convention Press, 1987). Southern Baptist Convention agencies collectively publish such a volume about every ten years, the purpose of which is to communicate their common understandings about the nature and the work of a church and its programs as the agencies agree to assist the local churches. There can be little reason to doubt that the emphasis on education has been a major contributor to the unusual growth of Southern Baptists.

CONCLUSION

When churches have remained free to teach and learn, to search the Scriptures, and to let biblical truth direct their life and work, the faithful have multiplied and the course of history has been improved. Truly history affirms the value of education.

CONCERNS FOR FURTHER STUDY

Consider these questions as you continue to reflect on history's affirmation of the value of education.

1. What are some positive lessons you observe in history which might help strengthen churches in their educational ministries?

2. What mistakes of the past should Christian educators avoid repeating?

3. What do you sense in current thought and events affecting churches
    which seem to parallel some of the historical experiences? Which of
    these suggest possible benefit? Which suggest possible harm?

CHAPTER 3

Needs of Persons

The wisdom and the way of God must come to bear on the experience of persons. This is what the educational ministry of a church is about. The Bible is the authority and guide for the educational ministry, and the primary subject matter base for Christian learning and development. The subject matter, the Bible, must relate to the experiences and needs of persons. Hence, an effective educational ministry is not only Bible-centered: it must also be life-centered.

Ministers and others who lead a church's educational ministry must have a basic and growing knowledge of the main subject matter. Likewise, effective educational leaders must be aware of and responsive to the needs of persons. The needs of persons—their needs for religious education—is the focus of this chapter.

THE NATURE OF PERSONS

One of the great psalms of praise asks the question, "What is man that thou art mindful of him, and the son of man that thou dost care for him?" (Ps. 8:4). This always has been a fundamental human question. From a theological point of view the truth of the answer remains the same. Our knowledge of mankind, however, constantly grows and develops.

A THEOLOGICAL VIEWPOINT

Each human is a person created in the image of God. This image of God is reflected in human personality, in the capacity and responsibility for being moral—for discerning what is right, and with God's help, doing right. It is reflected in the human capacity to plan. What animals do by instinct, people may do by intent. This image of God is reflected in our potential for eternity, and our capacity to respond in fellowship with God. Each person is of infinite worth and possesses the dignity of personhood.

Each person is a thinking, feeling, willing being. By nature the human person is both body and soul. The human will is free and cannot be coerced. Each person is competent under God to deal with God. Each must personally and voluntarily choose in matters of spiritual faith and moral choice.

Every person is a sinner. The human moral nature is corrupted by evil and inclined toward sin. Persons need salvation from sin, but are helpless to save themselves. They are utterly dependent on God's grace. At heart they hunger for God. This hunger is reflected in their search for forgiveness, for inner peace, for security, and for self-realization. They have the capacity to respond to God in faith and to be transformed through the redemptive power of God in Christ. By this transformation they become children of God. All are creatures of God, "But to all who received him, who believed in his name, he gave power to become children of God" (John 1:12).

The redeemed partake of the divine nature. This gives them immeasurable possibilities for growing and maturing in Christlikeness. Redeemed persons are indwelt by the presence of the Holy Spirit, whose judgment, power, instruction, guidance, and comfort are theirs to claim. They are not only citizens of the kingdom of God; they are lifelong disciples. They are members of God's family and joint heirs with Jesus himself.

AN EDUCATIONAL VIEWPOINT

Persons have inherent capacity for growing and developing physically, intellectually, emotionally, and morally. They hunger to know. They search for a meaningful understanding of life. They seek to belong, to adjust to the world around them. They seek to meet their basic physiological needs. They strive for safety, security, recognition, and power. They feel morally responsible. They yearn for God, and for assurance of life after death.

Persons are members of families, citizens of states, and related to the total human society. Their capacities and needs can be fulfilled in ways that are pleasing to God. Many of these capacities and needs require a family relationship and the experience of community.

Those who would minister to persons through education need to understand certain factors about persons regarding teaching and learning. Learning is gaining in knowledge, understanding, skill, attitude, appreciation, feelings. Teaching is helping in learning. Here are some factors about persons in the educational context that are foundational in religious education.[1]

Individuals can learn. God made persons intelligent beings. They can think and reason. They can recall the past, observe and act thoughtfully in the present, and anticipate and plan for the future. They can participate creatively in their own growth and development. They can choose purposes and goals, observe contrasts between these and their achievement, plan change in relation to these contrasts, and choose to direct their energies toward achieving goals and fulfilling purposes. Positive change is usually observable in their growth and in the improvement of their environment or their relation to it.

Learning occurs through experiences. Individuals are aware of the world through senses—seeing, hearing, touching, smelling, tasting. They are also impacted by revelation. On experiencing some impact of one or more sensory stimuli, or of revelation, persons can respond intellectually and emotionally. The experience might be planned or unplanned, and result in learning. Planned experiences might be chosen by the individual, by some other person or persons, or by some combination of these. The individual usually learns better by experiencing more than one kind of stimulus at the same time, such as seeing and hearing.

There are many kinds of experiences. Some are direct, real-life experiences. Some are direct, but they are made-up or play-like experiences. Some are indirect experiences, using words or other symbols. Some are indirect, using representations of real things. Direct experiences use more senses than indirect experiences. They also take more time than indirect experiences. Indirect experiences can speed up learning.[2] "No one type of experience is always best. The learner's differences determine the kinds of experiences that are best for him. When the learner has had many real life experiences, it is easier for him to learn from indirect experiences. Generally, the older and more experienced the learner, the fewer direct experiences he must have."[3] (Figure 1 is a graphic presentation of direct and indirect experiences.)[4]

The educational ministry of a church should seek to help individuals have experiences that direct their growth toward accepted goals. Learning may be improved by helping individuals participate in the choices of goals and the experiences for their attainment.

Knowledge is not usually the ultimate goal in religious education. More often, the ultimate learning goals should be increased Christlikeness in living and serving. Experiences that increase knowledge might provide tools with which to have other experiences on the way to Christlikeness. Persons rarely behave better than they know to act. Knowledge influences behavior. Any gap between knowledge and behavior, especially in matters moral or spiritual, becomes the concern of an individual's conscience.

Learning continues throughout life. Learning begins at birth. It develops during infancy and early childhood in proportion to experiences the child has alone, with parents, with other family members, with persons outside the family. The rate of learning is high during childhood and adolescence, but learning continues throughout life, though the rate of learning decreases in adulthood. The ability to learn and the rate of learning might be influenced at any age by the desire of the learner.

Group experiences contribute significantly to the individual's learning processes. Learning with others and from others is significant to the personal growth of the individual. Group experiences usually begin in family life. Parents are significant teachers in the young child's life. The general atmosphere of the home is educative. The family profoundly affects childhood learning because children spend their first and most impressionable years in the family. Persons learn through group experiences in the community, both in the immediate neighborhood and in wider experiences in the institutions, organizations, and activities of community life that influence their thinking, choices, and goals.

The classroom should be a community of learning, whether at church or at school. Group experiences in the classroom can contribute to learning by encouraging creative activities—expressing interests, ideas, and opinions, participating in group experiences related to life situations, and sharing information and experience.

Teachers influence learners. Teachers and other leaders exercise significant influence on individual learners. This is especially true in spiritual and moral education. The teacher's life and example are among the most effective and influential factors. In these areas more may be "caught" than taught.

The teacher and group members become partners in mutual growth. Freedom of expression is encouraged. Participation is anticipated and sought. The teacher seeks to know the members' problems and needs, to teach to meet those needs, and to guide members toward their maximum growth. Teachers seek to do this in an atmosphere of guided freedom. They must recognize and attempt to modify any lack of interest or concern, or any indication of idleness and inattention.

Spiritual resources are necessary to maximum growth. Persons have access to fellowship with God, and they may avail themselves of unlimited spiritual resources. At first they gain access to these spiritual resources by personal regeneration, becoming new persons in Christ and experiencing fellowship with God. In this way Christian education not only includes but also goes beyond the limits of mere intellectual understanding and activity.

NEEDS FOR CHRISTIAN TEACHING AND LEARNING

What do humans require to make it in life with meaning? Methods of classifying these many needs abound (for example, as spiritual, physiological, safety, social, esteem, and growth). There are developmental needs

Figure 1

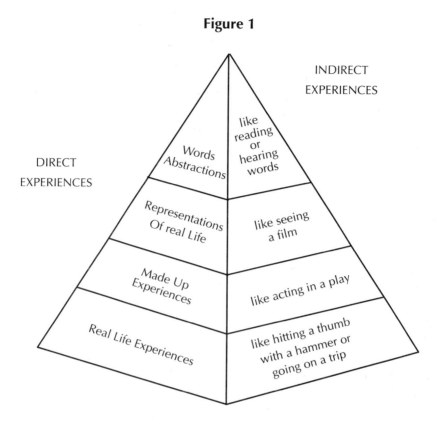

INDIRECT
EXPERIENCES

like
reading
or
hearing
words

Words
Abstractions

DIRECT
EXPERIENCES

Representations
Of real Life

like seeing
a film

Made Up
Experiences

like acting in a play

Real Life Experiences

like hitting a thumb
with a hammer or
going on a trip

Let's picture these experiences
as a "pyramid."

This pyramid shows learning experiences arranged according to how direct or indirect they are.

- The closer to the bottom of the pyramid, the more direct the experience.
- The closer to the top of the pyramid, the more indirect the experience.
- The closer to the top of the pyramid, the fewer senses are used.
- The closer to the bottom of the pyramid, the more senses are used.

that relate to the various stages of development from infancy through adulthood.

Crises, both personal and relational, create or reveal needs that often are occasions for significant ministries, including teaching and learning. Contextual factors in society—geographic, racial, ethnic, cultural, educational, socioeconomic, lifestyle, and others—significantly influence the experience of the various human needs.[5]

Educational leaders who really care about persons in a church must learn what they can about basic needs of persons. This is fundamental to an effective educational ministry in a church. Jesus' parables of the Good Samaritan and the Prodigal Son reveal an important lesson: leaders truly concerned for spiritual needs are also sensitive to other needs.

We shall attempt to describe people's needs in terms of their needs for Christian teaching and learning, and let our concern for their other basic needs be reflected in later suggestions as to how a church might provide such teaching and learning. The format for this review of people's needs with reference to the educational ministry of a church will be first to make an overarching concept statement of these needs, and then to show how the implications of this statement reflect the needs of persons in the major age groups in a church's educational ministry.

Here is an *overarching statement* of a person's needs for Christian teaching and learning: "A person needs to become aware of God as revealed in Scripture and most fully in Jesus Christ, respond to Him in a personal commitment of faith, strive to follow Him in the full meaning of discipleship, relate effectively to His church and its mission in the world, live in conscious recognition of the guidance and power of the Holy Spirit, and grow toward Christian maturity."[6]

What are some of the dimensions of this statement that apply to the individual? What does the individual need for this statement to be a guide?

The individual needs to experience Christian conversion. Each person needs to have the genuine experience of the forgiving and saving grace of God through Jesus Christ. No one can learn enough to earn salvation. But one must learn and acknowledge certain things before effectively availing himself or herself of salvation. This elemental learning centers around personal lostness and need for salvation, the inability to save oneself, the availability of new life in Christ, and the way to receive Christ for salvation.

The individual needs vital membership in a New Testament church. Each Christian needs to participate intelligently, actively, and devotedly in church fellowship as it functions in the world through worship, proclamation and witness, nurture and education, and ministry. Believers need to maintain relationship to the body, the church, just as parts of a human body must be functioning together in harmonious relationship if the body is to thrive and have unified purpose.

The individual needs experiences of Christian worship. Each person needs to experience encounters with God frequently and with some regularity. These encounters with God should deepen personal faith and strengthen commitment to serve God. Worship is always an individual experience, although it might occur in the company of others. Worship is essential for a believer's expanding experience as a Christian.

The individual needs growing knowledge and conviction. Each person needs to continue to grow throughout life in Christian knowledge, understanding, and conviction. A person should always be maturing as a Christian. The growth in knowledge one "holds" should result in the growth of right convictions that "hold" one and that lead one to live a more Christlike life.

The individual needs developing attitudes and appreciations. Each person needs to continue to develop Christian attitudes and appreciations that will enable him or her to have a Christian approach to all of life. One's knowledge, understanding, and convictions contribute to this development, as does the general behavior of fellow members, individually and in church life.

The individual needs growth in Christian living. Each person needs to develop habits and skills that promote spiritual growth and the application of Christian standards of conduct in every area of life. Christian living is the arena of education which registers the fruit of all the other areas of growth and development.

The individual needs to engage in Christian service. Each person needs to discover and exercise gifts for the good of the church and for extending the faith to others. A gift is free, not an accomplishment to brandish in some attempt to establish superiority over others. People need to discipline their gifts, to improve skills that strengthen their gifts, and use their gifts in Christian service.

Appendix 1 of this book details the "Needs of Persons in Major Age Groups" (page 235).

CONCLUSIONS

An effective educational ministry must be based on the needs of persons as well as on the Bible. Ministers and other church leaders need to know and to be sensitive to the needs of people. They need a clear understanding of people from a theological point of view. They also need to understand people from an educational viewpoint.

People's needs are many, and can be classified in numerous ways. It is important for an educational leader to know everything possible about people's basic needs and to reflect a sensitivity to those needs. The needs

of people and the educational objectives of a church should be closely correlated.

CONCERNS FOR FURTHER STUDY

Consider these questions as you reflect on the needs of people and their
importance to the educational ministry of a church:

1. What do you think of the idea that an effective educational ministry
    must not only be Bible-centered, but also life-centered?
2. What is the place of sensory experience in religious education? Of
    revelation?
3. What benefits might a minister realize from a careful study of the re-
    ligious education needs of people that takes into account human
    growth and development?

CHAPTER 4

Nature and Mission of the Church

The church has been given a unique place in the plan of God. Its place is at the center of God's redemptive purpose in Christ. In Ephesians 3:8–12 Paul declared that he was made a minister "to preach . . . the unsearchable riches of Christ . . . to make all men see what is the plan of the mystery . . . that through the church the manifold wisdom of God might now be made known." It is our intent here to focus attention on the nature of the church, its mission, and the implications of the nature and mission of a church for education.

THE NATURE OF A CHURCH

To consider the nature of something is to discern its essential character, to identify its distinguishing quality or qualities. What is the essential character of a church? What are the distinguishing qualities?

SOME BIBLICAL PORTRAITS

The Bible contains many references to the church. Some of these refer to the concept of church, and others refer to actual churches. None gives us a complete and definitive statement. As Daniel Aleshire writes: "Why, on such an important issue as the mission and nature of the church, does Scripture not provide a clear statement? As in many other issues of profound significance (i.e., the nature of redemption, the quality of the disciples' life), no one image is adequate to capture the scope and meaning of all the concept implies. Frequently, we discover that the Scripture provides multiple images of some reality; and, like the blending of sounds in a symphony, the true vision emerges from the strength of the several parts."[1]

The Bible portrays the church in a variety of phrases. Taken together, the biblical portraits provide a rich study of the nature of the church.

- People of God, "the Israel of God" (Gal. 6:16), "Abraham's off-spring" (Gal. 3:29), "a chosen race, a royal priesthood, a holy nation, God's own people" (1 Pet. 2:9).

- The church of God (1 Cor. 1:2; 10:32; 11:22; 15:9; 2 Cor. 1:1; Gal. 1:13; 1 Tim. 3:5), "the churches of God" (1 Cor. 11:16; 1 Thess. 2:14; 2 Thess. 1:4).

- God's flock (Matt. 26:31; Luke 12:32; John 10:16; 21:15, 17).

- A new humanity (Eph. 2:14–20), "a new creation" (Gal. 6:15).

- Bride of Christ (2 Cor. 11:2–3, Eph. 5:25–32; Rev. 19:7–9; 21:9).

- The pillar and bulwark of the truth (1 Tim. 3:15).

- God's field (1 Cor. 3:9).

- God's building (1 Cor. 3:9).

- The body of Christ (Rom. 12:4–5; 1 Cor. 12:12–27; Eph. 1:22–23; 2:14–16; 3:3–13; 4:1–16; 5:30; Col. 1:18, 24; 2:16–19; 3:15).

- A family (Mark 3:33–35).

- Branch of the vine (John 15:1–8).

- A fellowship (*koinonia*) (1 John 1:3).

- Children of God (John 1:11–12).

What an array of ideas! The church is people, new people, newly created by God. They belong to him. These biblical portraits indicate that a church is something very special.

One should be cautious, however, in taking these exalted ideas about a church to mean that any church is perfect or that it always acts as Christ would act if he were present in the flesh. Anyone who has been around a church (the people, not the building) would be aware of imperfections. The church's favored standing with God should not be taken to mean that some are chosen to be God's favorites, but should be understood to mean that some are given a special responsibility to share God's Word and way with the world.[2]

The meaning of the word "church" reflects its nature. The English word church translates the Greek word *ekklesia*, which means "the called-out ones," or "assembly." Before the New Testament period, *ekklesia* designated the assembly of citizens of a self-governing Greek city. "In this sense an *ekklesia* was a local assembly operating through democratic processes under the laws of the Empire."[3] It was also used in the Greek translation of the Old Testament, the Septuagint, to translate the Hebrew word *qahal*, "referring to the nation of Israel assembled before God and under his direct theocratic rule (Deut. 31:30, congregation; Judg. 21:8, assembly)."[4]

Nowadays the word "church" is used to refer to organized Christianity or to a group of churches, such as a denomination. Hobbs asserts that the New Testament never uses *ekklesia* in this sense. "It denotes either a local body of baptized believers or includes all the redeemed through all the ages. The greater emphasis . . . in the New Testament, is on the local church."[5]

The Southern Baptist Convention in session in 1963 adopted a statement called "The Baptist Faith and Message." Although not intended as a creedal statement, "The Baptist Faith and Message" has come to be a very influential document. It includes a descriptive statement about the church:

> A New Testament church of the Lord Jesus Christ is a local body of baptized believers who are associated by covenant in the faith and fellowship of the gospel, observing the two ordinances of Christ, committed to His teachings, exercising the gifts, rights, and privileges invested in them by His Word, and seeking to extend the gospel to the ends of the earth.

> This church is an autonomous body, operating through democratic processes under the Lordship of Jesus Christ. In such a congregation members are equally responsible. Its Scriptural officers are pastors and deacons.

> The New Testament speaks also of the church as the body of Christ which includes all of the redeemed of all the ages. Matt. 16:15–19; 18:15–20; Acts 2:41–42, 47; 5:11–14; 6:3–6; 13:1–3; 14:23, 27; 15:1–30; 16:5; 20:28; Rom. 1:7; 1 Cor. 1:2; 3:16; 5:4–5; 7:17; 9:13–14; 12; Eph. 1:22–23; 2:19–22; 3:8–11, 21; 5:22–32; Phil. 1:1; Col. 1:18; 1 Tim. 3:1–15; 4:14; 1 Peter 5:1–4; Rev. 2–3; 21:2–3.[6]

The church is not the entire kingdom of God, and membership in a church should not be equated with salvation. The kingdom of God is the reign of God in his creation. "The local church is an earthly colony of that kingdom."[7] Writing about salvation, church membership, and the two biblical ideas of church, Hobbs states: "Thus while salvation is synonymous with membership in the church general, it is not true with regard to local church membership. Nor is membership in the local church synonymous with salvation. 'Fellowship,' not 'membership,' is the New Testament word for Christian relations in the local church."[8]

Based on a study of the Bible, one can develop a personal understanding of what the nature of a church is to be. In keeping with the priesthood of all believers, this is both the privilege and responsibility of the individual believer. The individual has primary responsibility for what one believes and for how one's beliefs impact others. If the beliefs of one individual cause problems for the church, then the members must determine how they will accommodate the situation. All should seek to know and to obey the mind of Christ.

AN INTERPRETIVE MODEL

It is important to study the church as an idea. It is also helpful to look briefly at the nature of the church from an individual's viewpoint.

Church begins with Christ's calling individuals to discipleship. Many people might respond to his call in the same time and place, but each is called individually. This was true when Jesus called those first ones to himself. This call is recorded in Mark 1:17: "And Jesus said to them, 'Follow me and I will make you become fishers of men.'" He was calling two brothers, fishermen Peter and Andrew.

What did Jesus have in mind when he called these individuals to discipleship? What did he mean when he invited people to "Follow me"?

It would seem that he meant for those who would follow him to come and be in company with him. Since he invited several people, it would seem, too, that he intended that those who should follow him would also keep company with one another. Yet there must have been much more. He was not gathering about him a group of individuals just with the idea of having some introverted fellowship with him and with one another.

"Follow me" suggests much more than fellowship. It was a call to a discipleship that is more than companionship. It was a call to learn of him, to be his pupil. It was a call to his discipline for life. It was a call to live life his way in relation to the Father, to self, and to others. It was not a call to a standard of living in some material sense, but to a standard for life. The new relationship begins with reconciliation with God and is to be expressed in relationships with others. The Bible has much to say about both of these dimensions. They are core content for religious education.

One significant dimension of what the call to discipleship meant and still means is the latter part of the spoken call: "I will make you become fishers of men." The call to discipleship integrally means a call to live his way and to join him in the redemptive enterprise. So committed was Jesus to our joining him in the redemptive enterprise that he gave this task to his disciples, promising the indwelling Spirit to guide and to empower them. He also declared: "Truly, truly, I say to you, he who believes in me will also do the works that I do; and greater works than these will he do, because I go to the Father" (John 14:12). Surely disciples could not do works greater in kind than those done by the Master. Whatever else he might have meant, surely he meant that his disciples are to be faithful in doing the things which would be a blessing to others, the highest blessing being reconciliation to the Father through Christ. Learning and doing this is also the work of religious education—teaching and the rightful exercise of other gifts.

What does the call to discipleship have to do with the nature of the church? The call to discipleship is the nature of the church, when that call is lived out in its intended way. An individual disciple is one part of that body, the church. Discipleship involves joining the company of others who are also disciples and working together with Christ to bring people to God.

A church is built on the Rock. A church is more than a collection of people. It is a "building." It is not a building made of stones. It is a building made of people who are disciples of Jesus Christ.

Jesus came with his disciples into the district of Caesarea Philippi. He asked them who men were saying that he, "the Son of man," is. They mentioned John the Baptist, Elijah, Jeremiah, or one of the prophets.

> He said to them, "But who do you say that I am?" Simon Peter replied, "You are the Christ, the Son of the living God." And Jesus answered him, "Blessed are you, Simon Bar-Jona! For flesh and blood has not revealed this to you, but my Father who is in heaven. And I tell you, you are Peter [*Petros*], and on this rock [*petra*] I will build my church, and the powers of death shall not prevail against it. I will give you the keys of the kingdom of heaven, and whatever you bind on earth shall be bound in heaven, and whatever you loose on earth shall be loosed in heaven" (Matt. 16:15–19).

Hobbs explains, "A petra was a large ledge rock such as a foundation rock. A petros was a small stone broken off the large stone and partaking of its nature."[9] He continues, "In the Old Testament where 'rock' is used symbolically, it always refers to deity."[10] So, what should one make of this complex passage and of its meaning for the individual and the church? Consider this treatment: "Certainly the foundation of the church is Christ, not Peter or any other mere man (1 Cor. 3:11). . . . The writer sees 'rock' as referring to Christ. Peter was a petros, a small stone partaking of Christ's nature. The church is built on Christ, the building stones being all who, like Peter, confess him as 'the Christ, the Son of the Living God.' (See 1 Pet. 2:5.)"[11]

Individuals who respond to his call to discipleship and confess him as Lord, follow him and live his way in relation to God and other people, and share with him in the redemptive enterprise are his church. Each individual is a piece of the rock, the foundation stone of which the church is built. Each has equal opportunity of access to the Father. Each has a share of the privileges. Each has a part of the responsibility. Each has a voice and, when needed, a vote. Not all have equal influence, though all have equal opportunity to earn influence in the body. Such influence usually comes to those who are faithful with the responsibilities or opportunities they have.

Christ has supplied certain ones with gifts that are to be used for the good of the body as the church goes about the work of the kingdom. The gifts are for functional services that are to enable those in the fellowship, to equip them for the work of ministry. There are varieties of gifts, but the same Spirit, same Lord, same God. No part of the body, no member, whatever his or her gift may be, is to disdain another, or to set himself or herself over another as though he or she were of a higher order.

The nature of church is that of a living organism. Believers have new life. They are indwelled by the Spirit from the time of their new birth. Each is a "new person" in Christ, part of a new humanity. This new life is different from the old life. The believer is to live as Jesus lived in relation to the Father, to self, and to others. Banding together voluntarily under the lordship of Christ, individual believers comprise a church.

There is a sense in which the believers who are banded together to form a church have life in a corporate relationship. They become an entity of life. They take on qualities of an organism. In this instance, an organism is any highly complex thing or structure with parts so integrated that their relation to one another is governed by their relation to the whole. This seems to be the concept of church Paul advocated in 1 Corinthians 12:14ff. and Ephesians 4:11ff.

Just as he is the source of new life in the individual through the Holy Spirit, Christ is also the source of life and strength of the body of believers—the fellowship we call a church. He is to direct the life of the organism. He is to supply its power, its strength.

THE MISSION OF A CHURCH

The noun mission means first "a sending forth." It implies that there is some charge for which people sent forth are responsible. There is purpose to be fulfilled, an errand to be performed. There is a commission to be carried out. All of these elements grow out of the nature of the church. A church does what it does because it is what it is. What is its mission? What is a church to do?

MAKING KNOWN THE MANIFOLD WISDOM OF GOD

It is the mission of a church to make known the "manifold wisdom of God" (Eph. 3:10). The individual who comes to know the manifold wisdom of God, the "plan of the mystery" (v. 9), can respond in faith, receive Christ, and become a child of God. The people who have already received Christ are to make known the wisdom of God. This wisdom is the gospel, the good news.

Christ gave his church the responsibility of unbinding the gospel, letting it loose in the earth. But with this responsibility comes also the possibility that a church might not unbind the gospel, and by this very default bind it. Not all children obey the Father. Consider this comment about Matthew 16:19:

> The keys of the kingdom are the gospel which Jesus deposited in his church. If the church binds it on earth by not proclaiming it, heaven has

already decreed that there is no other way whereby men may be saved and enter into the kingdom of heaven. But if the church looses the gospel on earth by
proclaiming it, heaven has already decreed that men will hear it, some will believe it, and those who do will be saved or enter into the kingdom of heaven.
It is a privilege and a tremendous responsibility! [12]

It is essential to the nature of a church that its members be faithful in proclaiming the gospel. It is the only hope of salvation for mankind. As Peter declared, "There is salvation in no one else, for there is no other name under heaven given among men by which we must be saved" (Acts 4:12).

A FELLOWSHIP ON MISSION

A church is a fellowship on mission. It is a fellowship of disciples making known to all the gospel of Jesus Christ. Its mission is not to be a fellowship. It is a fellowship by its very nature.

Curriculum designers and program designers have done extensive work over recent decades in proposing accurate and practical answers to questions about the essential functions of a church on mission. Southern Baptist curriculum designers presently are working with this statement of a church's mission as their premise: "The mission of a church, composed of baptized believers who share a personal commitment to Jesus Christ as Savior and Lord, is to be a redemptive body in Christ, through the power of the Holy Spirit, growing toward Christian maturity through worship, proclamation and witness, nurture and education, and ministry to the whole world that God's purpose may be achieved."[13]

Colson and Rigdon believe that this statement is broad enough to include all of the educational activities in a church's curriculum plan and all the performance activities in its program plan. "The objective states the ultimate purpose for the church's total program and for each segment of it whether it operates in the community or throughout the world in cooperative efforts with other churches."[14]

Using this statement of a church's mission, we shall focus on the functional aspects as a valid expression of what a church does as it carries out its mission. A function is a basic activity natural to, characteristic of, and essential to the life of an organism. What are the functions of a church? They are four.

Worship. Worship is a basic activity. It is an individual "encountering God in experiences that deepen a Christian's faith and strengthen his service."[15] It is a natural expression of one's relationship to God. No one should be surprised to find a believer worshiping, for worship characterizes believers. It is essential to church life. Without regular and frequent worship, the organism cannot long perform its other functions. Worship supports proclamation, nurture, education, and ministry to others; that is more than mere humanism.

A word of caution might be important at this point. Corporate worship, with believers gathering together and experiencing encounter with God as a body of his children, is imperative (Heb. 10:25). It is a beginning point and a melding point for a church with regard to its development into a genuine fellowship. Moreover, those who comprise a church must also experience worship individually, apart from the corporate occasions. These times of one-to-one encounter sustain personal identity as individual disciples and contribute strength to relationship to others when they come together for worship or for other purposes. The caution is this: neither corporate worship, nor individual worship, nor both kinds together comprise the totality of one's responsibility to God or to his church. A body of believers whose members only worship cannot be a complete church. Conversely, to whatever extent the members neglect worship, to that extent they limit the total ministry of their church.

Proclamation and witness. It is natural that disciples of Jesus Christ should tell others what they themselves have seen and heard, what they have experienced with Christ. One who has had a vital experience wants to share the Word with others in order that they might also experience such joy and relatedness. It is essential that the faithful proclaim and witness, for the benefit of both those who proclaim and those who hear. Proclamation and witness are life-extending for the body.

A word of caution, too, seems in order regarding proclaiming and witnessing. Verbal proclaiming and verbal witnessing, both oral and written, are vital. One who has encountered Christ and experienced salvation has something to tell! But no amount of telling, even about a magnificent conversion experience, can adequately compensate for a careless lifestyle that seems to belie the care of Christ for people that a believer's life should reflect. One who runs roughshod over others, as though they were less than people for whom Christ lived, died, and rose to live again, cannot proclaim or witness with credibility. Also, not all of the verbal proclaiming and witnessing has to fall into one set pattern. Some disciples do not feel free to be as bold or as confrontational as do some others. Certainly these less bold ones should not be shamed or ridiculed by fellow disciples. All need to develop some ways of verbally proclaiming or witnessing, but in ways that are natural to their own personalities. In any case, the witness of one's life and behavior might be the most effective word spoken.

A church must proclaim and witness. To whatever extent it does, a church can expect increased vitality and new life—indeed new lives—to be added to the body. To whatever extent a church neglects to proclaim and witness, to that extent it can expect to suffer loss of vitality and the absence of new life.

Nurture and education. It is natural for a church to "nourish, modify, and develop individuals within a fellowship."[16] This is one expression of concern for people and their needs. It is natural for a church to provide for maturing and growing people in knowledge, wisdom, moral righteousness, and performance. None should be surprised to find a church engaged in activities to help people in these ways. Rather, it should characterize a church to be found faithfully working at nurture and education.

Again a caution seems in order. A church must engage its members in regular and frequent nurturing and educating experiences. But no amount of nurture or education can replace the conscious submission of one's will to the lordship of Christ for salvation. Nor can nurture and education supplant worship, proclamation and witness, or ministry.

It is imperative that a church nurture and educate. The God of all truth intends for his truth to be made known for the good of his creation. Nurture and education are ways this can be done.

Ministry. To minister is to do things needful or helpful—to aid people both in and out of its fellowship. Distinctively Christian ministering, such as a church renders, is that which is done for others in the name of Christ, through his power, in his Spirit, and for his glory. Just as those who comprise a church emulate Christ when they worship, proclaim, and educate, so they emulate him when they minister to those in need. And, while any church might hope that those to whom they minister would accept their highest expression of loving concern—the gospel of Christ for their salvation—such acceptance is not a condition for the help to be given. Individually and collectively, the church actively ministers to the spiritual, mental, and physical needs of people.

Ministry is largely made up of voluntary acts, acts that a church consciously chooses to do to help people because the people of the church love God, and because they love and care for others as they care for themselves.

Now comes another word of caution. Some sincere people might mistake the channel of ministry as the way to earn salvation. This is regrettable because Christian ministering comes from one who is first a Christian. Salvation is something given, not earned. Just as one cannot be educated into the kingdom, neither can one work one's way in by helping people. But there is a serious error at the other end of this spectrum. Many professed Christians proclaim and witness, study and learn, but never minister beyond the verbal. These Christians also need encouragement toward a fuller participation in the life of the church.

A church on mission is a fellowship on mission. One can tell when this is the case because a church will be observed doing with some regularity and balance of emphasis those characteristic, essential activities that are the functions of the organism we call a church: worship, proclamation and witness, nurture and education, and ministry.

HOW EDUCATION RELATES

Each dimension of activity of a church on mission is vital to every other dimension and to the total church. Worship is the essential beginning but not the end. Proclaiming and witnessing grow naturally from worship, but one cannot stop there. Ministering to people is an essential expression of the validity of proclamation and witness and worship, but it is inadequate if left alone. Aleshire was accurate when he wrote that "the distinctive task of education is its undergirding of all the other tasks."[17]

This is not to say that one function of the body is superior to all others or to any other. Each is the most essential function for that which it performs. Education contributes to each of the other functions in indispensable ways.

For worship to be most meaningful, the worshiper must know something of what worship is. Who is the worthy object of worship? What worship is pleasing to God? How may people most effectively engage in worship? Why should one worship? What are some hindrances to worship? How may these hindrances be overcome? What are some conditions on which worship depends? What worship is not fitting? What are some of the values to the person who worships? How are others helped to experience worship? These and many other questions must be answered if worship experiences are to fill their vital role in church life. Many of the answers must come through education.

Education must strengthen proclaiming and witnessing. One does not have to be a scholar to be a witness, but a witness can be a better witness if he or she is prepared. Peter wrote, "Always be prepared to make a defense to any one who calls you to account for the hope that is in you, yet do it with gentleness and reverence" (1 Pet. 3:15). Witness training is one of the most critical needs in any church. The basic facts of the gospel need to be known accurately by one who would witness aright. How a person receives Christ for salvation is essential subject matter for a witness. How best to present the witness is crucial. Education can help a witness develop into the quality witness he or she is capable of becoming.

Ministering to people in the name of Christ needs to be enriched and made better by education. Learning such things as how to discover people in need is important. Learning certain skills and knowledge about how to minister and to be received in order to minister is vital. Learning how to relate the resources of other ministering people and groups to help meet the needs of people is necessary in many instances. Education and training in ministry require teaching and learning.

The function of education itself requires the function of education. What should be the goals and eventual outcomes of education? What should be its content and its method? What are the needs of people that call for education? What supporting materials, supplies, equipment, furnishings, and other helpful items are needed, and how can they be provided? Who should teach? What training do teachers need? What should be the limits of the educational efforts? These and many other questions call for education about the education function itself in a church.

It is accurate to say, as Aleshire wrote of education in a church, "It informs and undergirds all the purposes of the church."[18] This is how education relates to the nature and mission of a church.[19]

CONCLUSION

A church is uniquely placed in the center of God's redemptive purpose in Christ. It is important to know the essential character of a church. The Bible presents some word portraits of a church that, taken together, provide rich insights into its nature. Essentially, a church is a group of the people of God on mission. It is important to describe a church further in order to understand it more fully, but this is its core concept.

It is useful to begin with an individual disciple and to think one's way to the church. Individuals are called to follow Jesus and to join him in the redemptive enterprise. Together with other people who have responded to this call to discipleship, these individuals become parts of God's "building," and Christ is the Rock on which a church is built. These followers meld into a living organism, with qualities of life as a unit. They live out their common life. They express the reality and validity of their corporate life by functioning together to worship, to proclaim and witness, to nurture and educate, and to minister.

Each of the functions of a church is the most important function for its purposes. All four are interrelated. Education informs and supports all the other functions, as well as itself.

The nature and mission of a church do, indeed, require education.

CONCERNS FOR FURTHER STUDY

Consider these questions as you continue to reflect on the nature and mission of a church, and on their requirement of education.

1. What are some of the reasons you would suggest about the importance of one's understanding something of the nature and mission of a church?

2. How would you propose to help members of a church fellowship learn more about the nature and mission of a church?

3. What are some ways you might go about educating people in a church regarding the functions of (1) worship, (2) proclamation and witness, (3) nurture and education, and (4) ministry?

a.

CHAPTER 5

World Conditions
and Trends

One might describe an era as the time required for a rather complete change to occur in the basic facts related to sustaining life at a reasonably functional level. Presently, many of the basic facts change several times in a single lifetime—facts related to technology, economics, sociology, politics, government, education, and other vital sectors of life. In prior centuries, such basic facts remained accurate over many generations. Who could challenge the assertion that such basic facts are changing at a dizzily accelerating rate?

Truth, unlike facts, remains true. One who aspires to influence others for good and for God must learn both facts and truth, and how to distinguish between them. This learning includes some awareness of world conditions and trends, if one is to be effective.

Sensitive people in almost any era could honestly say, "These are the times that try men's souls." Forces at work in the world, if not checked, seem destined to try men's souls—even to doom them. One writer said it this way: "I looked into the future, and it won't work!" Prophets of doom find ample evidence to support their prophecies. The glass is half *empty,* cracked, and leaking fast.

Yet some more promising forces are also working. With the poet Emerson it can be said, "This time, like all times, is a very good one if we but know what to do with it." The glass is half *full,* and filling.

What are some of the conditions and trends that can be so ambivalently construed? What about the church in such a world? What about religious education? We now turn our attention to these three questions.

WORLD CONDITIONS AND TRENDS

The world has always been changing, but change is coming faster than ever before. The rate of change is now so high that it challenges one's ability to tolerate it.

Individuals are made to feel inadequate and hopeless in the face of such a pace of change. This "changepace" seems to be an inevitable producer of anxiety and frustration, even of despair. Many cannot cope. How many changes will this generation experience? A glimpse at some of the major areas in which such changes are occurring will illustrate the problem.

Changing *technology* astounds even the most sophisticated at times. Superjets move large numbers of people over distances in a few hours that would have required months of arduous travel several years ago, yet most of the world's millions have never set foot on an airplane—a fact that is still true even in sophisticated America. Moving sidewalks start, stop, and move accurately in response to a computer-programmed pattern. Transportation tubes move large numbers of people quickly, encapsuled in underground carriers. Reusable space shuttles are almost commonplace realities. Motorized vehicles now pass from Britain to the European continent through a rail tunnel beneath the English Channel. Even passenger trains are bidding for a comeback in America, with plans for super-speed rail travel connecting major population centers, in competition with air travel.

Communication developments are making yesterday's science fiction today's reality. Edward R. Lindaman observes, "We blink our eyes with the sudden realization that, thanks to science, all the filters have been removed from between us and everything that happens anywhere in the world."[1] Events of the moment are available to the people of the earth with sight, sound, and living color. Distant wars, which many do not wish to see, are presented in graphic detail via television right into our homes as the events occur. Technology presently exists to make possible individual two-way verbal communication almost anywhere in the world with portable equipment approximately the size of a wristwatch, via communications satellites. While developing global communications almost defy description, there seems to be less understanding and willingness to accommodate to human differences than ever.

Medicine has experienced almost incredible changes. Major organ transplants are still news, but they are no longer uncommon. Even multiple organ transplants are being successfully performed with growing frequency. Preventive medicine progresses as techniques for early detection of disease are developed. Research to find the secrets of prevention and/or cure of dreaded diseases has virtually eliminated some diseases from the earth, and promises hope for others. Life expectancy continues to be extended, with large credit due to remarkable advances in medicine and medical care. Still, the multitudes do not have full access to adequate medical care, due in part to the enormous costs.

Agriculture has undergone a methodological revolution, and some of the benefits have reached the developing world. Fewer and fewer people now supply more and more people with farm products. Farms generally are larger than before, and many who formerly lived and worked there have migrated to urban areas. Still, it is estimated that from 40 to 60 percent of the people of the world suffer from malnutrition or from outright hunger.

Space exploration reflects some of the highest achievements of technological advance. Spacecraft fly near planets within seconds of their scheduled time while on multi-year voyages over billions of miles. They send back to earth numerous photographs of hitherto unseen sights, along with almost infinite data. They have mysterious operational problems corrected by remote control as they flash on their way to other rendezvous. While serious mishaps and spiraling expenses at times have slowed the pace of subsequent exploration, there will continue to be significant activity in that vast arena.

Computer science is now driving major advances in every field, occasioning a virtual contemporary Renaissance. Computers are changing business and commerce. Many are already using computerized shopping for everything from banking needs to food and clothing. The move is well underway to equip many households in America with their very own equipment to be used for everything from controlling heating, cooling, and lights to providing accounting services, education, news, and entertainment. More and more Americans no longer drive to work but work primarily from their homes via computers and fax machines. The new slogan is "Don't commute—communicate." Applications of computer technology to classroom education still lag behind those in many other sectors, though computers are rather extensively used in school administration. Still, the know-how is available to those with the inclination and the funding.

Erratic changes in *economics* keep the people of the world in a stir. Rampant inflation (in some countries as much as 200 to 300 percent per year) devastates monetary systems and personal lives and plans. In the United States, whose stable currency has long been the standard of international trade, there is a continuing struggle in the government and in the business sector, along with manufacturing and other areas, to try to find and maintain the needed balances between inflation and interest rates, imports and exports, and production modernization and obsolescence.

More and more people find it difficult to realize their "American dream" of owning a residence. Affordable health care for all eludes even the world's wealthiest nation. Increasing numbers of children in poverty, the continuing rise of the homeless multitudes, and the growing population of needy elderly challenge the economy, the government, and the very moral fibre of America.

Unemployment (inflation's economic counterpart in classic economic theory) incites violence and threatens to topple governments. In some areas and among some ethnic groups, the figure has approached 40 to 50 percent of the work force unemployed even in the United States. Mergers, "downsizing," reduced sales, production difficulties, managerial miscalculations, criminal activity of some in leadership positions, along with many other factors, contribute to massive layoffs of workers, and not a few forced retirements. Some of the old "laws" of the economy have been breached. For example, an economy such as that of the United States could in the past expect unemployment to go down as inflation rose, and vice versa. Now there have been times when both rose, bringing attention to a new kind of threat labeled "stagflation." As if that isn't complicated enough, enter high interest rates!

Even low *interest rates,* such as those experienced in the United States, cause havoc for many. Retired people who depend on interest earnings for their livelihood are suffering. Low interest also changes many of the patterns of investment, along with serious implications for international trade. As in other instances, the need seems to be to find balance to right the teetering economies of many nations.

Low growth of *productivity* as measured by the rate of growth in the Gross National Product has added fuel to the economic fires. Obsolete plants and machinery in some industries of America have contributed to the loss of many markets to international competitors.

Wages for most in America have barely managed to keep pace with the growth of the Cost Price Index, only to have most if not all of the gain wiped out by unprecedented tax increases. Still, Americans have more money left after taxes than do most other major industrialized countries. And the average American family has a share of the Gross National Product equal to more than twenty times that of families in the countries of the world outside of Europe and Scandinavia.

Concern for dwindling *natural resources* has mounted on a worldwide scale. Energy sources that come from fossil fuels virtually have been put on the "endangered species" list. Even water and air, previously considered free, abundant, and uncontaminated, are among the natural resources whose usable supply is a concern.

The price of *necessities* (food, shelter, clothing, healthcare, and transportation) has risen faster than the price of some of luxuries. All in all, the conditions in economics have been erratic and will probably continue to cause grave concern in the long term.

The pace of *social change* increases. "Explosion" is the word most often used to refer to the growth of the populations of the earth. Some expect world population to double within twenty-five years! Ralph Neighbour, Jr., writes: "It required the entire history of man to give birth to the first billion people, by 1830. It took only 100 years to add the second billion. The third billion came in thirty years. In fourteen more years, we added the fourth billion. By A.D 2000, we will add three billion more! Demographers are conservatively forecasting 7.2 billion by the end of the century."[2] The implications of such growth in population for every other area of concern—such as technology, economics, politics, education, and religion—are truly mind boggling.

Urbanization has resulted from the population explosion. According to Neighbour, 5 percent of the earth's people lived in cities in 1800. This is headed to 73 percent by A.D. 2000. From one hundred seventy-two cities of a million people in 1975, there are to be three hundred by the end of this century, with two hundred of these in Third World countries.[3] Providing means of subsistence for such areas of humanity challenges the world's resources.

Hunger is a reality for up to two-thirds of the world's people. It increases even though an estimated 60 percent of the wheat grown in the United States and one-third of all farm produce are sold overseas.

The United States has an *aging population*. Planners must anticipate this trend. Comparable numbers of the young are not entering the work force, thus creating havoc in tax-based support systems for the needy aged. A corollary development is the swelling population of young-old who find themselves responsible for assisting with the care of their fragile parents at the same time many of their own young adult children still need help. The stress on this "sandwiched generation" is taking a heavy toll on families and on their resources.

Antisocial behavior, including crime, alcohol abuse, drug abuse, tobacco use, sexual immorality, and family dissolution, continue to take heavy tolls in society. Security of people from violent crimes continues to diminish. Acts of violence formerly reserved for darkness are now common in broad daylight. Alcohol abuse is epidemic worldwide, destroying lives directly and consuming foodstuff as the world totters near starvation.

Drug abuse continues to victimize growing numbers of people. In the United States the "war on drugs" drags on, overfilling jails and prisons with short-term "clients of the penal system," resulting in streets and neighborhoods being intimidated by convicted criminals, some of whom have never had to serve sentences, and others who have had to be released prematurely to make room for more violent criminals. Courts are mandating the construction of new penal facilities faster than financially pressed government sectors can fund and build them. Law enforcement leaders attribute most urban crime to drug traffic, while the staffs of police forces need more people than strained city budgets can provide. And there are many more dimensions to this condition, such as the discussion as to whether certain drug use should be legalized as a strategy for relief from some of the problems.

The United States government subsidizes tobacco while warning of its potential for causing disease and premature death. Laws make it financially advantageous for some to live together without benefit of matrimony. Adultery is a social problem because the results of such behavior are borne by many people other than those who have given assent to such a style of life. Society continues to be bent on trying to evade moral responsibility for immoral living, attempting through comedy and other entertainment media to laugh away or to belittle righteous living.

Family structures are shifting. About half of the work force in the United States is female, although women receive less than two thirds the pay of men for their labor. Single-parent families have increased to well beyond ten million households. The rate of divorce as compared with the rate of marriage in the United States approaches one-for-one. While some are doubtless the victims of very difficult circumstances, others enter and depart the state of marriage with a casualness that is something of a social and moral felony. The debilitating effects of this latter group on family stability are indeed against the best interests of society. These trends, along with numerous others of a social-moral-religious nature (such as the millions of people who cohabit), leave social problems for all.

Political instability afflicts many nations of the world. The assassination of political leaders has become almost routine news. Violent terrorist acts strike frighteningly close to presumed bastions of security. Hostage-taking in many places occurs with alarming frequency. Joyful celebrations followed the fall of the real and symbolic Berlin wall and the scattering of the centralized power of the former Union of Soviet Socialist Republics. But the celebration was soon followed by wars, hunger, fear, and ethnic strife.

Politics and religion are now fused and confused. Some preachers try to influence the political system directly. Some proclaim that one who votes for candidates other than theirs would be doing a less-than-Christian act. Many politicians sound more like preachers or missionaries, and some of these are sincere. For many, though, there is an intensifying intolerance not only for different opinions, but also for the people who might hold them. A we-can-do-without-those-with-whom-we-differ attitude often has displaced any interest in respectful dialogue about issues.

Then there are the mullahs of Iran and the dictator of Iraq. Sectarian strife rends the garment of the "faithful" in country after country, with terrorist acts, firing squads, and outright war as the bitter fruits. Often Christian strives against Christian, or Muslim against Muslim.

The military-industrial complex in 1980 required more than one million dollars per minute, worldwide, for armaments and other military spending, according to the Stockholm International Peace Research Institute. The anticipated "peace dividend" following the dissolution of the Soviet Union and the fall of "The Wall" is still largely unrealized in the economies or the military postures of nations. There have been some two hundred wars since World War II, mostly in Third World countries. Overt and covert intrusions of nation on nation keep the world in dread that some situation will get out of hand and bring on a worldwide conflagration that will destroy all parties. The acronyms for strategies and weapons of war that became prominent in the language of the superpowers of the earth in the late third quarter of this century—ICBM (intercontinental ballistic missile), MIRVs (multiple independently targetable reentry vehicles), LOW (launch on warning), and MAD (mutual assured destruction)—are being replaced largely by fears of proliferating nuclear power for warfare among a larger number of mostly small nations whose leaders might not have the same concern for or knowledge of the awesome destruction potential they control.

Education has not kept pace with needs in the United States, much less in the world at large. Expenditures for education have not kept up with inflation, even in the United States. Even here the inflated number of dollars spent for education represents a diminishing portion of the Gross National Product. There continues to be concern for what these dollars are actually buying. Learning and development of skills for living generally are not at a level to satisfy what it takes to conserve and improve the quality of life many feel is eluding our grasp.

Sincere public educators are grappling with the problems, while many others just as sincerely continue to turn to alternative systems for schooling. There is a paradox in higher education: there are more than eleven hundred ethics courses in business schools of American colleges and universities, while many ethics teachers are focusing on the procedural realms, contributing, however inadvertently, to the growing lag of knowing what is right and doing it. A society can no more reach for ethical heights of which it doesn't know than can an individual. The immediate future portends to be pivotal in the patterns for educating a public in dire need of knowing all they can in order to cope with the fast-changing ways of life in these times.

RELIGIOUS CONDITIONS AND TRENDS

Religious conditions and trends cannot be disassociated entirely from the conditions and trends in the areas previously scanned. For instance, the entry of so-called conservative religionists into the political realm at the same time so-called liberal religionists are exiting that realm is a some-what curious phenomenon of the times in America.

On a worldwide scale, just under 40% of the world's population have no religious affiliation whatsoever. Christianity claims 23.3%, with 36.8% claimed by other world religions. The percentage claimed by Christianity is dwindling. We seem to be losing the pace race. Commenting on the sit-uation, Neighbour writes: "To keep pace with this expanding population, the Christian community will have to add 62,500,000 converts a year from now to the end of the century! The alternative to such evangelism is fright-ening. At our present snail pace of evangelism, some missiologists fore-cast a world Christian community of less than 1 percent of the total population by the end of the century."[4]

In the United States the trends of church membership and attendance are generally unchanged at the end of the 1990s. *The 1991 Yearbook of American & Canadian Churches* cites Gallup polls indicating that in 1990, 69% of adults said they were members of a church, synagogue, or similar congregation. In the 1980s the average membership was 68%, down from 70% in the 1970s. In the four decades before 1970 this figure was either 73% or 74% every decade.[5]

The Gallup studies for 1990 note also that "the highest claims of church membership are found among those who say they are 'born again' (82%) and the Catholic faithful (81%)."[6] Gallup reports that by regions the high-est proportions of the American population who are church members are the Midwest (76%) and the South (74%). In the East and in the West the figures are 69% and 54%, respectively. Women are more likely than men to be church members, by a margin of 72% to 66%.[7]

Four Americans in ten reportedly attended church or synagogue in a typical week in 1990. This figure is almost identical to those of the 1980s and the 1970s. The 1950s saw the high point when 46% of the adult pop-ulation said they attended church the previous week. Reports in 1990 indi-cate that Catholics are more likely than Protestants (50% to 40%) to have attended the previous week; and that the highest incidence of attendance is found among those who say that they have been born again (56%).[8]

Early indications in the 1990s suggest that the public might be turning toward the churches once again. But there has been no notable improve-ment in the low commitment of financial resources for religion and wel-fare, which still hover below the 2% figure of personal consumption expenditures for people in the United States. Per capita giving of members still rarely surpasses the percentage of total family income that was given during the lowest years of the Great Depression, even though many more dollars might be given in some denominations.

Research on trends in religion in America is more plentiful than ever be-fore. Following is a summary of ten key trends in the religious and spiritual lives of Americans, as indicated by numerous national surveys conducted by the Gallup Organization, Inc., the Gallup Poll, the Gallup Youth Survey, and the Princeton Religion Research Center:

1. Intensive spiritual search and a desire for individual spiritual growth.

2. Proliferation of religious groups to answer these spiritual needs—a clear warning to established churches that are sometimes not prepared to deal with religious experience.

3. Blurring of boundaries between various faiths and denominations.

4. Influence of charismatics and Pentecostals which is being felt across denominational lines.

5. Growing interest in interfaith dialogue.

6. Decline in the growth of most of the largest Protestant denominations; and the growth and revitalization of the evangelical churches, notably the Southern Baptist Convention. The percentage of people who have had religious training has declined sharply over the last quarter-century. In addition, the proportion of people who say they have no religious preference has increased from 2 percent in 1966 to 8 percent in the latest surveys—a fourfold increase.

7. Increase in secularity: people today believe religion cannot answer all or most of today's problems.

8. Increase in religiosity, described by Martin Marty as "a diffusion of religion into the larger culture."

9. Basic beliefs remain intact. Even those who are not church members are surprisingly orthodox in their Christian beliefs.

10. A growing gap between believing and belonging to a church. In many cases, churches seem unprepared to answer spiritual needs.[9]

FAITH, LOYALTY, AND CONGREGATIONAL LIFE

Some specific information regarding religious education conditions and trends could help one see the urgency of strengthening education in the churches. Search Institute issued a publication in 1990 entitled *Effective Christian Education: A National Study of Protestant Congregations—A Summary Report on Faith, Loyalty, and Congregational Life*. Peter L. Benson and Carolyn H. Elkin led in the three-and-one-half year study that commenced in 1987, and in producing the report, with participation of six major Protestant denominations and sponsorship of the Lilly Endowment.

Five denominations representing about 85 percent of the membership in what is commonly called "mainline Protestantism" were involved in the study—the Christian Church (Disciples of Christ), the Evangelical Lutheran Church in America, the Presbyterian Church (U.S.A.), the United

Church of Christ, and the United Methodist Church. The Southern Baptist Convention was invited by the five original partners to join the project. More than 11,000 individuals in 561 randomly chosen congregations provided in-depth, survey-based data on faith, loyalty, religious biography, congregational life, and the dynamics of Christian education programming. Teams of trained observers visited fifty-two congregations judged to have strengths in promoting faith.

The study focused primarily on formal Christian education, defined as the programs and events a congregation intentionally offers to teach the faith to children, teenagers, and adults. This included Sunday school, church school, Bible studies, confirmation, camping, retreats, workshops, youth ministry and youth groups, children's and adult choirs, auxiliaries for men and women, prayer groups, religious plays and dramas, Vacation Bible School, new member classes, and intergenerational or family events and programs.

A major assumption of the study was that the primary aim of congregational life is to nurture among children, youth, and adults a vibrant, life-changing faith of the kind that shapes one's way of being, thinking, and acting. The researchers attempted, secondarily, to understand the role of congregational life in promoting loyalty to one's congregation and denomination. One of the most important findings in this study is that congregations effective in promoting faith maturity reap the benefit of greater loyalty.

KEY CONSTRUCTS

Four key constructs were employed in this study:

- Maturity of faith—The degree to which people exhibit a vibrant, life-transforming faith marked by both a deep, personal relationship to a loving God and a consistent devotion to serving others.

- Growth in maturity of faith—The degree to which people report that their faith has grown in the last two or three years.

- Denominational loyalty—The degree to which people are committed to their denomination.

- Congregational loyalty—The degree to which people are committed to their congregation.

In addition to the report title listed above, there were published reports for the individual denominations that participated in the study. These reports are available from Search Institute, 122 West Franklin Avenue, Minneapolis, Minnesota 55404, phone (612) 870-9511. The report documents eighteen major conclusions, organized below into four major sections:

FAITH AND LOYALTY AMONG ADULTS

Major Conclusions

1. Only a minority of Protestant adults evidence the kind of integrated, vibrant, and life-encompassing faith congregations seek to develop. For most adults, faith is underdeveloped, lacking some of the key elements necessary for faith maturity.

2. Maturity of faith is strongly linked to age, increasing with each successive decade, and is most likely to be found among those over 70.

3. In every age group from the 30s on, women exhibit greater faith maturity than men.

4. While most adults report strong loyalty to their congregation and denomination, loyalty is less evident among those in the 20–39 and 40–59 age ranges than among those 60 or older.

Faith and Loyalty among Youth

5. A majority of adolescents fall into the faith type called "undeveloped faith." Faith is least well formed among 9th and 10th grade boys.

6. Less than two-thirds of adolescents express high denominational or congregational loyalty.

7. In each of the six denominations, a majority of adolescents evidence one or more at-risk indicators (e.g., chemical use, depression). Most youth report that congregations place little emphasis on chemical or sexuality education.

The Power of Christian Education

8. In examining the religious biographies of youth, the two experiences most associated with higher faith maturity are the level of family religiousness and the amount of exposure to Christian education.

9. In examining the religious biographies of adults, one of the two lifetime experiences most associated with higher faith maturity is the amount of exposure to Christian education.

10. Regarding the impact of congregational life on faith maturity, the congregational factor most associated with helping people grow in faith maturity is the degree of effectiveness in Christian education programming. This finding is true for both youth and adults.

11. Effectiveness in Christian education is also associated with greater denominational and congregational loyalty. This finding is true for both youth and adults.

12. Effective Christian education is as important for the faith development of adults as it is for youth.

13. Only about three out of ten mainline Protestant high school students (grades 10–12) and adults are actively involved in Christian

education. This finding, along with evidence of common biographical deficits in religious socialization, helps to explain the lack of faith maturity commonly found among adults and adolescents.

The Nature of Christian Education Effectiveness

14. Effective education for youth requires particular kinds of process, content, leadership, and administrative functions.

15. Many of these effectiveness factors for youth are lacking in a large percentage of congregations.

16. As is the case for youth, effective education for adults requires a range of definable processes, content, and administrative ingredients.

17. Many of these effectiveness factors for adults are lacking in a large percentage of congregations.

18. The more a congregation embodies these Christian education factors, the greater the growth in faith by youth and adults, and the greater the loyalty to congregation and denomination.

FACTORS OF EDUCATION EFFECTIVENESS

The Search Institute study reported these characteristics as positively associated with growth in mature faith for those who participate in Christian education activities, especially as pertains to adults and to youth:

Teachers

- High in mature faith
- Care about students (especially applicable to youth)
- Know educational theory and methods for the age group

Pastor

- Highly committed to educational program for age group
- Devotes significant hours to age-group program
- Knows educational theory and practice for education of age group

Educational process

- Emphasizes building understanding of faith applied to political and social issues and understanding of oppression and injustice (especially applicable to adults)
- Emphasizes intergenerational contact (especially applicable to youth)
- Emphasizes life experiences as occasion for spiritual insights
- Creates sense of community in which people help each other develop faith and values
- Emphasizes the natural unfolding of faith and recognizes each person's faith journey as unique

- Strongly encourages independent thinking and questioning
- Effectively helps youth to apply faith to daily decisions

Educational content

- Emphasizes biblical knowledge (and understanding, for adults)
- Emphasizes moral values and moral decision making
- Emphasizes multicultural awareness (especially for adults)
- Emphasizes global awareness and understanding (for adults)
- Emphasizes education about human sexuality (youth)
- Emphasizes education about chemicals (alcohol and other drugs, especially for youth)
- Emphasizes involvement in service projects (youth)
- Emphasizes responsibility for poverty and hunger (youth)
- Effectively teaches core theological concepts (youth)
- Effectively teaches how to make friends or be a good friend (youth)
- Effectively helps youth develop concern for other people

Peer Involvement

- Has high percentage of peers active in Christian education

Goals

- Has clear mission statement for education of the age group
- Has clear learning objectives

Church leaders might take note of the findings of this national study. Over time they might be able to enhance their Christian education ministries.[10]

AN APPROACH TO THE FUTURE

There is no turning back. Golden ages in the past tense usually are but illusions. Some who yearn for such either didn't "read" the past accurately, or they have poor memories. While no one can know all about the future with certainty, each person has a measure of that godlike capacity to anticipate a future and to think somewhat rationally about it.

There is a consensus, according to Lindaman, about the way a futurist approaches the future:

- The futurist makes explicit the assumptions others hold about the future. This equips society to connect the present with the future.
- The futurist examines human life and the world in general in the light of apparent trends and probable outcomes.

- The futurist looks beyond the trends and probable outcomes to imagine other possibilities, from which choices are made that determine our directions.[11] Leaders of a church's educational ministry must make this kind of approach in response to world conditions and trends.

Planning groups of the Southern Baptist Convention have taken a similar approach to the future. About once each decade during this half-century, they have identified challenges and opportunities that press on the churches. These should be of interest not only to Southern Baptists, but also to those of other denominations. The following sixteen areas have been noted on the list in almost every decade.

1. Family life—dealing with deteriorating marriages and changing families.

2. Mission involvement—a rising interest in missions and in presenting the gospel to every person on earth.

3. Leadership development—preparing and involving lay people in discipleship and leadership. The work force must be multiplied, taught, and trained.

4. Bible learning—taking advantage of the widespread interest in Bible study. This is an essential focal area if there is to be advance in reaching a world for Christ. Widespread interest and participation in Bible study have preceded almost every major advance of Christianity in history.

5. Church fellowship—preparing a caring fellowship that recognizes and develops the need for relations between people drawn to one another in Christ. It is the vital base from which evangelism and Christian discipline must spring.

6. Aggressive evangelism—witnessing to the unreached masses.

7. Efficient communications—using modern technological means to communicate the gospel. As the communications revolution sweeps the world, Christians must use all media capabilities to "make known the manifold wisdom of God."

8. Urban life—reaching the great cities with the gospel of Christ. The masses crowding into urban centers must receive the good news of forgiveness and salvation.

9. Human suffering—motivating Christians to help meet the world problems of human hunger and human rights.

10. Personal adjustment—helping people whose roles in life are changing to find personal fulfillment in their new circumstances. In view of the changepace and the often-resultant stress individuals experience, churches must respond by helping people to adjust.

11. Community life—ministering to the spiritual and moral needs of the community. The almost unbridled sense of individual rights over those of the community threatens the entire value system. Churches must help attain the essential and fragile balance between the individual and the society in the area of norms and values.

12. Christian morality—influencing society with Christian moral values. The Christian esteem for people, along with other values, has been the foundation of Western civilization. People are more than animals and need to behave on a higher plane than animals. Churches must help to identify and clarify moral values and use appropriate means to influence society in right directions.

13. Positive leadership—meeting the waves of social, economic, and political crises that threaten the stability of society. Churches must encourage Christians and others to give calm and resolute leadership when all about them seems to be in disarray.

14. Problem-solving—reconciling the mammoth discontinuities and conflicts that exist in society on a worldwide scale.

15. Cross-cultural expansion—establishing new congregations in ethnic and cross-cultural communities. Churches must take a new look at their mission obligations in America in view of the growing pluralism of the nation.

16. Women-power—finding new and creative ways for women to serve, especially in the ministries of churches.

The implications of these sixteen areas of challenge and opportunity for churches are numerous. The life and character of a local church is likely to change greatly. The organization of time and people to implement the life and work of the churches must be carefully examined and probably adjusted. Churches must give more effective help to the homes as they upgrade the responses of the homes for the spiritual formation of family members. Churches must find ways to strengthen their efforts in evangelism, increasing quality and volume of effort.

There appears to many to be a revival of religion in America. No doubt there are some good signs, as even some futurists declare.

Some churches are experimenting with varieties of worship styles, with early conclusions reporting successes. Most dramatic changes in worship involve the use of music thought to be more attractive to those born since 1955. Some churches are offering multiple worship services for "multiple congregations" featuring completely different styles, particularly in music, usually with one service featuring "contemporary Christian music with a beat," choruses, and praise songs while the other service is more "traditional," including hymns and anthems, often with much older dates of publication. Leaders in any such strategy must take care to avoid dividing the membership. Some feel the risks are offset by the attraction of larger numbers and varieties of participants.

Many congregations unable to offer more than one service might try to strike a balance of the "old" and the "new," and try to lead all members to be considerate of the needs and of the company of others. Potentially divisive practices of any kind in the church must be counterbalanced, if indeed they are practiced at all.

The members of a fellowship must become more engaged in the full scope of the life and ministries of a church. There are not and could never be enough vocational ministers to do all the work of a church. It would not be right for them to do it all, even if it were possible. Being a follower of Jesus Christ and sharing with him and with others in the redemptive enterprise are the responsibility and privilege of every believer.[12]

CONCLUSION

World conditions and trends clearly demand education. Leaders in a church must know something of the conditions and trends affecting the lives of people, both at home and around the world.

Religious education will play an essential role in any church that looks to the future to meet its challenges and opportunities. The people of God cannot do less than depend on God and give him their best effort. Jesus said, "We must work the works of him who sent me, while it is day; night comes, when no one can work" (John 9:4).

CONCERNS FOR FURTHER STUDY

Consider these questions as you continue to reflect on the idea that world conditions and trends demand education:

1. Think of the change that has had the most impact on your own life in the areas of (1) technology, (2) economics, (3) society, (4) politics, and (5) education. How have these changes affected your life?

2. What change in the area of religion has influenced you the most?

3. How would you describe the appropriate response of the educational ministry of a church to the challenges and opportunities presented in the decade ahead by world conditions and trends, and by trends in religious education?

PART TWO

BASIC COMPONENTS

There are many things a church might do; there are some things a church must do. One of the imperatives a church must do is to educate. Biblical precedent commands it. History affirms it. People need it. A church's nature and mission require it. World conditions and trends demand it.

There are also many things a church might do to educate. There are some things a church must do. Certain basics seem imperative in almost all churches. There are essential parts that make up the educational ministry of a church.

Education touches all that a church attempts to do as it moves toward fulfilling its mission. The model proposed for what a church should perform is set forth in this book in terms of certain tasks that "belong" to a church, but that can be structured into programs of ministry for assignment to responsible leaders. The intent is for these tasks to be "programmed" in relationship with other ministries, in order to be most effective. The church itself is the "basic unit" in planning and implementing the tasks through its ministry organizations.

A church task defines a basic continuing activity performed by a church to carry out its functions in accomplishing its mission. The tasks in this model are clustered into three kinds of ministry structures: base ministries, emphasis ministries, and service ministries.

A base ministry encompasses the work in a cluster of tasks that are basic, continuing, and of primary importance to the total work of a church. It has significant organization and seeks to involve the total church in its work in regularly scheduled, ongoing activity, as well as in short-term projects. It maintains a membership roll. It coordinates its plans with those

---

of emphasis and service ministries through the church-wide planning/co-ordinating group—the Church Ministry Leadership Team (called the Church Council in many churches).

BASE MINISTRIES

Six base ministries are presented in the model in this book. These are the recommended base ministries and their tasks:

CHURCH LEADERSHIP MINISTRY

1. Guide the church.
2. Proclaim the gospel.
3. Lead the worship.
4. Equip believers.
5. Care for people.
6. Undergird the work of the church and the denomination. (All base ministries have this "channeling" task.)

BIBLE TEACHING MINISTRY

1. Reach people for Bible study.
2. Teach the Bible.
3. Witness to people about Christ and lead people into church membership.
4. Minister to people in need.
5. Lead members to worship.
6. Support the work of the church and the denomination. (All base ministries have this "channeling" task).

DISCIPLESHIP TRAINING MINISTRY

1. Reach people for discipleship training.
2. Orient new church members for responsible church membership.
3. Equip church members for discipleship and personal ministry.
4. Teach Christian theology and Baptist doctrine, Christian ethics, Christian history and Baptist heritage, and church polity and organization.
5. Train church leaders for ministry.
6. Undergird the work of the church and the denomination. (All base ministries have this "channeling" task).

MINISTRY OF MISSIONS—WOMAN'S MISSIONARY UNION

1. Pray for and give to missions.
2. Do missions.
3. Learn about missions.
4. Develop spiritually toward a missions lifestyle.
5. Participate in the work of the church and the denomination. (All base ministries have this "channeling" task.)

MINISTRY OF MISSIONS—BROTHERHOOD

1. Engage members in mission activities.
2. Teach missions.
3. Pray for and give to missions.
4. Develop personal ministry.
5. Undergird the work of the church and the denomination. (All base ministries have this "channeling" task.)

MUSIC MINISTRY

1. Provide musical experiences in congregational services.
2. Provide church music education.
3. Lead the church to witness and minister through music.
4. Assist church programs in providing training in music skills and in consultation about music equipment.
5. Undergird the work of the church and the denomination. (All base ministries have this "channeling" task.)

EMPHASIS MINISTRIES

An Emphasis Ministry encompasses a task or cluster of tasks that deal with one or more continuing concerns of major importance in achieving a church's mission, but which need to permeate all church ministries as appropriate for their tasks. Because of its nature and importance, an emphasis ministry depends heavily on other ministry structures, especially base ministries, to provide education and information about emphasis concerns through their ongoing ministry groups, regular meetings (including congregational services), and other channels of information. An emphasis ministry has church-elected leaders as appropriate. It generally does not maintain an ongoing enrollment as base ministries do. However, the church may choose to approve emphasis project groups or continuing special interest groups relating to emphasis concerns. Emphasis ministry plans involving other ministries are coordinated with the plans of other

ministries through the churchwide planning/coordinating group—the
Church Ministry Leadership Team (e.g., the Church Council).

These are six recommended emphasis ministries and their tasks:

FAMILY MINISTRY

Minister to the distinctive needs of couples, parents and their children,
senior adults, and single adults.

STEWARDSHIP MINISTRY

1. Develop Christian stewards.
2. Involve the church in supporting Cooperative Program ministries.

EVANGELISM MINISTRY

1. Engage the church in evangelism by developing a comprehensive
   church strategy of evangelism.
2. Involve church members in personal evangelism.
3. Reach people for Christ through special events and mass evangelism.

MISSIONS DEVELOPMENT MINISTRY

1. Identify missions needs/opportunities.
2. Develop missions strategies to respond to unmet missions needs.
3. Establish new churches.
4. Support establishing and strengthening of Woman's Missionary
   Union and Brotherhood.

VOCATIONAL GUIDANCE MINISTRY

Educate in Christian vocation and guide people in church occupation
choice and adjustment.

STUDENT MINISTRY

1. Witness to people about Christ.
2. Lead students into responsible church membership.
3. Develop ministries to people.
4. Guide students in making life decisions.
5. Involve students in study of the Bible and Christian faith.
6. Involve students in missions.
7. Lead students to worship.
8. Build Christian fellowship.
9. Involve students in world issues and social action.

SERVICE MINISTRIES

There are three recommended Service Ministries in our model church, with these tasks:

MEDIA LIBRARY MINISTRY

1. Provide media and media library services.

2. Promote the use of media and media library services.

3. Train people in media skills.

RECREATION MINISTRY

Provide recreation methods, materials, services, and experiences that will enrich the lives of people and support the total mission of the church.

ADMINISTRATIVE MINISTRY

Assist the church to plan its ministries, manage its resources, and govern its life and work.

Ministry leaders and their staffs continue to refine and revise the statements of tasks by that they work to assist churches. Refinements and revisions of tasks should be and are under continuing scrutiny in the effort to increase the effectiveness of ministry and support to and through churches. The specific statements of tasks presented herein are presently processed through the Inter-Agency Council of the Southern Baptist Convention. Changes that are approved are then inserted into a working notebook called *The Church Base Design*. At each agency of the Southern Baptist Convention which relates to the base design of a church there should be one or more updated copies of this notebook at all times. People desiring to keep current regarding these task statements might refer to one of these agencies, such as the Baptist Sunday School Board.

AN OVERVIEW OF PART 2

We have stated the assumption that the Bible is the basic book for the educational ministry of a church. A church must begin and continue a ministry of Bible teaching and learning. For those who rely on the authority of the Bible as the primary guide in matters of faith and practice, such a ministry is not optional. It is the foundational dimension of the educational ministry. While all the other dimensions of a church's educational ministry might also engage in some Bible teaching and learning, a church needs a ministry in which Bible teaching and learning are the dominant features. That is the theme of chapter 6, "Ministry of Bible Teaching and Learning."

Training is a vital dimension of education that focuses on a rather specific kind of educating. Narrowly defined, it means "teaching to make one

fitted and proficient." A church needs to engage in such a ministry of training disciples. Chapter 7 sets forth basic concepts of this ministry of discipleship training.

A church must extend beyond itself if it is to fulfill its mission as a
church. There are certain understandings and skills Christians need to develop regarding missions. A church must pray for and give to missions. Its
members must do missions. They must teach and learn about missions.
They need to develop spiritually toward a missions lifestyle. They should
develop personal ministry. Chapter 8 describes a church ministry of missions education and action.

The Christian faith is a singing faith. Music is a basic part of Christian
worship. Increasingly, it is also an effective educational method. Too often
in churches the ministry of music is left to "musicians." But music, like
other means of praise and education, is too important to be left to the
"pros." A church needs to provide suitable musical experiences in congregational services. It needs to provide church music education. The church
needs to witness and minister through music. A church needs to provide
training in music skills and in consultation about music equipment. This is
the emphasis of chapter 9, "Ministry of Music."

There are other ministries that are essential to a comprehensive plan of
education in a church. Prominent among these ministries of enrichment
and support are the work of the media library, recreation, and administrative ministries. These service ministries support a church in achieving its
mission. They enrich the entire effort of a church by making its ministries
more effective, more meaningful, and more educational. Vital to a
church's educational ministry is its ministry to the distinctive needs of
couples, parents and their children, senior adults, and single adults. A
church has a responsibility to minister to the needs of families at all stages
of development.

Stewardship, evangelism, missions development, vocational guidance,
and student ministry are other emphases which merit our concern. Chapter
10 contains a brief presentation of some of these ministries of enrichment
and support.

The objective of Part 2 is to help people to identify and understand the
importance of the basic components of the educational ministry of a
church.

CHAPTER 6

Ministry of Bible Teaching and Learning

The ministry of Bible teaching and learning is the first of the basic components of the educational ministry of a church. The Bible is the source of multitudes of truths that make up the essential subject matter of religious education. Many other subjects relate to a "complete" religious education, but the Bible is the core subject.

Few, if any, have ever mastered the contents of the Bible. Many have memorized great portions of it. Some have learned many of its truths. All fail at some point to live by its teachings. Yet it remains the chief guidebook, setting forth models for faith and life for children of God. A church must begin and continue a ministry of Bible teaching and learning. This chapter will indicate why and how such a ministry might be performed.

THE BIBLE IS THE FOUNDATION

Education that is Christian must first be education in the Scriptures. The Bible is the unique and foundational text for the educational ministry of a church. James D. Smart wrote:

> God's chosen way of coming to us is through a Word, a word that sounded in the ears of the prophets and psalmists, in the fullness of time was incarnate in Jesus Christ, was heard and spoken by the apostles, and of which the record is preserved for us in the Scriptures. Through that record, the Word that was once heard and spoken sounds ever anew into the life of the world. The revelation of God in the Scriptures is unique; it is not one among many revelations of God which are to be set in line with each other and weighed and compared. God speaks to man through the Scriptures a word of judgment and mercy which, if it is not heard in this place, is not heard at all. Where else in all the ages of human experience is God made known as the Father Almighty, Creator of the heavens and the earth, as man's Lord and Redeemer, taking up our humanity into his divinity, and as God's own spirit, claiming the inmost self

of every man as his dwelling place. Close the Scriptures, and that God, who
alone is the God of Christians, is unknown. And where he is unknown, the life
that he alone gives to men through faith in him is unknown.[1]

James Marion Frost, whose concern for Bible teaching and learning
among Southern Baptists led to the founding of the Baptist Sunday School
Board in 1891, had a strong sense of the priority of Bible teaching through
the Sunday School. He said: "The work of the Sunday School is threefold:
First, teach the Scriptures; second, teach the Scriptures; third, teach the
Scriptures."[2]

AFFIRMING THE BIBLE

Southern Baptists are among those who have maintained a high interest
in the Bible. They affirmed in Convention sessions and in other ways:

> The Holy Bible was written by men divinely inspired and is the record of
> God's revelation of Himself to man. It is a perfect treasure of divine instruc-
> tion. It has God for its author, salvation for its end, and truth, without any mix-
> ture of error, for its matter. It reveals the principles by which God judges us;
> and therefore is, and will remain to the end of the world, the true center of
> Christian union, and the supreme standard by which all human conduct,
> creeds, and religious opinions should be tried. The criterion by which the
> Bible is to be interpreted is Jesus Christ.[3]

The Bible continues to be of unmatched interest in a church's educational ministry. Why should people be so drawn to Bible teaching and
learning? In their chapter "The Bible in the Curriculum," Colson and Rigdon indicate several good reasons.[4] They declare the Bible to be (1) the
record of God's self-revelation; (2) the repository of God's redemptive
message for the world; (3) inspired by God; (4) providentially preserved;
(5) God's gift to his church; (6) the only authoritative guide for Christian
life and work; and (7) the indispensable book that brings people to Christ.
They continue by showing the strengths of the Bible as based on its relevance to the needs of humanity, its authority based on the fact that it came
from God, and its power in individual lives and in society. They conclude
with guidance about using the Bible with integrity, how to interpret the
Bible, and how to use the Bible with children.

INTERPRETING THE BIBLE

Before we move into the suggestions about structures and curriculum,
it seems worthwhile to call attention to some principles of biblical interpretation (hermeneutics) that should be observed by those in a church who
lead in the ministry of Bible teaching and learning. Again, we have drawn
heavily from the form and order of expression presented by Colson and
Rigdon.[5]

1. Each individual has the right to come to the Bible for himself or herself. He might benefit by the efforts of others, but under God he must do his own thinking.

2. The student must attempt to discover what the text says, exactly. It is essential to understand what the passage meant to the people to whom it was first addressed, and then to interpret what God is saying through it to us now.

3. Consider whether the passage is to be taken literally or figuratively. To mistake either for the other might be misleading.

4. Try to determine whether the passage presents a permanent and universal truth or one that is only local and temporary. The dietary laws of the Mosaic code are examples of the temporary.

5. When dealing with narrative portions, the interpreter must recognize that beyond the event lies the witness of believers to the meaning of the event. The Exodus was not just a migratory trip; it was an act of God that demonstrated his steadfast love and his redeeming grace.

6. In long or short passages, look for the central message. Without this principle, one could study passages such as the parables and miss the main point.

7. Interpret Scripture by means of Scripture. Understand difficult or obscure passages when possible in the light of passages that are clear. In any case, a passage should be interpreted in the light of the Bible's message as a whole.

8. Examine the findings of the best biblical scholars, ancient and modern. This can keep a student from going too far afield from the consensus of Christian thought.

9. Recognize that Jesus Christ is the Lord of the Scriptures. An interpretation that disagrees with His teaching cannot be right.

THE BIBLE AND EDUCATIONAL MINISTRY

The Bible is the foundation of a church's educational ministry. There are at least three ways a church's educational ministry should be examined by the Scriptures to determine the validity and the rightness of the plans.

1. Determine whether the Bible explicitly calls for or supports the matter under consideration. For example, it seems clear that the admonition to "make disciples of all nations. . . . teaching them to observe all that I have commanded you" (Matt. 28:19–20) presents a permanent and universal truth to be obeyed by the faithful.

2. Determine whether the Bible forbids the matter under consideration. If so, do not proceed to do it. For example, James 2 is clear in its teaching against showing partiality.

3. If the Bible seems not to speak either for or against a matter, deter-
    mine if it is compatible with other biblical teachings. Many of the
    methods available to Christians today in the work of ministry were
    not known to those who were God's instruments in producing the
    Scriptures. If these ideas do not violate the spirit of the Scriptures and
    if they are useful, there should be no hesitancy to use them. There are
    many things that are neither advocated nor prohibited in the Bible,
    but that seem compatible with its spirit to use—church buildings,
    electricity, visual aids, air conditioning, lesson helps, and many other
    things.

The Bible is the foundation, not only in that it is the principal text, but
also in that it is the standard by which all of a church's educational ministry should be appraised. Ignorance of the Bible is a bane to the church and
to the world. Knowledge and practice of it are a blessing to all. Teaching
and learning the Bible must be the first concerns of a church's educational
ministries. We shall look now at some structures for a church to use as it
engages in a ministry of Bible teaching and learning.

STRUCTURES FOR BIBLE TEACHING AND LEARNING

There are many ways a church might plan for Bible teaching and learning. One of the ways that is most obvious is through increased use of the
sermon for teaching the Bible and its doctrines. In the 1980s the authors of
A Church on Mission forecast a trend in this direction for the church.[6] Certainly preaching must be strongly infused with the Bible if it is to be effective. Our purpose here, however, is to focus on the intentional teaching and
learning a church might engage in beyond the pulpit.

USE THE SUNDAY SCHOOL

The most important structure for many churches of many denominations for Bible teaching and learning is the Sunday school. This remains
true even in the face of serious problems that some denominations have experienced in recent years with Sunday school. Overall enrollments in
American Sunday schools in general have dropped by 25 to 40 percent in
recent decades. Some denominations that once strongly supported their
Sunday schools have suffered the greatest losses—Methodist, Presbyterian, and Episcopal. Some experts feel that the Sunday school is in a struggle
for its very existence. This probably has always been true.

The Sunday schools of America remain the largest single voluntary enterprise in the nation. Some denominations and some congregations within
other denominations are not only holding their own in Sunday school but
are improving and growing in participation and in effectiveness. It is estimated that up to ninety percent of the new church members in non-

Catholic churches have come from the work of Sunday schools. Among the Southern Baptists, whose Sunday schools continue to grow, there is a historical ratio of one in three people enrolled in Sunday school becoming a Christian and church member. The ratio of those who profess faith and join the church without coming via the Sunday school has been approximately one in two hundred forty. Sunday school outreach is a major strategy of Southern Baptists and accounts for a large measure of their growth. They have learned some important concepts about growing churches through growing Sunday schools. Chapter 14 includes information about some of these concepts. Some of these concepts of growth also apply to other church ministry structures.

A church has many basic, continuing activities of primary importance that it must perform to carry out its functions and to accomplish its mission. If a church had no ministry organizations within its body to carry out these tasks, the church would still need to find some way to do them, because the tasks belong to the nature of the church itself. Certain tasks of a church, as it performs its educational ministry, can best be implemented through the Sunday school.

Tasks of the Sunday School. Six tasks define the continuing activities a church performs to carry out its functions in accomplishing its mission.

The first task of a Sunday school is to *reach people for Bible study.* This means that the Sunday school begins by getting as many people as possible engaged in Bible study. It often is easier to get people to take part in a Bible study group fostered by a Sunday school than it is to get them into the church for worship. There are many non-Christians, many unchurched Christians, many church members themselves (nonresident or inactive regarding church), and many children of these who are not being reached for Bible study on any regular basis. The first business of those who work in the Sunday school is to reach out to these.

The teacher, more than anyone else, has the responsibility to provide pupils to teach in Sunday school. Teachers, if people are to be reached as they must, have to accept responsibility for enlisting their own classes, along with help from others. (In chapter 14 we shall describe ways that organizations in a church might be organized for growth.) People must be reached in order to be taught, and a Sunday school, properly designed to include people of all ages and conditions, is in the best position to accomplish the church's task of reaching people for Bible study.

The second task of a Sunday School is to *teach the Bible.* Here the emphasis is to engage people in the study of the biblical revelation in Scriptures and in the application of its meaning for all of life. The Bible is the text. Other lesson materials might be used with profit in learning and in teaching, but it is the Bible and its truths that must be taught.

This teaching is with the hope and purpose that those who have not yet received Christ will, as appropriate in their own readiness under the leadership of the Holy Spirit, receive him for the forgiveness of sin and salvation. Too, the hope and purpose for those who are already Christians is that they will follow the leadership of the Holy Spirit and respond to God with maturing faith, love, and obedience. Believers and nonbelievers are taught together in their classes. Most of the Bible teaching and learning sponsored by Sunday school takes place in church buildings on Sunday morning. (We shall mention later other approaches that have come into use in recent years.)

The third task of a Sunday School is to *witness to people about Christ and lead them into church membership.* This means that members of a Sunday school who are Christians will join with those who are leaders in sharing the faith with other members and potential members who have not yet received Christ. They will try to lead them to receive Christ and to join the fellowship of a church. Faithful performance of this task is one of several evidences of effectiveness in teaching. At the same time this task is being performed, others are to be brought into Bible study who are in need of Christ and the church.

The fourth task of a Sunday School is to *minister to people in need.* Sunday school leaders and members are in a unique position to help one another and others in the church and community. This is not only a vital service itself, but gives essential validity to the real learning that is taking place in the Bible study. It is putting into practice the teachings of the Bible. The authors of *A Church on Mission* write: "It means every Sunday School member should be encouraged to meet the needs of other people in the spirit of Christ. This may take the form of personal service, concrete acts of caring expressed in material support, encouraging words, affirmation, or simply taking the time to listen. This task is at the heart of a loving, caring fellowship."[7]

This continues to be the posture for the best Sunday schools. In many churches, the close relationships that develop in the relatively small Sunday school groupings provide the natural setting for the kinds of mutual support and help that often might not be known about or met in the larger body, the church. A Sunday school class or department often is a church's "front line" of pastoral ministry in situations of need among members and nonmembers.

The fifth task of a Sunday School is to *lead members to worship.* Worship is the foundational function of a church. The Sunday school should regularly interpret the biblical teachings on worship and provide materials for use in personal worship. In many churches the Sunday school is the best organization through which to distribute materials to motivate individuals and families to worship and to guide them in doing it. Too, the Sunday school usually meets in conjunction with the morning worship services of a church. This gives leaders and members in the Sunday school good opportunities to encourage participation in the church worship service. In addition, there should be regular occasions in Sunday school, and in outside activities that it might sponsor, to provide opportunities for worship experiences. No other organization is in as good a position to implement this important task as is the Sunday school. Worship is another of the normal results of good Bible teaching and learning.

The sixth task of a Sunday school is to *support the work of the church and the denomination.* This means that the Sunday school should be available as appropriate to present the goals, plans, and activities of the church and the denomination, and to explain their significance. It also means that the Sunday School cooperatively supports the work of the other church ministries and those of the denomination. Each basic church organization shares this task. They are not organizations apart. They are parts of a church that is part of a denomination.

Harry Piland, national leader of Sunday school work among Southern Baptists until 1994, wrote: "The Sunday School has more members than any other program organization. It has more leaders and prospects than any other. It has the organization and structure through which to do its work and much of the work of the church. Therefore, it is logical that it should interpret, support, and undergird all of the work of the church and denomination."[8] However, no church ministry organization should be so regularly or so completely co-opted for interpreting or promoting the work of groups other than itself that its own work is neglected. The information or support that might be presented or called for in an organization should be essential, compatible with the interpreting organization, and in keeping with the age, maturity, and need of the recipients. For example, a church budget subscription plan would not be appropriate for presentation to younger preschool children in the Sunday school.

Special projects of Bible teaching and learning. Among the important elements of a comprehensive ministry of Bible teaching and learning are special projects. Several short-term projects are usually extensions of a Sunday school. They can render valuable service in Bible teaching and learning. Some of the projects, by virtue of the nature of the opportunities they present, are engaged in tasks not only of the Sunday school, but also of other ministry organizations of the church. Some of these special projects perform other tasks like these: (1) lead the church to witness and minister through music; (2) equip church members for discipleship and personal ministry; (3) teach Christian theology and Baptist doctrine, Christian ethics, Christian history and Baptist heritage, and church polity and organization; and (4) teach missions and engage in missions.[9]

Major projects that relate to this facet of the Bible teaching and learning ministry are a church Vacation Bible School, which is usually designed along lines of the Sunday school; a mission Vacation Bible School, usually designed for people who do not attend a Sunday school; and Backyard Bible Clubs, which are small Bible schools usually designed for children ages six through eleven, and conducted in yards, carports, patios, or open areas in a community. Other projects and Bible teaching and learning opportunities will be identified later in this chapter.

Organization for Sunday School. A well-organized Sunday school most often makes the largest impact for Bible teaching and learning. Effective operation requires appropriate organization. There is no suitable alternative to good organization if the Sunday school is to perform its tasks. It is impossible to function at near maximum potential in the present or to anticipate reasonable growth without proper organization.

Even the smallest Sunday school needs to be organized to function and to grow. Larger Sunday schools need more organization than smaller ones. It is imperative to distribute the work load through the organization, to place responsibility where it belongs, to avoid confusion, and to minimize or eliminate unnecessary duplication of work. An effective Sunday school is an organized Sunday school in which leaders use the organization to accomplish the tasks of the Sunday school.

Sunday school members, prospective members, and leaders need to be organized. With reference to members and prospective members, it is the members who are organized; the prospective members are "allowed for" in the design of the organization. Otherwise, growth that includes prospective members is not likely to occur. Leaders also need to be organized so they can work together more effectively in planning, conducting, and evaluating the Sunday school.

Figure 2[10] describes the "Sunday School Grouping–Grading Plan." Updated versions of this plan may be found in each year's version of the *Sunday School Plan Book*, published by Convention Press. This plan for organizing and grouping people for Bible teaching and learning in a Sunday school is based on age grading. There are other principles on which to grade people for Sunday school purposes, but none serves as well in almost all instances as does the principle of organizing by age. By using the age basis, teaching can be geared more easily to meet pupil needs. Further, age grading helps to place responsibility for outreach where it belongs— with leaders and members of the group where the prospective member would belong on being enrolled. Neither compatibility, intelligence, achievement, nor even common interest unrelated to the life stage of the learners comes close to being as advantageous as the age principle for organizing a Sunday school.

Notice in Figure 2 the brackets that designate the groupings. Consider the situation of a small Sunday school. Reading column 1 (vertically), it is suggested that there be at least four groupings: a division each for

Figure 2: Sunday School Grouping–Grading Plan[a]

Division Titles	Divisional Grouping Patterns			
	I.	II.	III.	IV.
Preschool Division	Birth–1 1 2 3 4• 5•	B–1 1 2 3 4 5	B–1 1 2 3 4 5	B–1 1 2 3 4 5
Children's Division	6 (Grade 1) 7 (Grade 2) 8 (Grade 3) 9 (Grade 4) 10 (Grade 5) 11 (Grade 6)	6 7 8 9 10 11	6 7 8 9 10 11	6 7 8 9 10 11
Youth Division	12 (Grade 7) 13 (Grade 8) 14 (Grade 9) 15 (Grade 10) 16 (Grade 11) 17 (Grade 12)	12 13 14 15 16 17	12 13 14 15 16 17	12 13 14 15 16 17
Adult Division	18 (high school graduation and up 34 Adult 65	18 (or high school gradu-ation) Young Adult 34 35–64 (or retirement) Adult 65 Senior Adult	18 (or high school graduation 1 Young Adult 2 34 35 1 Adult 2 64 (or retirement) 65 (or retirement) 1 Senior Adult 2	18 (or high school gradu-ation 1 Young Adult 2 3 4 34 35 1 2 Adult 3 4 64 (or retirement) 65 (or retirement) 1 2 Senior Adult 3 4

a. The size of your Sunday School is a factor in your use of the four patterns shown. The smallest Sunday School would begin to use column one with all members of one age group in one unit. The Sunday School next in size would probably use pattern two with one age group divided into two units. (Example: In pattern two, children would be in two units instead of one because of the number enrolled.) Larger Sunday Schools would select the pattern for each age group that provides for the enrollment.

preschoolers, for children, for youth, and for adults. In the Preschool Division there is a department (preferably not called a class) for children ages birth through five years; in the Children's Division there is a department for children ages six through eleven (or school grades one through six); in the Youth Division there is a class for youth ages twelve through seventeen (or school grades seven through twelve); and in the Adult Division there is a class for people age eighteen (or high school graduation) and up.

Continue to think of a small Sunday school while reading the chart in figure 2 from left to right within each age division. Observe the changes in location of the brackets that designate the groupings from left to right. These brackets suggest the most appropriate subdivisions within an age division as the need arises to create more groups.

Obviously it is advantageous to reduce the age span of groupings in any age division as soon as the number of members and prospective members warrants new groups (departments or classes). In order to determine more specifically when the need for new units (departments or classes) exists— along with such matters as suggested maximum enrollments of classes and departments, recommended teacher-pupil ratios, consideration of prospective members, and other considerations—study carefully Figure 3, "Organization Planning Chart.

The chart in figure 3 also suggests separate groupings of males and females, beginning with age ten (or grade five), or at the latest with age twelve (grade seven) and continuing through the Adult Division. In recent decades many churches have grouped some of their youth and adult classes as "co-ed classes." Some of these classes have had good experiences in numerical growth and fellowship growth. However, for more individualized teaching to meet specific needs, for more effective outreach, and for supplying more class members to join the work force and serve in other groups as teachers, it is usually more effective in the adult division to follow the plan of separate classes instead of co-ed classes. Leaders in a church should study their own needs along with the best experiences of others and design the most effective organization for their situation.[11]

A special word might help those in small Sunday schools: each department in the Preschool and Children's divisions should have at least two workers. Normally one teacher per class can meet the needs in the Youth and Adult divisions.

It is critically important that a school of any size maintain a reasonably small teacher–pupil ratio. At the beginning of a new Sunday school class and annually at the beginning of a new church year, it is important to allow room for growth in each class or department, rather than to begin with a unit that already has reached its suggested maximum size according to the chart in figure 3. To allow for reaching as many prospective members as possible, leave 25 to 40 percent room for growth in each unit. For example, in an adult class in which the suggested maximum enrollment is twenty-five, begin with an enrollment of fifteen to twenty, not twenty-five or more. The number of prospective members and the attendance pattern of present members are other factors to consider when determining at what size to begin a unit. But it is important to remember that unless growth is allowed for in the organization design, it is not likely to occur.

Leaders in a Sunday school need to be organized. In a small Sunday school all teachers and other leaders might need to meet in one group on a regular basis to plan and evaluate the work of the total effort. A weekly workers meeting is recommended as the best pattern. At least a monthly meeting of the Sunday School Leadership Team (which in many churches is called the Sunday School Council) should bring together all the workers of the small Sunday school. If several work together in one department, those workers need to meet frequently as a department to plan and evaluate their work. Again, the weekly meeting pattern is far more productive than any other pattern. (More attention is given to the work of the Sunday School Leadership Team in chapter 13 of this book.)

In larger Sunday schools a weekly workers meeting is recommended also. However, the format for the meeting should allow both for general meeting time for all workers and for separate departmental meetings. In large schools the Sunday School Leadership Team in its monthly meetings probably should include only heads of departments and divisions, along with general leaders of the Sunday school.[12]

Earlier we alluded to allowing room for growth in Sunday school units at the beginning of a new church year. Normally it is healthy for a Sunday school to capitalize on the new church year to restructure the organization along recommended lines. This has been found to be the most advantageous time to begin new classes and departments (though they might be started at other times). With age as the basis of grading, this is the best time to "promote" those who should move to another age group. Sunday schools that are growing rapidly often begin new units throughout the year. Churches that use the "Growth Spiral" (see chapter 14 for more about this tool for growth) often start some new units each quarter.

Annual promotion on the basis of age, at the beginning of the new church year, has many advantages for use in Sunday school. Harry Piland, in *Basic Sunday School Work*, lists ten values of annual promotion on the age basis. He said it (1) provides for normal advancement through the natural stages of life; (2) encourages a person to adapt to changing conditions; (3) provides (for the individual) guidance and influence of a larger number of consecrated teachers; (4) creates new places of service for many class members; (5) brings fresh interest in prospects by assigning them to new workers; (6) removes the vacuum in which cliques often develop;

Figure 3

ORGANIZATION PLANNING CHART

Member Classification Age (Grade)	Enrollment M	Enrollment F	Prospects M	Prospects F	Total Possibilities M	Total Possibilities F	Suggested Maximum Enrollment	Departments Needed	Suggested Maximum Enrollment	Classes Needed	Suggested Worker / Member Ratio[2]	Approximate No. of Workers Needed
Cradle Roll							35		x	x	1/6	
Babies							9		x	x	1/3	
Ones							9		x	x	1/3	
2							12		x	x	1/4	
3							16		x	x	1/4	
4							16		x	x	1/4	
5							16		x	x	1/4	
Special Education							20		x	x	1/4	
6 (Grade 1)							30		x	x	1/6	
7 (Grade 2)							30		x	x	1/6	
8 (Grade 3)							30		x	x	1/6	
9 (Grade 4)							30		x	x	1/6	
10 (Grade 5)							30		x	x	1/6	
11 (Grade 6)							30		x	x	1/6	

Column groups: Pupil Possibilities (Enrollment, Prospects, Total Possibilities); Department; Classes; Workers.

Divisions: PRESCHOOL (Birth–1: Cradle Roll, Babies, Ones; 2; 3; 4; 5); CHILDREN (Special Education; Grades 1–6).

ORGANIZATION PLANNING CHART (Continued)

		Col 1	Col 2	Col 3	Col 4	Col 5	Col 6	Col 7	Col 8	Col 9
YOUTH	12 (Grade 7)					60		12		1/8
	13 (Grade 8)					60		12		1/8
	14 (Grade 9)					60		12		1/8
	15 (Grade 10)					60		12		1/8
	16 (Grade 11)					60		12		1/8
	17 (Grade 12)					60		12		1/8
ADULT	18–24 (College)					125		25		1/5
	18–24 (Single)					125		25		1/5
	25–34 (Married)					125		25		1/5
	25–34 (Single)					125		25		1/5
	35–44 (Married)					125		25		1/5
	35–44 (Single)					125		25		1/5
	45–64 (Married)					125		25		1/5
	45–64 (Single)					125		25		1/5
	65–up					125		25		1/5
	Weekday S. S. Classes					X		25		1/5
	Adults Away					75		5	x	1/5
	Homebound					75		5	x	1/5
	Outreach Bible Study Group	x				x		x		x
	New Sunday Schools	x				x		x		x
	Pastor/Staff/Gen. Officers	x	x	x	x	x	x	x	x	x
	Total	x	x	x	x					

a. Adult ratio in Column 9 includes care group leaders in the classes

(7) brings new friends, new relationships; (8) brings new life; (9) means a "new beginning"; (10) makes possible new growth.[13]

ENCOURAGE AND GUIDE OTHER
BIBLE TEACHING AND LEARNING

A church might consider possibilities for enabling individuals and groups to participate in Bible teaching and learning. Beyond the Sunday school and special projects directly related to Sunday school there are several approaches that might be available to a given church or individual.

Seasonal study of Bible books. A comprehensive plan should include seasonal Bible book study. There is considerable interest among church members, both those in Sunday school and others, as well as the unchurched, in opportunities to study books of the Bible in concentrated time frames. For instance, the annual Winter Bible Study conducted among Southern Baptist congregations for more than fifty years has become the largest project of its kind in that denomination. Materials are available for Bible study for all ages—a book of the Bible for adults and youths, and age-graded units or books for children and preschoolers. A change in the early 1990s has all age-groups focusing on the same Bible area in these studies. Some conduct this study in a single week, beginning on Sunday and continuing through Wednesday evening. Others schedule the sessions as appropriate to their needs, such as a series on Wednesday evenings. Often a church's pastor uses this occasion to teach the adults of the congregation. There has been a warm reception of the plan for many years.

Bible conferences. The study of Bible books or themes in Bible conferences by people of a single congregation or by groups of congregations is a viable supplementary Bible study activity. These conferences might be conducted in a church or some other convenient location.

Bible study by correspondence. Many individuals are participating with great interest in Bible study by correspondence. Several denominations have plans for guided correspondence Bible study. In this plan the individual learner follows a Bible study guide and progresses at his or her own pace. On completion of a unit of study, the individual completes a review form and returns it by mail to the people guiding the study. The correspondent receives a response to the review form and material for the next unit of study. At any given time there are hundreds of thousands of people engaged in this process worldwide.

Many courses in Bible study, as well as in many other subject fields, are available. A student may enroll for either college-level home study or for the noncredit "Basic Series" of Bible study. The noncredit series include multiple certificates students can earn, each recognizing completion of ten courses of study from a variety of subjects including the Bible. There are available diplomas in college-level series, each requiring completion of sixteen courses.

Study at extension centers. Each year thousands of pastors and other church workers continue their education in Bible study and other ministry areas in various extension centers. These centers include church members who are not in vocational ministry, as well as many people who are. A student may enroll for a single course, or he may pursue a long-range study plan. For instance, the Seminary Extension of the Southern Baptist Convention presently operates in more than three hundred such Seminary Extension centers located throughout the United States and in several foreign countries. Normally a group of churches establishes and conducts these centers. Certain of their courses might be applied to college or other levels for credit.[14]

Bible study fellowships. Numerous Bible study groups are conducted in homes of church members with encouragement, guidance, and support of churches. These groups usually meet during the week rather than on Sunday. Some meet at places other than homes. They are especially helpful in engaging non-Christians in Bible study in a setting to which many respond openly. In the informal and friendly atmosphere of a home Bible fellowship, many people receive Christ and move into the fellowship of a church.

Weekday Bible study. A church might sponsor an ongoing weekday age-graded Bible study that extends through the public school terms. In some public school systems these courses have been conducted at a church during released time from school. More often they now are conducted after school hours at church.

Other church-sponsored Bible study courses. Many churches sponsor either class studies or individual studies (or both) using special study materials, requirements, and recognition. A class or an individual alone might study a Bible survey series. Such courses might be scheduled in relation to the seasonal study of Bible books. Individuals can engage in such Bible study at their own pace.[15]

Study in new Sunday schools. Many churches offer Bible study on Sunday (using Sunday school study materials) in locations where there is no other organized Bible study. Some of these study groups are in areas where the possibilities for further growth (such as their becoming a church) are limited if not impossible. A nursing home is an example. In some instances, however, the location might be conducive to later development into a congregation. In these places, the Bible teaching and learning provide a suitable foundation on which to begin a new congregation.

Creative leaders in churches small or large will seek and find ways to involve as many people as possible in Bible teaching and learning. The near future will offer even more options. Advances in cable television and communication by satellite have great potential. Almost the entire nation could be serviced with software (program materials) for religious education. Leaders must be aware of these and other options for Bible teaching and learning.

CURRICULUM FOR BIBLE TEACHING AND LEARNING

There is no doubt that the Bible should be the basic curriculum material in a church's educational ministry. There is no better text than the Bible. But the Bible is admittedly a very difficult book even for adults. There is an evident need for curriculum materials that support and improve Bible teaching and learning.

Occasionally a pastor might decide to lead a congregation to "just use the Bible" in Sunday school and in other Bible teaching and learning efforts. The pastor then usually supplies the teachers with Bible teaching outlines, interpretations, and other teaching suggestions so that they can "just use the Bible." Often these teachers fail to observe that they are, in fact, using materials in addition to the Bible—those materials supplied to them by the pastor. Further, such materials usually reflect the limitations of the gifts of only one person, the pastor, instead of reflecting the gifts of many people who are dedicated to and skilled in providing materials of remarkably high quality. Generally a church would be well advised to select curriculum materials from a reliable publisher, freeing their pastor (and others) from the responsibility of producing curriculum materials. Then the pastor can perform those important pastoral duties that inevitably would be neglected if his time were consumed in curriculum production.

In no instance should curriculum materials displace the Bible. Some curriculum planners doubt the wisdom of even printing the Bible study passages in the periodical study materials ("the quarterly") or other study guides. They are concerned that people might neglect to use their own Bibles in their study. Others perceive the deletion of the printed Bible passages in study guides as an attempt to minimize the use of the Scriptures. This dilemma remains unsolved. In any event, it is the intent of those who publish curriculum materials to augment and improve Bible teaching and learning. Harry Piland stated this fact clearly: "Curriculum materials can never be considered a substitute for a study of the Bible. Bible study materials are prepared to provide for each age group a systematic plan of study to provide tools for learning for both teachers and pupils. They are designed to help people understand, appreciate, and apply the Bible in their daily lives."[16]

Many denominations provide curriculum materials for the congregations in their constituency. Some provide multiple lines or series of materials, which makes it necessary for local congregation leaders to try to choose what is best for their constituents. Secure catalogs from the publisher or publishers from whom materials might be desired. It is almost always best for congregations to look carefully first to see if they can use the materials supplied by their own denominations. Select the curriculum series that best meets the wants and needs of those who will use the materials.

Usually it is best to use the same series for all within one age division. Doing this makes it easier to do coordinated planning and preparation for all those in the same division. Plan to stay with one series long enough to achieve maximum value from it rather than switching frequently back and forth from one series to another. This kind of consideration will assist the Sunday School Leadership Council in giving appropriate leadership in selecting curriculum materials for Bible teaching and learning.

CONCLUSION

Teaching and learning the Bible are the first of the basic components of the educational ministry of a church. The Bible is foundational. Some organizational designs promise more success than others. The Sunday school offers tremendous opportunities for effective Bible teaching and learning if it is well organized and operated.

Essential to an effective Sunday school is an understanding of its tasks. The curriculum is vitally important in Bible teaching and learning. The Bible is the text. Church leaders, such as the Sunday School Leadership Team, should very carefully select other materials that will best meet the wants and needs of those who will use them.

CONCERNS FOR FURTHER STUDY

Consider these questions as you continue to reflect on the ministry of Bible teaching and learning.

1. What has been your observation/experience regarding the attractiveness of the Bible as a subject for study among (1) church members and (2) nonmembers?

2. What do you think about a church's using its Sunday school to carry out the tasks suggested in this chapter? Consider each task in light of this question.

3. What do you think you might recommend to your own congregation growing out of your study of the suggestions in this chapter about (1) structures and (2) curriculum for Bible teaching and learning?

CHAPTER 7

Ministry of Discipleship Training

A church's ministry of discipleship training is a unique part of its over-all educational ministry. It is unique in that it involves a specialized approach to education. It is concerned with equipping all of God's people for the work of Christian service, to build up the body of Christ (Eph. 4:12)— new church members, church members, and church leaders. Yet discipleship training may be the most neglected area of educational ministry in the church.

Early Christians took seriously the responsibility of leading and directing the growth of one another in what it means to follow Jesus, to live his way in relation to the Father and to others, and to join with him and with others in the redemptive enterprise. This emphasis on specialized instruction became the exception rather than the rule during the Middle Ages.

Leaders of the Reformation strongly advocated and practiced discipleship training. As a result, vital Christianity surged ahead as never before. But much of this vigor seems to have waned among churches in recent decades.

Today concern among Christians for effective discipleship training is reemerging. Such a reformation could not come too quickly. A church that continues to neglect its needs for discipleship training limits its vitality as a part of the body of Christ and threatens its very existence. Conversely, a church that develops and continues faithfully a ministry of discipleship training enlivens and enriches its present fellowship and helps to assure its own extension into the future.

TRAINING NEW CHURCH MEMBERS, CHURCH MEMBERS, AND CHURCH LEADERS

A person becomes a member of a church on that church's acceptance of the person's affirmation that he or she has received Christ for forgiveness of sin and for salvation, and following baptism. This profession of faith is often spoken of as being "born again," using the language Jesus used in conversation with Nicodemus. The newly born Christian then is baptized into the fellowship of a church. He is a new member. He is also a "babe in Christ." Most churches also have ways of receiving new members who already are Christians.

A church's training ministry should provide immediate care and follow-up for new Christians, and, for different reasons, for other new church members who come from other churches. New Christians need to understand their conversion experience and their commitment to Christ. They need help in using the Bible as their guide and the source of authority for their new lives. They need to begin a personal plan of growth in what it means to be a disciple of Jesus Christ, including daily disciplines of study, devotion, and prayer.

New Christians need encouragement and guidance in sharing with others their relationship to Christ. At this time, they probably know more non-Christian people than they will ever know well for the rest of their lives. They need to be received with warmth and care into their new family, the church. Parents of young converts also need guidance in understanding the experience of children and in nurturing their development.

New Christians need to know more about the meaning of church membership. They need to know that their change in commitment should be reflected in changes in the way they live. They need to develop an appreciation for the fact that being in the family of God is different from being a part of the world at large. They need to learn of their own church, its covenant, its beliefs, its history, its governance, its ministries, its organizations, and its leaders. They need to be educated to become involved (at the level of their readiness) in the church's life and work. They need guidance in discovering and developing their gifts, and in finding ways to exercise them for their good, for the good of the church, and for others.

New members who have joined after having been members of another congregation need an opportunity to affirm among their new church family their own commitment to Christ and to his church. They might need some of the same instruction as that needed by new Christians, depending on how they have progressed in their growth as disciples. They at least need and deserve information about their new church that will help them to be assimilated effectively into its life and work.

Church membership either means something or it means nothing. Too often when one joins a church, it seems to mean very little. Weldon Crossland, a great writer in Methodism in an earlier generation, was painfully accurate when he observed that it is easier to join a church than it is to get on a bus. And he made this statement before riders had to have correct change in order to get on a bus! Churches need to reach people for discipleship training.

The education given at the entrance point to church membership could help raise awareness of the meaning of church membership. On mission fields there is often a waiting period following one's profession of faith so that the convert might be instructed and prepared for church membership. The rationale for this is that people often are crossing such great cultural and social barriers to become Christians that time is needed for them to be instructed and prepared for participation as members of the church. Otherwise, they might actually become a detriment to themselves and to the church by defaulting on their commitment and reflecting negatively on the Christian faith.

In what culture of this world is this not true? Does anyone really believe there is such a thing as a Christian country where such care is unnecessary? Ancient churches trained converts for periods ranging from one to three years before allowing them to enter the full service of worship. We do not advocate rigidity, but surely a few weeks of careful guidance would help the new Christian—even a new member by transfer. And it would also help the church. A church should determine what its expectations are in terms of what it will offer to new members and what new members are to do to satisfy the church's expectations.

Church members who are not new members need training in discipleship and personal ministry on a continuing basis. They need guidance through training in continuing to grow in their own spiritual development. They need to continue to grow in personal skills essential to following Christ, living Christ's way in relation to the Father and to others, and sharing in the redemptive enterprise. They need to develop in their abilities to perform personal ministries to others.

Church members need to develop and to continue developing their personal understandings of Christian theology and Baptist doctrine. They need to know and to appreciate the great teachings of the faith, the doctrines as understood by their denomination. They need to continue to study what the Scriptures teach about ethics, what is right and wrong in the issues and circumstances of life today. They need to know about church history, about the great ways, and those not so great, in which God's people have come to the present. They need to be informed about their own denominational heritage. They need to learn and to continue to examine their own church's polity—its theory and form of government—and their church's organization. A church member never outgrows the need to train and grow as a disciple. This is a lifelong need for every individual. A church must help its members meet their needs.

A church should offer training for its members who are leaders. Leaders need help at times in discovering their gifts for leadership. They need the added knowledge that will enrich their leadership potential. They need specific skills that will make them as effective as they can become.

The leaders must continue to lead the way by their own growth as disciples and effective servants of the church lest those they lead either overtake them or stumble and fall on the nongrowth of the leaders. Leaders must lead, usually by being in front of followers. A church should provide continually the kinds of leader training that will assure that its leaders have ample opportunity to grow and develop as disciples and as leaders of other disciples.

TASKS OF THE DISCIPLESHIP TRAINING ORGANIZATION

It is helpful in a church to have an organization whose assignment is to lead in implementing a church's training tasks. Some churches are too small to sustain a separate organization for training in discipleship. Such churches might designate one person, or a small committee of people, to do what they can to advance the church's training activities. Some have done this by having one person given this responsibility exclusively, as an additional "general officer" of the Sunday school organization. In any event, there are certain tasks which a church must find ways to fulfill.

The *first task* of a church's ministry of discipleship training is to *reach people for discipleship training*. This means to discover, enlist, and enroll church members, their families, new church members, leaders, and other concerned people. This means helping disciples live under the lordship of Christ in a growing, lifelong commitment to his person, his teaching, and his spirit. It includes offering planned experiences to enable people to grow as disciples. All of this must begin with reaching people—discovering, enlisting, and enrolling them.

The second task is to *orient new church members for responsible church membership*. This means to acquaint all new church members— new converts, transfer members, others—with the situation of their new relationship and to help them get suitably assimilated. It means to help them become functioning members of the living body of Christ, the church. Responsible church membership is the New Testament expectation of all Christians.

The third task is to *equip church members for discipleship and personal ministry*. Equip means to make complete, to fully furnish, to put into proper working condition. Discipleship is the Christian's lifelong commitment to the person, teaching, and spirit of Jesus Christ. Life under Jesus' lordship involves progressive learning, growth in Christlikeness, application of biblical truth to every area of life, responsibility for sharing the Christian faith, and responsible church membership. Personal ministry is an individual's specific, ongoing expression of the spiritual gift(s) in redemptive, loving service for people in the name and spirit of Christ.

The fourth task is to *teach Christian theology and Baptist doctrine, Christian ethics, Christian history and Baptist heritage, and church polity and organization.* This is designed to involve learners in meaningful exploration of the realities of the Christian faith and life. Disciples need to develop a valid system of beliefs about God and his relationship to people, including distinctive denominational insights. They need to grow in Christian character and the ability to express and apply it in every relationship of daily living. They need to discover and appropriate meaning and values in Christian history and denominational heritage. They need to explore church polity and organization, and ways of working together in achieving Christ's objectives for churches.

These essential content areas, if not systematically taught in a ministry of discipleship training, might not be taught in any other educational organization. No other church educational organization systematically addresses these subjects. A church with no distinct organization to carry out this task needs either to begin one, or to find some other good way to accomplish it.

The fifth task is to *train church leaders for ministry.* Training church leaders includes general training for any type of leadership role commonly held by church members: potential leaders, new leaders, and experienced leaders. Training results in the trainee developing increased competence to serve effectively and efficiently. Training also enables the trainee to develop an understanding of the type of leadership roles, both formal and informal, in which he or she is likely to be most effective. Specific training for a particular ministry organization's leaders is done by or in consultation with the leaders of that ministry organization for the purpose of strengthening that ministry.

God has made potentially available to a church the leaders and other resources needed to accomplish whatever he wants the church to accomplish. The church must take the initiative to identify its needs for leaders, help members to discover their gifts for leadership, and provide the necessary kinds of training for leadership.

This task suggests that potential leaders must be equipped for possible leadership before they are enlisted to serve in specific places of responsibility in a church's ministries. Such training should be offered not only to adults but also to older youth.

Youth need not forfeit their participation in their own peer group experiences in order to begin contributing as leaders in a church's ministries. They can and should have opportunities to assist in leading in special projects, church committee assignments, and other activities where their gifts are not only useful, but are needed both for the sake of the church at large and for the sake of the ones who render the service.

This is not to suggest that adults should fail to perform their leadership responsibilities. Nor is it to suggest a "youth takeover" of a church. It is to suggest that youth who are a part of the membership need opportunities, in keeping with their individual readiness, to grow while leading, and to feel that they are members in fact and not just in theory. A church can benefit greatly by their leadership. Having opportunities for genuine service during the youth age span is a significant factor for many youths in hearing God's call to commit themselves to vocational ministry.

Potential leader training is designed to provide basic knowledge and understanding and to develop basic skills in the general area of church leadership. Courses are offered primarily for older youth and adults who are not yet enlisted for specific places of leadership.

New leader training is designed to enable a person to function in a specific leadership role and is conducted in conjunction with other church ministry organizations. It may be given when a person expresses an interest in a specific role, after a person has been elected to a specific leadership position but before he has begun to function in that position; or as soon as possible after a person has begun to function in a specific leadership position.

Experienced leader training enables a person who is already a leader to improve or gain additional knowledge, understanding, skills, or attitudes, or to develop as a leader beyond the point of functioning in a specific job. Some experienced leader training cuts across ministry organization lines. Some training, for instance, might be needed by all children's workers or by all youth workers. Other training might be needed by all who have administrative responsibilities or who need to develop skills in group leadership.

The sixth task is to *undergird the work of the church and denomination.* The same suggestions made in the previous chapter about this task apply in principle also to the training organization. A church ministry organization should be available as appropriate for this task. But in view of the fourth task of discipleship training (which calls for teaching denominational doctrine, denominational heritage, church polity, and organization), the training organization has unique opportunity to relate to this interpreting and undergirding task. Its curriculum should carry appropriate helps to educate and to lead church members in their understanding of and support for their church and denomination.

ESTABLISHING THE DISCIPLESHIP
TRAINING ORGANIZATION

Probably the way for most churches to conduct their ministry of discipleship training is to establish and maintain a continuing Discipleship Training organization. This would seem best even for the very small church that might have only one person or a small committee who could lead the training tasks. The principal activities of this organization could be conducted in connection with the Sunday evening worship service, either before or after the service. Most churches do far better by having the training prior to the evening worship service. This time can be protected from other conflicts, and having members present for training can contribute significantly to attendance in the worship service.

Step 1: Establish the need for a Discipleship Training organization. A church whose members are informed and convinced of the values of a ministry of discipleship training will more likely respond to efforts to establish such a ministry. This becomes the first step in establishing a Discipleship Training organization. Through sermons, testimonies, special Sunday school lessons, articles, bulletin and newsletter inserts, invitational meetings with the pastor and prospective leaders and participants to discuss the idea, and other means, members must be informed and convinced that they need a Discipleship Training organization. If this step is successful, church leaders should proceed with the other suggestions. If, after a reasonable time of informing and convincing church members, there is a definite sense that they will not at least give the idea a good experimental try, it would be wise to wait and try again at a later time.

Step 2: Request the church officially to endorse the forming of a Discipleship Training organization. At this same time, ask the church to establish the principal time for its operation, and to assert that that time is to be protected from conflict with all other interests and groups in the church's life. This is an indispensable part of the church's decision to form the organization. Even the Sunday school, which is usually given the prime time on a church's calendar—Sunday morning—would not do as well if it had to compete with church committee meetings, leadership team meetings, lack of church staff presence, meetings of music groups, mission education groups, or others. Such conflicts draw people out of possible participation in the Discipleship Training ministry, and indicate that the church is not quite serious about the importance of its ministry of discipleship training.

Many Discipleship Training ministries have been weakened greatly, and in some cases eliminated, by the failure of their churches to give them almost absolute priority during their allotted time. Exceptions to this exclusive priority for Discipleship Training time must be genuine exceptions and should be allowed only rarely. The same support should be given to any other church organization that is conducting an all-age ministry at a regularly stated time in the church's calendar.

Step 3: Select and enlist a Discipleship Training director. In a very small church this person might be the only one leading in the Discipleship Training ministry. This leader would do all one person could do to encourage individuals to use training materials for their growth and development. The director assists the pastor in scheduling and promoting the discipleship training for new church members. The director might personally lead an ongoing group of adults or youth and adults. The director might also supervise individual training plans for church leaders, placing training materials in their hands and following through with individual encouragement. The director could also promote training emphases to be included in Sunday school class monthly business meetings and in similar meetings of other groups.

In larger churches the Discipleship Training director works with the pastor and others to lead the organization in carrying out its tasks.

Step 4: Identify the needs for training and discipling in the church. The pastor, other ministers, the Discipleship Training director, and other leaders such as the Discipleship Training leadership team and the Church Ministry leadership team can use various means to identify individual and corporate needs for training. Surveys and individual conferences are helpful in identifying the needs.

The frequency of the addition of new church members will suggest the needs for their discipleship training. Each one should have individual attention immediately after coming into the fellowship. Continuing training of new members in an ongoing group might be needed in churches with frequent additions of new members. The sessions can be designed so that new members can enter and complete the cycle of sessions at any point, and then move into ongoing training groups for regular membership training. In churches with few additions, the group training of new members should be conducted as needed.

Step 5: Decide on the most practical ways to organize to meet the needs and interests that have been identified. There are many alternatives. A very small church might have only a Discipleship Training director as described earlier. Larger churches will have more elaborate organizations to meet their training needs.

The Sunday school roll serves as a source of prospects for enrollment in Discipleship Training. If there are two groups in Sunday school for a given age, there might be one in Discipleship Training, with the enlistment efforts focused on those on the Sunday school roll. Provision should be made for short-term training groups. These are usually undated units of study that supplement ongoing training and are designed to meet special interests or needs. In a large organization, ongoing groups usually keep right on with their dated curriculum materials, while certain ones participate in short-term training groups. In small churches the short-term training probably would substitute for the ongoing training for a time. Members then would go back to the regular ongoing training once the undated studies are completed.

Step 6: *Select and secure training materials and record-keeping materials.* Denominational publishers' catalogs should supply the information needed to accomplish this important step.[1] Be specific in ordering the items chosen, and allow sufficient time for materials to arrive and for those who will lead in their use to become familiar with the study materials.

Step 7: *Enlist and train leaders.* The Discipleship Training director, with guidance from the pastor and any other ministers related to the program, should work with the church's normal procedures for enlisting leaders. Many churches use a church nominating committee to match people with the leadership needs and to approve the enlistment of certain potential leaders.

After approval by the church's nominating committee, such enlistment is best done by the person who would be closest to the potential leader in the organization, the one who would lead that leader in the work. This simple procedure sequence avoids the confusion of having a person contacted for enlistment as a leader by two or more people. This creates confusion and often does not achieve the desired matching of individual gifts with church leadership needs. Many churches then formally elect these leaders to their office, and some have an appropriate installation service that includes a charge to the leaders regarding their responsibilities.

New leaders must begin and continue their training for leadership. At the start, an orientation workshop might be all there is time for. If so, do it well. Then follow up with continuing education and training for the leaders, frequently consulting with them about their progress and needs for more training. On-the-job training should continue for as long as one serves as a leader.

Step 8: *Launch the new organization well.* Publicize it through every good channel. Secure individual commitments to participate. Use the other church organizations to interpret and to support the promotion, even as the Discipleship Training organization stands ready to assist other ministry organizations in their similar needs.

It is important to time the beginning of a new organization well. Usually a church ministry organization is begun best at the beginning of a new church year. Another good time is at the mid-year point. If the ministry is to be only seasonal, then any season can be suitable to begin. Also, it is important to get enough time at the right time of day for an effective Discipleship Training program. A full hour could be well used, and probably should be set prior to the evening worship service. No other regular activities should conflict or take away from this vital ministry.

MAINTAINING THE DISCIPLESHIP TRAINING MINISTRY ORGANIZATION

Once begun, a Discipleship Training ministry organization requires regular and routine maintenance to assure its continued effectiveness. This maintenance includes complete records information to inform the leaders of the progress of the organization and its members and groups. Regular meetings with other leaders as a group are necessary to check on needs and progress, and to plan together to meet the needs. This is the work of the Discipleship Training leadership team. Further, leaders in a supervisory position should regularly confer with individual leaders and members to see that the work of the organization goes as it should. In all instances, the pastor and any other ministers related to the Discipleship Training ministry need to be informed of the status and the needs of the organization. Church members should have regular reports in sufficient detail to keep them aware of the organization, its needs, and its plans.

Leadership vacancies should be filled promptly so that training groups might continue without serious delays. This need makes it all the more important for the leader training segment of Discipleship Training to function effectively, and for supervising leaders to keep closely in touch with all leaders in order to anticipate needs for replacement or for expansion of organization that will require additional leaders.

Once a church has a well-operating, ongoing Discipleship Training ministry organization, great care should be taken regarding how short-term or other special training projects are correlated with the ongoing program. If such opportunities are to be supplementary to the ongoing program, take the steps necessary to avoid displacing the ongoing training. For example, if a church has several groups of adults in ongoing Discipleship Training with the use of dated units of study, consider offering only one group of a short-term or special-project nature to compete with the ongoing groups. Even then, care should be taken to assure that no ongoing group is permanently weakened. This can be done by limiting the number who enroll from any ongoing group, and offering to schedule the short-term or other special-training project again when others might participate. People completing these temporary sessions return to their regular ongoing groups, unless they become leaders.

If the need and interest in the short-term or special project warrant it, another procedure is to adjourn the ongoing group or groups for definitely specified time, with firm plans including dates for returning to the regular format. Let these plans be well known before interrupting the ongoing groups. Care must be exercised by not making a frequent practice of this formal adjournment procedure, lest the ongoing Discipleship Training suffer irreparable damage. Good, regular educational groups are more easily weakened than they are strengthened or restarted. Eventually, all types of training suffer from the effects of continually starting over and the accompanying confusion and uncertainty about what is to be offered.

TRAINING THROUGH SPECIAL PROJECTS

There is a place in a church's ministry of discipleship training for special training projects. They should be chosen to meet special needs and interests, and carefully correlated with the church's ongoing training. As a matter of fact, the training ministry in a very small church might take on the appearance of being altogether made up of special projects. If that is what can be done, that is what should be done. In many churches, however, the special projects are chosen to be offered for a specified time only, and often for just certain people needing the training.

SEASONAL TRAINING

In a church that does not have a continuing training plan for new church members, such a group or groups (or even the training of individuals, if there are not enough to form groups) might be treated as special training projects. If possible, there should be a group for each age division. This allows the training to be conducted in keeping with the human growth and development needs of the new members. True, they are all "babes in Christ" if they are all recent converts, but the learning readiness varies widely among children, youth, and adults. Such training groups usually include those who join the church by transfer of membership from another church, though some special provision might be made for them if it is useful to do so.

SPECIAL GROUPS

Many special groups in a church need training for their leaders. Much of this training can be provided by the leaders in a church who specialize in setting up and conducting training events. For example, an annual training event for church committees is a good way to launch the new church year's work that is done through committees of a church. A short series of training sessions can be scheduled for those who serve in this way. Other special needs, such as training ushers, media personnel, and people to witness and to lead others to witness can be met through leader training sessions. These training projects are in addition to the other leader training that a church might conduct.

SPECIAL TRAINING PROJECTS FOR ALL AGES

From time to time, such as once or twice a year, a church can enrich the training for its members by offering special training opportunities for all ages. For example, the subject areas of doctrine, ethics, or other discipleship training areas can be good training subjects for an emphasis in which provisions are made for all age groups. The format might be to begin the study on Sunday and to continue through Wednesday, meeting each evening for training. Other schedules might suit some churches better.

Insofar as is possible, such studies should be in addition to the regular training offered to members, rather than being in lieu of their regular studies. Great doctrines like the doctrines of God, the church, salvation, missions, and others could greatly support discipleship growth among members.

CURRICULUM FOR DISCIPLESHIP TRAINING

It might surprise some to know that the basic text for discipleship training in a church is the Bible. The use of the Bible in Sunday school is largely for exegetical studies. In discipleship training the studies are more topical, or more skill oriented, with the Bible related often as supporting and elaborating data. Often in skills training, the skills themselves require apt use of the Bible. In all cases, what is being taught in discipleship training must be compatible with biblical truth. The place of the Bible in discipleship training must not be overlooked.

Church leaders, especially those who make up the leadership of the Discipleship Training leadership team, should lead in choosing the curriculum materials for this ministry. The "Curriculum Selection Checklist" (page 216) could help in evaluating and selecting curriculum materials for discipleship training. Catalogs of denominational publishers should be among the first resources to examine. There are numerous dated and undated materials from which to choose. Generally, dated materials should form the base of materials a church uses. Undated materials are used to supplement and to enrich the program.

Professional-quality curriculum materials for discipleship training of all kinds are usually far to be preferred over any other kind. Members participating in the training groups need materials of their own that involve them in study and preparation for the sessions and for participation in the learning activities. Otherwise, the training leader becomes the only resource of the learning experience; at best, this limits possibilities for effective learning. Using quality curriculum materials helps to assure that the training will come much nearer toward realizing its potential.

CONCLUSION

Discipleship training is an indispensable ministry in a church. To make it optional is to neglect the training of new Christians, other new church members, church members, and church leaders. A church cannot have a vital present nor an assured future without it. The bare survival of many churches is testimony to the need for effective discipleship training.

With carefully correlated ongoing church member training, new church member training, and church leader training, a church can have an effective ministry of discipleship training that will enrich its present life and work and help to assure its future. As someone has said, "Christian conversion is the end of the Christian experience—the front end." New members must be nurtured. Church members must continue to grow in orderly development. Church leaders must learn to serve more effectively. This is the challenge of the ministry of discipleship training.

CONCERNS FOR FURTHER STUDY

Consider these questions as you continue to reflect on the ministry of discipleship training.

1. To what extent do you share the author's view that the area of discipleship training as described in this chapter is probably the most neglected area of educational ministry in the history of churches?

2. What difference do you think it might make in your church if you had an effective ministry to train (1) new church members, (2) church members, and (3) church leaders?

3. What do you see as some advantages of using professional quality curriculum materials in a church's training program?

CHAPTER 8

Ministry of Missions Education and Action

A church is a fellowship of Christians on mission. Its mission is to make known the manifold wisdom of God—the gospel of forgiveness, grace, and salvation through Jesus Christ, the Lord and Savior. What a church does to express genuine Christian love for those people outside its membership, those who are not presently enrolled in its programs or in its fellowship, is the external mission of a church.

Mission means "a sending forth." It implies that there is a commission for which those who are sent forth are responsible. The Great Commission is obeyed: "And Jesus came and said to them, 'All authority in heaven and on earth has been given to me. Go therefore and make disciples of all nations, baptizing them in the name of the Father and of the Son and of the Holy Spirit, teaching them to observe all that I have commanded you; and lo, I am with you always, to the close of the age'" (Matt. 28:18–20).

This compelling command of Christ is for a church not only with regard to itself, but to all who have not yet received him. "Missions is what the church does in keeping with the Great Commission of the sovereign Lord to extend the witness and ministry beyond itself (its community of faith) to bring all people to Christ and thereby glorify God."[1]

A church is to send forth those who will go both near and far to do the work of fulfilling the commission. There is a correlation between knowing and going. There is a correlation between missions education and mission action. Either missions education or mission action might be the starting point. Some people might not be interested in doing missions if they know nothing or little about missions. Others might not want to study missions until they have had a mission action experience. Leaders should be aware of the validity of different starting points for different people, and try to meet the needs of all. Wherever a person begins, there is a need for education in missions.

It is redundant to speak of a missionary church. By nature, a church that is a church is missionary. Being missionary is inherent in being a bona fide church. While some churches are more active than others in missions, a church is not fully a church if it is not obedient to the command of the Lord of the church in this area. It is imperative that a church manifest life in missionary terms. It is also imperative that a church do all it can to advance the knowledge and understanding of its members regarding missions. This emphasis on missionary education is a major strategy for leading members to become involved in missions.

Of major concern to many Christians is the relatively small number of church members who are regularly involved in missions education. We should rejoice that many are engaged in Bible teaching and learning, for example, but wish to see comparable numbers engaged in the study and the practice of missions. Fortunately, one cannot be engaged in Bible teaching and learning without being exposed to the missionary message of the Bible. The need for a sharper focus on the missions aspects of biblical truth is obvious. Church leaders would do well to reflect on their personal needs for a stronger participation in missions education and action.

STRUCTURES FOR MISSIONS EDUCATION AND ACTION

In many denominations the work of promoting and supporting missions (both direct missions and representative missions) has been led by the mission-minded women of the church. They have led in missions education. They have done a disproportionate share of mission action. They deserve the deep respect and gratitude of all. In some denominations men have joined the women in this effort. The most common expression of organized effort in many churches today is in the form of separate organizations for women and for men, although some churches are able to involve more people by forming co-ed organizations. Cooperation between men and women and organizations for missions education and action are increasing in many churches. Regardless of who does the work, it is a church's responsibility to advance the cause of missions.

A church should provide ample opportunities for those who are informed and concerned for missions to work together to get the job done. Perhaps in some churches this would mean a churchwide approach to missions in which every person is given an opportunity to participate. In others, missions is best accomplished through separate organizations for men, women, boys, and girls. Each church should examine its own needs and provide missions education and action via plans and structures that will fit those needs. It would seem wise first to attempt to work together even from different organizational bases, and then, if the occasion warrants, merge into a single structure. Pursue that path very carefully.

For our purposes of presenting a model of missions education and action, we shall describe a women's organization and a men's organization—Woman's Missionary Union and Brotherhood, both of which are recommended for churches cooperating with the Southern Baptist Convention. Other denominations have their own unique models for missions. The tasks of Woman's Missionary Union and Brotherhood are very similar. Their approaches to their work are similar. Often they work together from their separate organizational bases.

How a church organizes for missions education and action is important to its success in these endeavors. More important, however, are a church's answers to such questions as these:

- Are we providing opportunities for each person in the church family to be involved in missions?

- Are we keeping the entire congregation aware of evangelistic efforts worldwide?

- Do we encourage financial support of cooperative missions causes locally, statewide, nationally, and worldwide?

- Are we planning exciting churchwide events and activities that teach global missions concepts and introduce learners to missionaries and their work?

- Do we create experiences so the whole church family can participate in prayer for missionaries, nationals, and volunteers?

- Do we nurture lifestyles that demonstrate the Great Commission?

- Do we offer organizations for children, teenagers, and adults that focus on missions learning, giving, praying, ministering, and witnessing?

- Are we evangelizing people who do not know Christ as Savior?

- Do we participate with other church leaders in accomplishing the goals of the church?

- Are we creating an environment where the Holy Spirit can easily be heard by individuals whom God is calling out for mission service?[2]

Consider these questions as you read about the illustrative model organizations.

WOMAN'S MISSIONARY UNION

Woman's Missionary Union (WMU) exists in a church for the purpose of helping the church involve all its members in missions, especially women, girls, and preschool boys and girls. To be involved in missions means that people will be committed to, and carry out, the missions imperatives of the Bible. This church organization does its work through five tasks.

Task 1: *Pray for and give to missions.* The authors of Woman's Missionary Union *Guide* wrote: "WMU motivates people to support missionaries and mission work through praying and giving. No church can individually minister and witness to the whole world. By praying for and giving to missions cooperatively, people in a church can be involved in representative missions all around the world. Their prayers and money make it possible for missionaries to share the Savior with a lost world, one by one."[3]

The organization encourages people to give through the church, individually and as families. The focus is on cooperative missions giving. Regarding praying, the WMU *Guide* states: "Missions praying takes place as individuals, family groups, prayer partners, missions groups in church, and the entire church family pray for missions. Prayers are offered regularly in personal study time, WMU organizational meetings, and other times. In addition, special seasons of prayer include all of the church."[4]

Task 2: *Do missions.* The focus is to provide opportunities and motivation for people to be directly involved in ministering and witnessing to non-believers. People in a church should be involved in ministering to other people because they want to follow Christ's example of being concerned about the whole person, not just spiritual needs. . . . The goal of witnessing and ministry is to bring the person into a saving relationship with Jesus Christ. . . . Witness and ministry can take place locally, where individuals live, or in other parts of the nation or world as the individual goes to other places.[5] Some of the people of special need or circumstance to whom a church, led by WMU, ministers are: prisoners, juvenile delinquents, alcoholics, drug abusers, migrants, military personnel, latch-key kids, the poor, language groups, internationals, nonreaders, the aging, unwed parents, the sick, the abused, minority groups, and the institutionalized. The witnessing aspect of this task focuses on people often overlooked by the church. Christians are taught and led to share the gospel with others, and to encourage them to confess Jesus Christ as Savior and Lord.

Task 3: *Learn about missions.* "Learning experiences can instill concepts, change attitudes, increase knowledge, and develop skills helpful in supporting missions."[6] The authors of *A Church on Mission* wrote: "The in-depth study of missions helps a church achieve its reason for being, encourages church members to understand their world responsibility, cultivates concern, and motivates the investment of life and resources in missions."[7]

How vital is it for a church to learn about missions? Carolyn Weatherford, former executive director of Woman's Missionary Union, writes:

Mission study embodies four basic personal truths I started learning before I went to school. . . . Simply stated, those truths are: (l) Jesus loves me; (2) Jesus loves all the children of the world; (3) Some children do not know Jesus loves them; (4) Jesus wants me to tell them. . . . What happens when I study missions? I become knowledgeable about what God is doing through His people in the world today. I see the part my church has in carrying the gospel to the ends of the earth. I understand how Southern Baptists have chosen the idea of voluntary cooperation so churches together can do what no one church can do alone.[8]

In addition to teaching missions in a variety of groups within the organization, WMU joins with Brotherhood in certain joint study projects. They promote special mission study projects for the whole church, or for one age group in the church.

Task 4: *Develop spiritually toward a missions lifestyle.* WMU helps people grow in their understanding of who God is and what he is calling them to do. . . . That growing relationship with God will result in a lifestyle that is increasingly more aware and sensitive to the needs of others. Spiritual development affects a person's response to personal opportunities to minister and witness, prayer life, and use of resources of time, energy, and money. People in the church can be involved in spiritual development opportunities that lead to a missions lifestyle. WMU will be able to give special attention to the spiritual development of all people who are a part of the WMU age-level organizations.[9] Resident in this task is the potential for developing a most powerful and effective multiplier effect in bringing people to God through Jesus Christ. No other human factor can match the possibilities of multitudes of believers living the Christ life and loving others to God through Him.

Task 5: *Participate in the work of the church and the denomination.* This is a task that is common to all of a church's ministry organizations. Each organization should implement this task as appropriate to its other assignments. For WMU this means to help make people aware of and involve them in the work of the church and denomination, especially in the areas related to missions. . . . WMU members and leaders are to also be involved in the broader picture of the entire church in worship, proclamation, evangelism, discipleship, education, and ministry.[10]

Age-graded missions groups for women, girls, and preschool boys and girls reflect the structured approach for Woman's Missionary Union. Recommended groupings are:

- Women on Mission, an organization for women 18 years of age and older (grouped as needed by either age, task, common interest, or needs);

- Acteens for girls in grades 7 through 12, or aged 12 through 17 (grouped on the basis of the number and ages of girls involved);

- Girls in Action for girls in grades 1 through 6 (with at least two groups, one for older girls and one for younger girls);

- Mission Friends for preschoolers, babies until first grade (with multiple classes as possible for Younger Mission Friends—babies and ones, Middle Mission Friends—twos and threes, Older Mission Friends—fours and fives until first grade, or one class for all Mission Friends).

The WMU *Guide* suggests the additional possibility of co-ed organizations for all members of the church to be a part of an ongoing missions organization, and offers detailed information about Adults on Mission, Youth on Mission, and Children in Action organizations. Also, there should be provisions for providing missions opportunities and experiences for churchwide audiences such as the entire congregation, targeted audiences of specific groupings of people already formed in the church, and small groups created by people with similar interests or needs for a particular activity, project, or event. A very small church can have an effective program of mission education and action. Many small churches excel in this regard. In churches of all sizes, the mission organizations advocate a close working relationship with the pastor and with any other staff ministers a church might have. Whatever the size of the church, the WMU *Guide* suggests the recommended structures for the leadership teams and for each type of group.

In addition to working through its own structures, Woman's Missionary Union makes special efforts to relate appropriately to the educational plans for all other ministry organizations in a church: Sunday School, Discipleship Training, Brotherhood, Music Ministry, and Church Leadership Ministry. It is important for all church ministry organizations to work together to help a church fulfill its mission and perform its functions. The tasks of all church ministry organizations must be programmed in relationship.

BROTHERHOOD

Men and boys are the constituency of the Brotherhood organization. Through Baptist Men, the unit for men 35 and older; Baptist Young Men, for men 18–34; Challengers, grades 7–12; and through Royal Ambassadors for boys in grades 1–6, Brotherhood purposes to help a church involve men and boys in missions. This purpose is expressed in missions activities, mission study, mission support, and personal ministry.

Significant work can be done in small or large churches with very little organization, especially in the beginning. For example, a Brotherhood might function for a time with only a Royal Ambassador section. In such an instance the Brotherhood director would serve as the Royal Ambassador director and personally lead the work with the boys. Models of additional organization may be found in the current leadership materials for Brotherhood work.

Leaders work to inform, to motivate, and to involve men and boys in living their faith, having personal experiences in witness and ministry, and giving and praying to support people involved in missions. This organization for men and boys in missions education and action is structured to work through five tasks.

Task 1: *Engage in missions activities.* These activities include mission action, personal evangelism, mass evangelism, and special mission projects. Brotherhood defines mission action and personal evangelism as does WMU. It adds mass evangelism. In special projects, it might be visible in such activities as Scripture distribution; disaster relief; the erection or renovation of church buildings; or survey work and mission Vacation Bible School work in pioneer areas, perhaps in a partnership relationship with a state convention.

Task 2: *Teach missions.* The content areas are the missionary message of the Bible, the progress of Christian missions, and contemporary missions. The Brotherhood approach is to try first to involve people in some mission activity (as in task 1) and then, having activated their interest, move them into study. This approach seems especially well suited to men and boys, but certainly not exclusively.

Task 3: *Pray for and give to missions.* Brotherhood gives major emphasis to support for the Cooperative Program. It also joins with WMU to promote the two annual special missions offerings and offerings for state missions. Giving to missions is seen as a way people are helped to grow in being missionary and help to fulfill the Great Commission.

Task 4: *Develop personal ministry.* This means "to discover and implement a service to others which a person is uniquely and spiritually gifted to perform."[11] Pastors are encouraged in this task in their equipping ministry. It is important that those involved in personal ministry be affirmed by the pastor and other members of the fellowship.

Task 5: *Interpret and undergird the work of the church and the denomination.* Accomplishing this task strengthens not only Brotherhood work but also that of the church and the various agencies of the denomination.

CURRICULUM FOR MISSIONS EDUCATION

The teaching task of missions education includes four content areas:

1. The biblical basis of Christian missions. The organization is committed to the concept that the study of the missionary message of the Bible forms the basis for any understanding of missions.

2. The progress of Christian missions. This study of missions history shows how churches have progressed in carrying out the Great

Commission, leading them to understand better the plans and methods of contemporary missions.

3. Contemporary missions. This area receives by far the most attention. A study of missions in the present tense enables people to respond and to relate personally to missions.

4. Spiritual development of the learner, especially as it relates to missions. "It includes prayer guides, helps for personal meditation, stewardship, personal witnessing, mission action, career mission service, non-career mission service, and the role of women in missions."[12]

In missions, as perhaps in few other areas, it is important in the curriculum experiences to see the connections between education and action. Whichever comes to an individual first, education or action, each stimulates interest in the other, if the experience is authentic. Genuine education in missions results in a desire to help make some needed things happen. Getting involved in helping make some needed things happen stimulates interest in knowing more about the situation. Education is change. Involvement in mission education and in mission action changes people. This is a powerful combination of forces in the lives of people.

Guided curriculum experiences, whether the beginning point is in a study group or on some mission action occasion, are significant in the ministry of a church. The leadership teams (councils) of a church's missions ministry organizations should give careful attention to study plans and resources, as well as to mission action experiences. In cooperative undertakings between these organizations, their councils jointly should plan and select curriculum materials and experiences.

The denominational sources should be the first place the leaders look for help. Leaders should contact the appropriate sources within their own denomination to secure catalogs and sample materials to consider in their planning. The "Curriculum Selection Checklist" in chapter 16 of this book could be useful in choosing the resources that are best.

The association of education and action in missions is intentional. Missions education manifests itself in mission action and in other forms of mission support. Two of these we mention here.

The work of the emphasis program of Missions Development requires close coordination with the major missions education and action ministry organizations—WMU and Brotherhood. The Church Missions Development Team, comprised of a director, a missions survey director, a WMU representative, a Brotherhood representative, and project leaders as needed and approved by the church, lead in coordinating plans through the Church Ministry Leadership Team for accomplishing the Missions Development tasks. Many churches continue to use the term "missions committee" to do these and/or similar tasks.

Considerable educational opportunities emerge as the ministry of Missions Development addresses these tasks:

Task 1. *Identify missions needs/opportunities.*

Task 2: *Develop missions strategies to respond to unmet missions needs.*

Task 3: *Establish new churches.*

Task 4: Support establishing and strengthening WMU and Brotherhood.

Developing missions support through Christian stewardship—especially with regard to the areas of earning, spending, giving, and the final distribution of possessions—is of vital importance in missions education and action. This is a part of the responsibility of the emphasis ministry of Stewardship (see the task statements for this ministry on p. 134 of this text). While all church organizations should assist in communicating stewardship concepts and information, a church stewardship committee should lead this work. This committee should work year round to help develop Christian stewards and to support the ministries cooperatively undertaken by their church with other churches. See chapter 10 for more about the Stewardship ministry in a church.

Mission action is supported by human resources and financial resources. Education in missions depends on education and development of human resources and financial resources in order to move into mission action directly on the home front, and through representative missions—others going where all cannot go—in other lands around the world.

CONCLUSION

It is the mission of a fellowship of Christians who form a church to make known the manifold wisdom of God, near and far. This must be done within a church for those who are part of a church and its families. It also must be done beyond the "walls" of a church, for those who are not presently enrolled in a church's ministries or fellowship. This latter area is usually understood as "missions."

A church needs a ministry of education and action in the area of missions. It is an expression of the bona fide nature of a church to involve itself in missions education and action.

In missions there are strong ties between study and action, when either is authentic. Missions uniquely implies doing something about concerns of which one knows. A church comes very near fulfilling its mission as a church when it conducts an effective ministry of missions education and action.

CONCERNS FOR FURTHER STUDY

Consider these questions as you continue to reflect on the ministry of missions education and action.

1. What is your response to the statement that "by nature a church that is a church is missionary"?

2. In view of the relatively small number of people involved in regular missions education and action in many churches, what do you think a church might do to involve more of its members in these vital activities?

3. What are some ways in which missions education and action might appropriately be included in the activities of other church ministry organizations?

CHAPTER 9

Ministry of Music

Music is an integral part of making known the manifold wisdom of God. Just as one may speak or listen to another speak, so may one sing or listen to another sing the good news. And one may listen to musical instruments as they express the devotion, skill, and commitment of the performer (the doer of music, not just a presenter of a show of music) and as they aid the listener to have experiences pleasing to God. Music is a medium with a message. Christian music is a medium of Christian messages.

The people of a church need a ministry of music. Those outside a church whom a church seeks to reach need a ministry of music. All need the messages communicated by appropriate Christian music. There is an eloquence in the use of good music that, when presented to God and to one another with the right spirit and attitude, transcends barriers of communication and understanding that might not be overcome by other mediums.

God would have his children make use of music. Paul wrote the church at Corinth, "I will sing with the spirit and I will sing with the mind also" (1 Cor. 14:15b). "The mind" is also translated "the understanding." This suggests "that the singing should be Spirit-filled and that the singing should be understood by the singer. . . . If there is no understanding, the singing has no meaning."[1] All who hear need to be able to understand. Again, Paul wrote, "Let the word of Christ dwell in you richly, teach and admonish one another in all wisdom, and sing psalms and hymns and spiritual songs with thankfulness in your hearts to God. And whatever you do, in word or deed, do everything in the name of the Lord Jesus, giving thanks to God the Father through him" (Col. 3:16–17).

The authors of *A Church on Mission* suggested that this passage outlines the direction, dimension, declaration, and desirability of a church's music ministry.[2] Robert Orr writes that "biblical instruction, coupled with the

needs of people, reminds us of the importance of an effective Music Ministry to a church. The purpose of the Music Ministry is to glorify God, edify
His children, and lead people to a saving knowledge of Jesus Christ."[3]

The ministry of music in a church has many possible facets. *Congregational* music includes music of adoration, praise, prayer, proclamation, invitation, confession, forgiveness, faith, love, hope, victory, joy,
thanksgiving, commitment, and other offerings and responses. *Music performance groups*, such as choirs and instrumental groups, can be meaningful both to the participants who perform and to those who hear and see
them. *Music activity groups,* like preschool choirs and others whose primary purpose is the experience they might have with music (as over
against performing), have their place. *Music study groups,* working together to learn musical skills, history, appreciation, and other music interests, contribute. *Individual musicians*—vocalists, music directors,
pianists, organists, other instrumentalists—can render vital services while
they themselves grow and develop.

Music in other church organizations led by trained musicians and that
which is employed as an educational method by people who are not necessarily musicians in a highly technical sense are areas of potential value
hitherto only slightly realized. Churches have only begun to utilize the vitality and strength of good church music, and to use it boldly and skillfully
in the church's mission.

Church leaders and members, musicians and nonmusicians alike,
should take a vital interest in the ministry of music. The gifted and trained
musicians should be depended on to give worthy leadership in this ministry. But, as with all other areas that are important parts of the faith—Bible
teaching, theologizing, nurturing, proclaiming, witnessing, for example—
music is too important to be relegated exclusively to the professionals. The
priesthood of all believers applies to music as it does to the other vital areas
of concern in the faith.

MUSIC AS AN EDUCATIONAL METHOD

The place of music in worship has been firmly established not only in
New Testament Christian history, but also in the Old Testament. The place
of music in education is not yet as clearly seen, apart from the educational
values to those who lead and perform for others. Surely this latter value is
no small educational consequence. The arduous hours of rehearsals, private practice, and performances certainly have their impact on the diligent
musicians.

Harry Eskew and Hugh T. McElrath assign high priority to hymn instruction in the music ministry of a church. "Through hymn instruction
one is able to teach the message of the church, to help people worship, to
provide guidance in Christian living, and to present the vast heritage of the

church, including knowledge of outstanding leaders in its history and a significant portion of its devotional literature and music."[4]

They go on to suggest hymns in the curriculum of each of a church's educational organizations. They also recommend learning new hymns in a variety of ways, including a hymn of the month, hymn study classes, and hymns in the home. They cite James R. Sydnor's suggestions for encouraging family hymn singing.

> 1. The church office can keep a supply of hymnals to be sold to members.
>
> 2. A list of suggested uses of hymns in the home can be published in the church bulletin.
>
> 3. Children can be provided music appreciation and training (e.g., recordings, private music study, and membership in a children's choir) which will result in improved hymn singing.
>
> 4. Parents may request piano teachers to include hymn playing in the private music studies of their children.
>
> 5. A hymn stanza frequently can be used as a table grace (e.g., the Doxology, "For the beauty of the earth," "Now thank we all our God").
>
> 6. Parents can use an evening hymn as they tuck their children into bed.
>
> 7. Families can enjoy informal hymn singing, either by themselves or with invited friends.[5]

"The music experiences which the church provides for preschoolers and children (grades one to six) are largely educational in purpose."[6] Preschool groups are seldom involved in performing in congregational services. But both groups form concepts related to Bible truths about God, Jesus, the Bible, church, the family, self, others, and the natural world as they participate in the regular music activities of a graded choir program. They experience wonder, joy, feelings of well-being and personal worth, beauty, relaxation, rhythmic response, outlets for emotions, and personal creativity.[7]

For youth there are added educational values in music education. "Choir retreats and choir tours are new areas of keen interest involving musical, social, witnessing, and mission endeavors that build strong morale."[8] Youth do respond to good, consistent leadership. Their lives are enriched and enhanced in many ways through music education and participation. Many receive Christ through their participation in music. And adults have these experiences and others through music, including unique opportunities by special adult groups—single adults, singles again, and senior adults.[9]

The graded choir program offers the fullest opportunities for the educational use of music in a church. However, we would voice as strong an appeal as possible to the music leaders and to other members of a church to work together to capitalize on and to maximize the opportunities for using music in the other organizations of a church. This appeal involves extending the present use of music leaders and instrumentalists into every possible group where music would be appropriate. But even more strongly, the appeal is to educate and train the workers of other church educational organizations in ways music can be used to teach and to lead the growth of their constituents.

Obviously, it would be desirable for everyone who uses music in teaching to be able to do a highly acceptable job musically. Yet almost any teacher or leader who can "make a joyful noise" could find ways to employ this marvelous method to instruct, and to have other growth experiences in education. For example, almost anyone could use a recording!

Music leaders who supply curriculum materials for the graded choir programs for churches, and others of influence in the programs of education in the churches, must do more to bring together the resources of music in the educational ministries of churches. Already they have bridged the gap of using superior educational methods in music groups.

Let the flow between music and education go in all directions. Let there be not only good educational methods in music groups, but also good music in educational groups—even that which is done by nonmusicians.

STRUCTURES FOR THE MINISTRY OF MUSIC

There are tasks of the ministry of music in a church. These are basic continuing activities of primary importance in helping a church fulfill its mission.

Task 1: *Provide musical experiences in congregational services.* The music ministry has responsibility for planning, rehearsing, arranging, performing, and leading music for the congregational services. Congregational services include any corporate gathering of a local church congregation for worship, witness, proclamation, nurture, ministry, or fellowship.

Several actions are essential for those who lead the music ministry in performing this task. They include: (1) assisting the pastor in planning the congregational services; (2) leading in evaluating, selecting, creating, arranging, rehearsing, and performing music for congregational services; (3) leading the congregation in musical experiences that are relevant, meaningful, and inspiring, and that contribute to the thrust and mission of the church; (4) motivating the church constituency to want to be involved in musical experiences and to grow in their understanding of the value and role of music in the congregational services; (5) providing resources for musical experiences of the congregation.[10]

Task 2: *Provide church music education.* The church Music Ministry will plan and implement a definite schedule of teaching/training/performing activities to (1) develop a positive attitude toward church music; (2) increase knowledge and appreciation of the purposes and benefits of church music; (3) and guide people in developmental learning and performing experiences.

"Target groups for music education include all church members, their families, and other prospects. . . . Content for this task includes a curriculum with a balanced approach to music education and music performance, designed to meet the needs of the age group involved."[11]

Task 3: *Lead the church to witness and minister through music.* The Music Ministry has the responsibility of leading people to witness and minister through musical experiences and activities in the church and community. That means the Music Ministry is to use the music resources of the church in ministering to the human and spiritual needs of the church constituency, and actively seek ways to witness and minister through music to believers and unbelievers.

The Music Ministry implements its task through (1) regular and special congregational services, (2) music productions or services, (3) aid or support to other churches or missions, (4) mass media channels, and (5) the use of individual and group music talents in a variety of ways.

Task 4: *Assist church ministry organizations in providing training in music skills and in consultation about music equipment.* Through this task the Music Ministry assists those ministry organizations whose leaders want to use music to enrich their work. The leaders in the Music Ministry, especially the church's music director/minister, may serve as developers of skills in musical areas such as singing, playing instruments, and songleading; and as sources of information about other music needs, such as hymnals, keyboard instruments, and sound equipment. The Music Ministry leaders can provide music skill training through short-term class or group sessions, ongoing class sessions, or private instruction.

Task 5: *Interpret and undergird the work of the church and the denomination.* One of the major contributions the Music Ministry makes through this task is to relate and interpret the emphases of the church and the denomination to those who are primarily the members of the Music Ministry. How this is accomplished should be appropriate to the Music Ministry.

Churches of all sizes have a ministry of music. A very small church might have only a pastor, a volunteer (nonpaid) music director, and a volunteer pianist. These, together with the congregation, from whom there might also be individual vocal or instrumental contributions, make up their music ministry structure. Obviously, larger churches require more organization.[12]

For churches in which there is the possibility of graded choirs, the recommended basis for grouping and grading is to use the same age divisions as for the other program organizations in a church: Preschool, ages four and five; Children, ages six through eleven (or school grades one through six); Youth, ages twelve through seventeen (or school grades seven through twelve); and Adult, ages eighteen (or high school graduation) and up. Most large churches have multiple groups within these age divisions.

A church might have almost any number of other music groups, depending on the resources among the membership and in the community. And, with or without the possibility for much group work in the music ministry, almost any church can give encouragement and other help to individuals who have the interest and the potential for music development and growth.

CURRICULUM FOR THE MINISTRY OF MUSIC

Curriculum for the ministry of music in a church calls for uniquely complex sensitivities. Added to the many considerations regarding the texts of the music are many other criteria regarding the music itself, and, of course, the text and the music together. Add to these considerations the suitability and acceptability of the many situations in which music is called for, and it is not difficult to see the complexity.

There is diversity of musical tastes among churches. There is often diversity within a given church. With the help of the Holy Spirit, leaders in a church's music ministry must find ways to use appropriately and effectively the talents and the resources available to them, thus meeting the needs of the members and of others who are their concern.

Music texts should be compatible with biblical truth. In many instances the texts are passages of Scripture. The texts must be theologically and doctrinally sound, especially in light of the educational values of music. Relevance to past, present, or future experience is often a desirable feature of good texts.

The texts should communicate meanings that are clear and accurate, suited to the purpose of a church and to the occasion of their use. The language should be appropriate to the abilities of the participants, both the performers and others involved. Highly abstract, figurative language is usually inappropriate and might mislead children and even some literal-minded adults. Good grammar and poetic form are important in most instances. The overall literary quality of the music text should grace its message.

The music itself should be technically acceptable, calling forth responses appropriate to the text or to the witness of the church. It should be within reasonable range of the capabilities of the performers to perform and of others to receive with appreciation. It needs to be interesting. At times it should be stimulating. It helps if the music is pleasing to an appropriate extent. Appropriateness as to taste, rhythm, beat, tempo, difficulty, and length are among other considerations for the music.

The curriculum of a church's Music Ministry must take into account the many areas of knowledge, skills, attitudes, and understanding in which both performers and others need education and experiences. Writing of this need, the authors of *A Church on Mission* called for a curriculum with a balanced approach to music education and music performance.

This material involves sequential and progressive learning and performance activities based on mental, physical, and spiritual readiness of individuals. This task leads participants in the music ministry to make use of their musical skills through structured educational and performance activities that result in personal development, Christian growth, and the use of talents to support the mission of the church. The curriculum is contained in leader and member age-graded periodicals, Church Study Course materials, and related products.[13]

Music Ministry leaders, such as the Music Ministry Leadership Team, should oversee and supervise the selection and use of music curriculum in a church. Often they need to work together with leaders of other church organizations and with church staff members. Probably the single most important choice of materials, assuming the Bible is already a church's basic text, is selecting the church's principal hymnal.

According to Eskew and McElrath, "The teaching of the hymnal has yet to become a significant part of the educational program of most congregations."[14] These music scholars make an excellent case for teaching hymns in a church. In addition to the fact that hymns communicate the message of the church, they state that some hymns are based on specific Scripture verses, and others are paraphrases of Scripture. Hymns effectively convey theology. Singing hymns involves the congregation in active participation. Hymns are sung over and over again, year after year, and teach effectively through repetition. Their melodies linger in the memory and carry the thoughts connected with them into the mind and the heart. In worship, they help individuals express their feelings that they otherwise might have difficulty expressing.[15]

In addition to the regular use of hymns for singing, there are available hymn study sheets that are excellent aids in teaching hymns. These sheets usually explain how a hymn came to be written, what the text means, and something of the background of the tune, and refer to particular Scriptures that might relate to the hymn. One plan that involves the systematic integration of hymns into the children's choir curriculum consists of two three-year hymn cycles, one for grades one through three, and another for grades four through six. This plan is being used by the Church Music Department of the Sunday School Board of the Southern Baptist Convention, and is in their periodicals.[16]

Other music supplies and equipment, ranging from recordings, players, and teaching aids of various kinds to musical instruments that may be simple or complex, are of interest and importance to a church's Music Ministry. In all a church provides by way of its ministry of music, the power and the potential for good should be taken seriously by those who lead.

God in his Word exhorts us to praise him, to "come before his presence with singing." In his church, in all its activities, music is a vital experience. It voices praise, it testifies to the power of the gospel for salvation, it bears witness to the vitality of the Christian life. It reaches the unreached, it goes beyond closed doors, it communicates Christian love and understanding, it calms and heals and comforts. Those who have leadership responsibility in all areas of church life will wisely seek ways to use musical resources to help the church achieve its mission.[17]

CONCLUSION

A church's ministry of music is an integral part of its mission to make known the manifold wisdom of God. People in and out of the church need this ministry. Its tasks are complex. Its participants, performers, and listeners vary greatly in their needs and readiness and tastes. A ministry of music must give attention to the needs of all the members.

One of the major areas of yet-untapped potential is the fuller use of music as an educational method, not just for those who are to be the music leaders and performers, but for all the people of a church. Not only must music leaders be found and trained to lead them, but also the "nonmusician" people who teach and lead in church ministry organizations must receive help and training in the use of music as a method. Musicians already make large use of educational methods in music; nonmusicians need to make good use of music in education.

Churches of varying sizes have a ministry of music. The organization of a church's Music Ministry should be suited to a church's needs and resources. When possible, the use of graded choirs should be a major part of this ministry. Music Ministry leaders have an opportunity to structure the organization and to lead in the selection and use of appropriate experiences and materials in music. Wise leaders in a church's ministry of music can help a church in significant ways as it achieves its mission.

CONCERNS FOR FURTHER STUDY

Consider these questions as you continue to reflect on the ministry of music in a church.

1. What is there about music that makes it, perhaps above all the other arts, such an important aspect of the Christian faith?

2. What do you see as some advantages and some disadvantages in attempting to minister to the variety of musical tastes among church members?

3. How would you seek to increase the use of music as an educational method by the "nonmusicians" who work in other church ministry organizations?

CHAPTER 10

Ministries of Enrichment and Support

Most churches have many ministries. They have a ministry of Bible teaching and learning. Many have a ministry of discipleship training. Many also have a ministry of missions education and action. Almost all have congregational music, and many have larger ministries of music. All have church leadership ministries. These are the "base programs," foundational ministries of the model church structure in this text.

In addition to base programs, there are other important ministries that enrich and support a church in fulfilling its mission. Some of these are called "emphasis ministries." These include Family Ministry, Stewardship, Evangelism, Missions Development, Vocational Guidance, and Student Ministry. These emphasis ministries are interpreted and channeled by all appropriate church base ministries. Some others are called "service ministries." These include Media Library, Recreation, and Administrative Services. These supporting ministries help a church operate and conduct its overall ministry more effectively.

This chapter focuses on five such service ministries: Family Ministry, Stewardship, Media Library, Recreation, and Administrative Services. Our approach to each shall be to describe or define what it means, relate the importance and the essence of its work, illustrate the kinds of things it might do, and observe ways it might go about its work.

FAMILY MINISTRY

The family is God's first institution in time. He provided that man and woman meet each other's needs for companionship in marriage. He designed the family as the setting for procreation. When God wanted to convey his relationships with the highest order of his creation, mankind, he used the idea of the family. God is the Father; Jesus is the Son; those who receive Jesus are the Father's children and are joint heirs—brothers and sisters—with Jesus; Jesus is the bridegroom of the church, the bride.

Both the Old Testament and the New Testament affirm the special place of family in the values of the Heavenly Father. Parents were given clear and strong admonitions to train their children religiously. This parental responsibility has not been rescinded. In numerous ways Jesus sanctioned, blessed, and advocated the sanctity of marriage and family.

The New Testament writers had much to say about the family. Paul was especially strong when he wrote to Timothy: "If any one does not provide for his relatives, and especially for his own family, he has disowned the faith and is worse than an unbeliever" (1 Tim. 5:8). This provision covers all the needs of a family. Just as the Heavenly Father ordained and commanded that man and woman in a family should "be fruitful and multiply, and fill the earth and subdue it" (Gen. 1:28), the Son extended the Great Commission (Matt. 28:18–20) to the family of God, the church. One should conclude that the family is of unique interest to God.

Families today are in severe stress. So serious are the evidences of family trauma that some have concluded that the family as a unit cannot survive. Some of the indicators of this stress were identified in chapter 5. Statements of the needs of families abound, such as are found in *A Church on Mission*, an important book for the decade of the eighties for leaders and others in the Southern Baptist Convention; and in the comparable book for the latter eighties and the nineties, *Being God's People*.[1] This denomination has determined to place priority emphasis on family ministry. The Roman Catholic Church in the United States also designated the eighties as the decade of the family, with special programs to strengthen families. Along with these two largest of America's denominations of Christians, other church groups are working diligently to minister to the needs of families.

TASK AND NEEDS

Individual congregations must bear the responsibility for most of what might be done to assist families. It is urgent that a church give major attention to its ministry to families. The task of Family Ministry is: *minister to the distinctive needs of couples, parents and their children, senior adults, and single adults.* Its purpose is to help enrich family life—marriages, parenting, senior adulthood, and single adulthood—by meeting family-related needs of these groups in the church and its programs.[2]

Needs related to development and crises. Two major groups of considerations that a comprehensive ministry to families must include will illustrate both the critical needs and the complexity of family ministry. First are developmental and crisis needs. The Family Ministries leaders of the Baptist Sunday School Board have identified fifteen areas of such needs:

- Development and learning tasks within a family system
- Capability skills, discipline, nurture, and meeting needs
- Sexuality needs and adjustments
- Christian education, values, worship, service
- Relationship and communication skills
- Divorce, widowhood, separation adjustment
- Marital growth and development
- Parenthood skills development
- Financial management, vocational change adjustment
- Self-esteem and personal competency development
- Health and nutrition
- Personal and spiritual enrichment
- Affirmation, confrontation, forgiveness, reconciliation
- Remarriage adjustment
- Physical, emotional, and terminal illness adjustment.

Churches need leadership development, ministry designs, materials, and other help in developing and sustaining a ministry to these developmental and crisis needs of families.

Needs related to stages of the life cycle. A church's ministry to families must take into account all of the stages of people in the family setting: birth, infancy, childhood, youth, young adulthood, median adulthood, older adulthood, and death. The family at each stage has its distinctive needs. Church leaders must be aware of these distinctive needs and be prepared to help.

Often the occasion for special ministry to families arises just prior to, during, and just after the passage from one stage of life to another. Marriage, birth, and death are examples of opportunities for ministry to families. Always in these change points are times when values might be reviewed, and vows and new levels of commitment made or strengthened. Timely ministries at these change points can help strengthen families, and often help them avoid having crisis turn to tragedy, such as the breakup of the family.

Church leaders must be aware of the potential for ministry in the times of transition crises in families, and be prepared to minister to families effectively. Likewise, families need to be aware of the possibilities in their own needs, and be encouraged to look to their church for strength and support.

A church should minister to people because people need help. A by-product of appropriate ministries to people often is a strengthening of the relationship between individuals and their church. This is not the primary motivation for such ministries, but is a fortunate by-product for individuals and for the church.

FAMILY MINISTRIES PLAN

There are so many possibilities a church might consider when developing a ministry plan for families that it is essential to focus on priority concerns of families.

> Priority concerns of families usually include marriage preparation education, marriage enrichment, family relationship development, parenting skills development, family crises ministry, mid-life and empty nest adjustments, preretirement planning, and adjustments to retirement and to the later years of life. The family ministry program of a church may be a variety of special projects designed and conducted to meet these specific priority needs. Ongoing activities may also be a part of the program.[3]

An individual church leader, such as the pastor or another concerned person, might begin to awaken a church's sensitivities to the needs for a family ministries plan. One approach might be to conduct a family needs forum. This event could be conducted in one evening, and would be designed to secure ideas and suggestions regarding the needs in a church for family ministries.

Family Enrichment Committee. Such an event could result in the formation of a Family Enrichment Committee to lead the suggested ministries. If a church already has such a committee, this group could conduct the forum. Suggested purposes of the committee might be: (1) to assist the church ministry organizations in providing for the needs of families; and (2) to provide family enrichment programs for couples, parents, and other family members. Members of the committee might number from three to twelve, depending on the size of the church. The committee should have some balance of married adults and parents and of ages and interest (younger, median, senior adults; parents of preschoolers, children, and youth, including single parents). These should be elected by the church through the church nominating committee.

Duties of the Family Enrichment Committee should include: (1) to increase the church's awareness and understanding of the needs and concerns of families; (2) to survey the needs of couples, parents, and other family members; (3) to develop a comprehensive plan for meeting the needs of families; (4) to plan and conduct family life projects or programs through which family needs are properly met, including "Christian Home Emphasis;" (5) to encourage and assist the programs of the church in meeting the needs of families; (6) to lead the church to develop a ministry with intergenerational groups; and (7) to coordinate plans and activities through the Church Council[4] (the Church Ministry Leadership Team).

A church might also form other leadership groups as needed, such as a Senior Adult Leadership Team and a Single Adult Leadership Team. These groups should have representation on the Family Enrichment Committee, and on the Church Ministry Leadership Team. Detailed instructions regarding these organizations are available in specialized materials from the Baptist Sunday School Board, Nashville, Tennessee.

Special emphases. Certain Sundays in the church year might be chosen for special emphasis days. Family Worship Commitment Day, Family in Bible Study Day, Couples Commitment Day, Parent Commitment Day, Senior Adult Day, and Single Adult Day, as well as Mother's Day and Father's Day, illustrate occasions that might be used to focus on families.

Conferences, workshops, retreats, and special study programs offer formats for more depth in ministry. These formats might be the vehicles for such concerns as marriage enrichment, parent enrichment, Christian education in the home, spiritual growth, personal relationships, ministry to others, stewardship of life, continuing to learn, and other needs to be met.

Christian Home Week, Growing in Oneness project, Parents Building a Christian Home project, Family Fest, Your Family a Witness for Christ, Single Adult Revival, Senior Adult Clubs or Groups, and intergenerational projects are some of the events a church might include in its family ministry plan.

Deacon Family Ministry Plan. A significant part of a church's ministry to families can be conducted by way of the Deacon Family Ministry Plan. In this plan a deacon is assigned responsibility for a specific number of church member households (ten to fifteen at most) with whose families the deacon establishes and maintains contact on a year-round basis. Special events in the lives of family members, and other occasions in the life of the church itself, give opportunities for the deacon to be aware of needs and to minister to the family members. In addition, the deacon can be the communication link between the family and the other resource people and groups in a church. Since a large percentage of the membership of most churches do not participate regularly in any of the church's organizations (even Sunday school), this pattern for organized ministry to all church members might be the only vital link between these members and the larger fellowship.

Other church organizations render valuable ministries to families. Sunday school classes, for example, often minister very effectively to their members at critical points in the members' lives. Base ministry programs, emphasis ministry programs, and service ministry programs—these groups are important in the overall ministry of a church to its families.

Most churches do not have a formal educational organization (more than a committee) for family ministry or for family life education. Perhaps a suggestion to the church's major educational ministry organizations would help: Give special care in planning regular, extracurricular, and supporting events (planning meetings, special program events, and rehearsals, for example) to assure that families are considered. Otherwise it is possible, even likely, that church ministry organizations might become an inadvertent contributor to the problems families experience.

A practical expression of this special care for families would be to minimize the number of meetings that are designed to provide only for one family member, and to try to schedule essential and useful experiences for other family members when such meetings are necessary. This is not an easy concept to implement, but churches must come to grips with this problem. A church must not be part of the problems families have, but part of the solution to their problems.

Perhaps every event's planning procedure should include consideration of the event's impact on families and what provisions are planned to maximize the contribution to families. Family Ministry is a vital emphasis ministry. It is of primary importance to a church in achieving its objectives. Its program is most often interpreted and channeled through the other ministry organizations. Through a plan for family ministry, a church must minister to the distinctive needs of couples, parents and their children, senior adults, and single adults. Implementing such a plan is a major educational and leadership challenge for a church.

STEWARDSHIP MINISTRY

Stewardship of life and possessions is a significant emphasis ministry in a church. This ministry in a church should lead people to an understanding of and commitment to biblical concepts of individual and corporate stewardship. It should be based on the doctrines of the ownership of God, the lordship of Christ, the mission of the church, and the accountability of Christians.

TASKS

The Stewardship ministry in a church has two specific church tasks:
1. Develop Christian stewards;
2. Involve the church in supporting Cooperative Program ministries.

To develop Christian stewards we must clarify the meaning of stewardship in the total lives of church members. It is to lead them to adopt growth and commitment as basic stewardship qualities. It is to lead members to raise the level of individual and corporate giving to standards consistent with the highest ideals of biblical stewardship. It is to educate members regarding what stewardship means both in concept and in practical applications in their lives individually and corporately.

To involve the church in supporting Cooperative Program ministries is to relate church members to "doing together what we cannot do alone."

This means to support the mission ministries outside the local church, at each judicatory level. For Southern Baptists this is done primarily through the associations, the state conventions, and the Southern Baptist Convention. The Cooperative Program is the vital central plan for financial support of mission, educational, and benevolent undertakings beyond the local church.

Developing Christian stewards and involving the church in supporting cooperative ministries of the denomination call for continuing work on a year-round basis by church leaders to inform, to motivate, and to commit church members to the tasks.

There must be educational efforts throughout the year as appropriate, often through the base ministry organizations, the worship services, prayer meetings, and during special times of stewardship emphases. Even the processes of planning and implementing the financial operations of the church—budget planning, record keeping, reporting, and financial management procedures—can be developed and communicated in ways that are educational and motivating, and can lead to deeper commitment. To realize these possibilities requires good leadership and planning.

STEWARDSHIP COMMITTEE

A church needs a standing (year-round) Stewardship Committee to lead in educating its members and in implementing all phases of stewardship development. This committee would lead in budget development, promotion, and commitment; and ensure sound procedures in operational areas of church finance, including receiving, counting, depositing, recording, disbursing, reporting, and auditing church funds. The committee would also relate to any special fund-raising, such as for building funds; and to the education and support for cooperative ministries beyond the local congregation. The committee needs to relate at times to other church ministries and to the Church Ministry Leadership Team (Church Council) in order to coordinate effectively the accomplishment of its work.

Help is available for the vital work of Stewardship in a church cooperating with the Southern Baptist Convention via the national Stewardship Commission, 901 Commerce Street, Nashville, Tennessee 37203; and through each state convention office. There are annually updated materials for each church, distributed by state convention stewardship leaders. Local church leaders in stewardship should contact these sources for help.

MEDIA LIBRARY

Decades ago churches began seriously to use what was called the church library to enrich and support the various ministries of the church. The church library was a repository of books, for the most part. The church library ministry has grown tremendously, and its outlook has changed from that of a book depository to that of a Media Library.

TASKS

The Media Library in a church is designed to unify a church's efforts to involve media in the life of its members and the work of its programs. A church needs to use the most effective media available for communicating. This service ministry in a church, the Media Library, performs three tasks:

1. Provide media and Media Library services.
2. Promote the use of media and Media Library services.
3. Train people in media skills.

THE MEDIA CENTER

The Media Library is located in a media center in a church. It might have a very small staff, such as a director, a technical processes director, and a promotion director. In very small churches, one person might do all of these basic jobs.

Churches use a variety of media in their ministries. Some of the materials included in a full-service Media Library ministry are: printed materials—including books, periodicals, newspapers, tracts, leaflets, and clippings from newspapers or magazines. Projected visuals and audiovisuals are among the first additions beyond printed materials. These include slides, filmstrips, overhead transparencies, motion pictures, videocassettes, videodiscs, and microfiche. Audio materials, such as disc and tape recordings, are part of a full-service Media Library. So is a variety of audiovisual equipment, such as 8mm, 16mm, and 35mm projectors, opaque projectors, overhead projectors, tape recorders, record players, disc players, cassette duplicators, video monitors, portable public address systems, and microfiche readers. Nonprojected visuals—including maps, charts, flipcharts, sentence-strip charts, posters, flat pictures, framed art pieces, games, and globes—contribute significantly to a Media Library ministry. Other miscellaneous materials are useful, such as multimedia kits, costumes, permanent flower arrangements, props for drama groups, and other objects. Music resources might also be requested by the music ministry.[5]

Many churches operate their Media Library with the small staff listed earlier. Some have a larger staff. They might add to the three positions already stated these others: a circulation director, a media maintenance director, a media education director, and a special services director. The staff select media needed for individuals and church programs; secure media from stores and agencies; record messages for use when needed; process, catalog, and store media; and circulate media by lending, selling, or giving.[6]

The staff of the Media Library try to determine the needs of the various target groups. They study information about dated curriculum, special events, seasonal interests, and the personal concerns of individuals. They promote through audiovisual previews, bookmarks, book talks, brochures, bulletin boards, bulletin inserts, church bulletins and papers, letters and cards, media fairs, Media Library Emphasis Week, posters, signs, displays, and skits. These and numerous other activities and services are useful in advancing the educational opportunities in a church. It is important that media resources be seen as valuable aids in learning, growing, teaching, ministering, and witnessing.

The media field is complex. Materials and equipment can be expensive. It would be poor stewardship generally for individual leaders or church organizations to provide their own media, even if they could do so. It makes good sense for media services to be provided through a Media Library staff and a Media Library.

In Bible study, missions education, discipleship training, outreach, music ministry, and in many other ministries of a church, media can be used to stimulate interest, maintain attention, and generate better learning experiences. The challenge of the times calls for the use of every appropriate means to reach people for Christ and to help them grow and develop as Christians. A vital Media Library ministry can be a significant part of a church's efforts to fulfill its mission.[7]

RECREATION MINISTRY

Recreation is the use of leisure time for activity that is "designed to create, to restore, and to refresh the individual."[8] Leisure time as a generally available "commodity" is a relatively recent phenomenon. Most people throughout history have not had large blocks of unoccupied time when they were free to do what they chose. For most of the ages, people's energies have been required to eke out an existence. This fact remains true today for many in the world.

Technological developments since the beginning of the Industrial Revolution have afforded an increasing number of people increasing amounts of discretionary or leisure time. Many have chosen to use their discretionary time to busy themselves in alternate occupations for added pay, to increase materially their standard of living, or to support more adequately the standard they already try to maintain. Many others have chosen to use some of their newly found leisure time to create, to restore, to refresh themselves in recreation activities.

Most church members and their families can choose to use portions of their leisure time for recreation. This has given rise to a vibrant and growing ministry opportunity for churches, the ministry of Christian recreation. In addition to the positive factors which favor a church's involvement in

ministry through Christian recreation, there are forces almost too numerous to catalog which vie for the recreation time and other resources of society at large as well as church members and their families. Many of these
forces add to the misery and suffering of Christians as well as of the total
society. Church members, their families, and those whom churches are trying to reach need some constructive and Christian recreation alternatives
which churches can provide.

Robert A. Orr wrote succinctly about the service role of recreation in a
church.

> First, it can play a conductive role as the functions of a church find expres-
> sion in the recreational activities themselves, as when a Christian drama is
> used to proclaim the gospel and call people to decision. Second, by providing
> ideas, tools, and methodologies for use by other church programs, it supports
> the activities of other programs and the entire congregation. Christian disci-
> pleship includes stewardship of time including leisure time, those blocks of
> unoccupied time in which a person is free to do what he chooses. Church rec-
> reation can help a faithful Christian steward use leisure in constructive and
> healthy ways.[9]

TASK

The task of Recreation Ministry is: *Provide recreation methods, materials, services, and experiences that will enrich the lives of people and support the total mission of the church.*[10] In serving to enrich and support a
church's ministries, recreation services can be a catalyst in outreach, a ve-
hicle for ministry and mission action, a tool for teaching, an environment
for fellowship, and an avenue to abundant living.[11]

ACTIVITIES

Churches engage in a variety of recreational activities as part of their
Recreation Ministry. Social recreation has long been part of a church's leisure time options. Parties, banquets, fellowships, picnics, and other similar
activities can contribute to quality interaction of people with people.

Sports and games offer enjoyment, competition, fellowship, and exercise. Christ-centered and properly directed sports programs can provide
opportunities for individuals to give or receive a positive Christian witness, have joyous Christian fellowship, and develop desirable personal
qualities of honesty, self-control, responsibility, sportsmanship, and team-
work that contribute to building Christian character. Included could be
such activities as team sports, lifetime sports, individual sports, and dual
sports.[12]

Christian drama includes storytelling, clowning, puppetry, monologue,
improvisation, creative dramatics, choral drama, mime/pantomime, tab-
leau, music drama, play production, fun drama, readers' theater, and multimedia. These can be a powerful recreational force for those who

"present" and for those who "spectate." Relatively few churches have maximized this potent medium, but more and more are beginning to realize what it can do. It is one art form that churches should investigate with confidence and care. Rightly used, there are few methods that equal its possibilities for good.

Camping of many types uses the resources of the natural environment for Christian education, fellowship, evangelism, ministry, and personal growth experiences. Among these types are retreat camping, travel camping, day camping, resident camping, wilderness camping, backpacking, primitive or pioneer camping, Christian stress camping, family camping, and adventure recreation. An excellent resource in this specialized area is the book by Bob Raus, *Ministry Through Camping* (Nashville: Convention Press, 1990).

Other recreation services that a church can provide include recreation music, retreats, arts, crafts, hobbies, physical fitness, and therapeutic recreation. A church might conduct a recreation interest survey, such as the one detailed in Ray Conner's book, *A Guide to Church Recreation* (Nashville: Convention Press, 1977)[13] to determine the interests and needs for particular forms of recreation in its church and community. The types and amount of recreation activities, the different age groups and target groups to be included, the number of people available to train and qualify as recreation leaders, and other resources together would indicate to a church just how they should organize for this ministry.

THE RECREATION DIRECTOR

The pastor, or other appropriate person, should lead the church to secure a recreation director. This person might be unpaid, or employed part-time or full-time. A very small church might have only one person leading its recreation ministry. Other churches might have, in addition to a director, others who direct one or more areas of recreation—crafts, camping, drama, retreats, socials, sports, for example. Some churches might find it useful to have age-group or special target group representatives to assist directors in interpreting needs and opportunities of their groups.

The best organization is the one that best accomplishes the work needed and desired by a given church. Those who lead a church's recreation ministry should work through their relationships to other church organizations and through the Church Ministry Leadership Team to enrich and support the total mission of their church.

ADMINISTRATIVE SERVICES

A church as a whole can rarely attend to all its administrative needs. Most often the church body should limit its administrative work to making policy and governance decisions, and should delegate to individuals and to groups the responsibility to study, plan, and recommend procedures and solutions to detailed administrative concerns. Those individuals, such as church officers, and those groups, like church committees or the Church Ministry Leadership Team, render administrative services to a church.

RESPONSIBILITIES AND TASK

Numerous church administrative responsibilities require consideration, study, decision, and action by or under the direction of the church itself. Responsibilities like these include:

- Govern the life and work of the church under the lordship of Christ
- Determine the church's ministries, emphases, and administrative services
- Establish organizations to conduct and/or coordinate the church's ministries, services, and emphases
- Determine the church's cooperative work with other churches
- Establish and maintain appropriate external relationships
- Select pastor, staff and volunteer leaders and assign responsibilities
- Provide and allocate resources for the total work of the church

Out of the responsibilities listed above grows the Administrative Services task: *Assist the church to plan its ministry, manage its resources, and govern its life and work.*

ADMINISTRATIVE GROUPS

Church committees, elected by and accountable only to the church, represent one of the major types of administrative service groups. The nominating committee, church property and space committee, stewardship committee, family enrichment committee, flower committee, food service committee, history committee, personnel committee, preschool committee, church weekday education committee, public relations committee, ushers committee, and audio services committee are among those commonly found in churches.

The Church Ministry Leadership Team is a key administrative services group that plans and coordinates the ministry work of a church. See chapter 13 of this text for a discussion of its important work.

Perhaps through a temporary study committee, a church should identify the areas in which it needs committees. Appropriate committee titles should be chosen, and the responsibilities of each committee clearly stated in writing. The church nominating committee or a committee on committees should enlist the chairperson of each committee, and work with each chairperson to select committee members to be enlisted by the chairpeople themselves. Chairpeople and members should be elected by the church.

Committee members should serve on a rotating basis, perhaps on three-year terms. The first year one-third of the members of a given committee would be elected to serve for one year, one-third for two years, and one-third for three years. Those completing their tenure would be replaced by newly elected members, thus providing a revolving service and growth opportunity for more church members. Normally it is wise to choose new chairpeople from among those who have served one or more years as a committee member.

Each year there should be a church committee workshop to train all committee members. One good format for this workshop is to have a general meeting of all committees for a presentation suited to their needs as they begin a new year of work for the church. Following a general session, individual committees should meet briefly to get acquainted and to set the time and agenda for their first working meeting of the new church year or calendar year. Training helps for this workshop are available.[14] The continuation of this kind of service and training, with new personnel coming into service each year, provides opportunities for growth and learning by committee members that no other means provides. It should be a worthy part of a church's educational ministry.

Some of the same suggestions might be applied to officers of a church, such as the moderator, trustees, church treasurer, and church clerk. The idea of annually rotating members who serve in these offices should not apply. Rather, there might be fixed tenures with additional terms allowed by election. Their training might best be done on an individual basis.

ADMINISTRATIVE SERVICES AND EDUCATIONAL MINISTRY

Administrative services are part of the educational ministry of a church. Some dismiss administrative services as certain responsibilities (even disdainful chores) that must be performed so the church can get on with its ministry. Instead, let us see two significant values of administrative services for the educational ministry.

Value 1: Administrative services are integral to the successful completion of the church's ministries themselves. The church needs assistance in guiding, governing, and maintaining itself. This assistance is provided by administrative services in a church. Without these services, a church will not function at the optimum effectiveness or efficiency.

Value 2: Serving in administrative services enriches the lives of those who serve. People usually need and sometimes receive special training for their task. This training itself can be a very worthy contribution to the growth and development of the individual. The very acts performed while serving often cause growth and development of significant value to the individual. Personal insights and insights about others, as well as knowledge, skills, and relationship opportunities often are real compensation for serving. There is also the joy of knowing a service has been rendered to others, to the church, and to the Lord. Such personal growth and development opportunities should be pointed out to those who are asked to serve, and to others, to the end that administrative services are seen for what they are really worth both to the church and to individuals. They should not be unduly magnified, but they should never be ignored.

CONCLUSION

Many churches have multiple ministries they attempt to maintain. They have Bible teaching and learning, discipleship training, missions education and action, music ministry, and church leadership ministries—called base ministries or programs. Churches also have other significant ministries that are essential if these base ministries are to be most successful: emphasis ministries, like family ministry, stewardship, evangelism, missions development, vocational guidance, and student ministry; and service ministries like Media Library, recreation, and administrative services.

The educational opportunities in these emphasis and service ministries are abundant. In Family Ministry it is urgent that churches consider very carefully the impact on families of fragmented scheduling, as well as considering the positive needs of families that they might plan to meet. These needs can be seen in terms of developmental and crisis needs, and must be viewed from the life cycle perspective. A Family Enrichment Committee should give leadership in this emphasis area.

In Stewardship the educational needs are vast, ranging from the needs to study the biblical bases for living and giving as good stewards, to knowledge and training in the appropriate operational aspects of a church's financial resources management, and on to informing and enlisting people for cooperative missions support. A Stewardship committee leads in this essential work.

The service ministries—Media Library, Recreation, and Administrative Services—are organized differently. The Media Library and Recreation function like a staff organization. Administrative Services works through church committees, individual church officers—the moderator, the trustees, the church treasurer, and the church clerk—and the Church Ministry Leadership Team.

Each of these services offers indispensable assistance to other church ministries, while providing growth and development for those who serve. Hence, these are vital parts of a church's educational ministry, and should be seen as such.

CONCERNS FOR FURTHER STUDY

Consider these questions as you continue to reflect on the ministries of enrichment and support.

1. What do you think a church might do to maximize its ministry to families?

2. What are some basic approaches you would consider for beginning to address the stewardship tasks in a church?

3. Assuming you had an interest in and a commitment to being the Media Library director in a very small church, what are some of the things you might do to establish and maintain this important ministry?

4. What rationale would you give to support the idea of a comprehensive ministry of recreation in a church?

5. What would you suggest as possible ways to put more education into the administrative services—church committees, church officers and the Church Ministry Leadership Team—of a church?

PART THREE

LEADERSHIP PERSONNEL

The educational ministry of a church requires leadership. Very little that is prized or cherished is accomplished in the ministries of a church by accident. Someone, or preferably several someones, must lead intentionally.

A leader is one who has others following. What the leader does intentionally to get others to follow is leadership. There are certain things to be done for which churches historically have sought leaders who have experienced a call from God to minister. The vast majority of churches have only one staff position for which they seek such a person—the position of pastor. Most churches determine who will be their pastor. Hence, the pastor has a call from God and a call from the church. What the pastor does to enable the church to be the church and to do the work of the church we call ministry.

Some churches grow to the point that they call others who also have experienced a call from God to share the pastoral responsibilities to minister. These people might also minister where the pastor alone could not possibly have time, knowledge, or energy to minister. What these other ministers do is just as surely ministry as that which a pastor might do.

Ministry is ministry because of what is done rather than by whom it is done. Fortunate is a church that has the services of a team of gifted and called ministers who give their best energies to leading the church to fulfill its mission. What these and others do to lead in the church's ministries comprise what we call the Church Leadership Ministry, a "base ministry" in a church.

There are others in addition to the called ministers who lead in a church's ministries. Their name could be "Legion," for they are many—though not yet enough. They are volunteers. The volunteers are ministers, too, though churches seldom formalize them into a status with the designation of minister. These volunteers are the leaders who are asked by the church to serve without financial compensation. They teach classes in Sunday school, lead individuals or groups in discipleship training, mission education and action, or music ministry, or work in one of the emphasis or service ministries. There is a sense in which all who serve are volunteers. But those who serve with no financial compensation form the classic category for which we use the term volunteers.

Part 3 has three chapters in which we shall present the work of the pastor, other ministers, and volunteer leaders in education in a church. One of the major organizational approaches to leadership, leadership through a church's leadership teams (councils), will be presented. The objective of part 3 is to help people clearly to understand the roles and working structures of those who lead the educational ministry of a church.

CHAPTER 11

Pastoral Role in Education

A church needs to be guided, protected, and nourished in order to grow, develop, and reproduce itself in the world—to fulfill its mission. God has provided ways acceptable to himself for these needs for loving, caring concern to be met. His way is through the variety of gifts he has given to the church. "And his gifts were that some should be apostles, some prophets, some evangelists, some pastors and teachers, to equip the saints for the work of ministry, for building up the body of Christ, until we all attain to the unity of the faith and of the knowledge of the Son of God, to mature manhood, to the measure of the stature of the fulness of Christ" (Eph. 4:11–13).

God has given to some, from among all who respond to his call to discipleship, certain essential functional abilities that are to be used within the church. The abilities are gifts. Those people who are recipients of his gifts become his gifts also, as they develop and use worthily the functional abilities they are given. The gifts are not personal accomplishments; they are gifts to be used to minister, not to exalt or to achieve status among those who comprise the church. God has given pastors and teachers, deacons, and other ministers—servants—who are to bless the life and work of the church by exercising their gifts in ministry.

Many churches have only one vocational minister: a pastor. Other churches have a larger staff of ministers. Often churches choose volunteer workers to lead some ministry areas. Whoever make up the ministry team, theirs is the opportunity and responsibility to work together to lead the ministries of a church. The pastor, other vocational ministers, and church-chosen volunteer leaders are to work together as equippers of the saints to do the work of ministry. Theirs is a Church Leadership Ministry. In churches large or small, the pastor is the leader of the church leadership team.

AN OVERVIEW OF CHURCH LEADERSHIP MINISTRY

There are six basic tasks for Church Leadership Ministry in support of the ongoing life of a church: (1) guide the church in the accomplishment of its mission; (2) proclaim the gospel to believers and unbelievers; (3) lead in worship; (4) equip believers; (5) care for people; and (6) undergird the work of the church and the denomination.

Guiding the church in accomplishing its mission is a pastoral leadership task. It involves working with other church members and leaders to develop the vision, the direction, and the motivation for the church and its ministries. It may be accomplished by working with the Church Ministry Leadership Team (the Church Council), organizational leadership teams, officers and committees of the church, and the church itself, to plan, conduct, and evaluate short-range and long-range church projects and programs. Those who guide the church's ministries help develop processes for administering, planning, problem solving, and decision making by the church. They guide the coordination of church ministries. They lead in communicating the work of the church and in all of its relationships. They encourage and inspire responsible participation in the life and work of the church. They try to lead the church to be the church, and to do the work of the church.

The task of leading the church to proclaim the gospel to believers and unbelievers is a pastoral responsibility. "Those who lead are expected to develop skills to achieve maximum effectiveness as proclaimers. They seek to lead all church members to become proclaimers to the extent of their ability and opportunity. They seek to discover and use all possible avenues in communicating the gospel."[1] Preaching is the primary approach in public proclamation of the gospel. Teaching the Bible is another approach. Witnessing is still another.

There are other approaches through which proclamation might occur. Discovering and developing the interests and skills of church members in the use of all legitimate means and media for proclamation of the gospel is the challenge of this task. It is a church leadership ministry to lead the worship. This task includes planning and conducting congregational worship. It also extends to encouraging worship by families, small groups, and individuals. The experiences of individuals encountering God in authentic worship provide the energizing of almost all that is worthy in subsequent endeavor. Church ministry leaders are to equip believers. They do this task first by modeling Christian discipleship and service. This modeling is indispensable in the realm of spiritual and moral leadership. Then and only then can leaders move effectively to enable people to discover and use their gifts in ministry. Included in this task, too, is that of teaching or mentoring people for life direction and vocation.

It is a pastoral task to lead the church to care for people. "A church is at its best when it is known as a community of believers who express the love of Christ to people in need."[2] This task calls for enabling people to minister to individuals, groups, and families. It includes encouragement of individuals and groups to pray. It might provide for church discipline through a ministry of restoration. It includes referral of people for specialized help. Church groups, such as Sunday school classes, WMU groups, Brotherhood, and deacons (especially through the Deacon Family Ministry Plan), can be significant in a church's plans to care in specific ways for those in need.

As with all other ministry programs in a church, the church leadership ministry has the responsibility to undergird the work of the church and the denomination. Following reasonable achievement and maintenance of success as a Christian person, and as a married person, and a parent person (for those who experience these relationships), the pastor as leader in the church leadership ministry succeeds when the church succeeds. "Good preaching or competent counseling alone will not build a church. Part of the success of pastoral ministries depends on interpreting and undergirding the work of the entire church."[3] It is important to all concerned that ministry leaders maximize the opportunities appropriate to them to advance the work of the church and the denomination.

THE UNIQUE LEADERSHIP ROLE OF THE PASTOR

From the days of the early churches, the role of the pastor has been vital. In the church leadership ministry the pastor is the leading servant of a church. The pastor has the primary individual responsibility, privilege, and sometimes burden of being the one person to whom the church looks for significant guidance in the life and work of the church. There are times when the complexities and the magnitude of the office of pastor weigh heavily on the person in that office.

The predicament of the pastor often is like that of Moses as he was leading the children of Israel from Egypt to the Promised Land. Moses' father-in-law, Jethro, said to Moses, "You and the people with you will wear yourselves out, for the thing is too heavy for you; you are not able to perform it alone" (Exod. 18:18). Jethro then proceeded to tell Moses how he could be the leader and share the responsibilities with other qualified and trained people. Together they could get the job done, the people could go their way in peace, and Moses and the people could endure. There are many worthy lessons in this biblical experience for those who minister.

There are certain aspects of ministry that the pastor normally must perform. For example, the pastor must be the chief proclaimer and the leader of others who proclaim. Through proclamation the pastor not only presents the truths of the gospel, but also the vision of the implications of the gospel for the church in its ministries. Through proclamation the pastor leads the church to do the work of the church. Such proclamation is the cutting edge of pastoral leadership. Without it a church is not likely to come close to reaching its potential as a church.

Effective leadership by the pastor cannot end with proclamation. The pastor must also lead the church in doing its work. A major part of that work is the educational ministry of the church. The pastor is also the chief educator of a church. One of the biblical qualifications for one who aspires to the office of pastor is to be "an apt teacher" (1 Tim. 3:2). But again, what pastor can do all that is needed in teaching a church? Not even the pastor of the very small church can do it all. It would not be wise or right to attempt to do it alone.

The basic approach that seems to offer hope for a pastor in the unique role of leading educator in a church is threefold in its dimensions. First and of most vital importance is for the pastor to be a growing Christian person. In the arena of spiritual and moral leadership, this is fundamental.

One promising model for this dimension is described by Ernest E. Mosley in *Priorities in Ministry*. In order for one to be an effective pastoral leader Mosley suggests the arrangement of priorities according to the chart in Figure 4.[4] He offers four principles in priority management by using concentric circles. (1) The control, or constraints, in priorities must always be from the inside out. (2) Whenever an inside circle is weak, the potential in the circles outside is limited. (3) Whenever an outside circle takes priority over an inside circle, look out for trouble. (4) When the order of priorities is maintained, greater satisfaction is experienced in a minister's life, and greater effectiveness is experienced in work.[5]

With regard to the idea that the pastor must first be a growing Christian person, Mosley suggests a simple but profound acceptance of the areas identified in Galatians 5:22–23, the "fruit of the spirit," as the criteria for evaluating one's growth: "love, joy, peace, patience, kindness, goodness, faithfulness, gentleness, self-control."

The personal example of the pastor as a growing Christian is an important element in the effort to help others grow. And, to be sure, the need for being a growing person cannot be limited properly to the pastor. But no pastor can lead effectively in the growth of others without trying to set an example.

A second dimension for a pastor in the unique role as the leading educator in a church is that of being an enabler of others. The pastor must not attempt to carry the responsibility alone. There are others in a church who have gifts of teaching. They can be identified, trained, and given the responsibility. The pastor can remain faithful to the admonition to teach and,

Figure 4

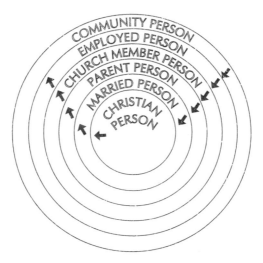

at the same time, focus major attention on the strategy of being an enabler of others who teach.

Some ministers have difficulty sharing what they perceive to be their responsibility for the gospel of salvation. Seward Hiltner spoke to this concern.

> There is no reflective Christian who has not at some time asked the question, "Was God out of his mind to entrust this most precious treasure to people like us and churches like ours?" And if he has answered the question rightly, he has finally said, "Yes, we are as bad as that; but God was willing to risk it, and he must know what he is doing."

> If even God felt it wise and right and essential to risk his purposes and his love through fallible human instruments, who is a minister to be unwilling to acknowledge that his ministry must be risked through fallible human beings who are, in actual fact, no more fallible than he?[6]

The pastor must encourage and lead in the discovery and development of others who can help in the educational ministry.

The third dimension is that of the pastor's personal leadership and support. The pastor must actively demonstrate leadership and support for the educational ministries. This is not to say that the pastor should make all of the decisions or try to do all the work. Harry Piland illustrated how a pastor can relate to the Sunday school in order to demonstrate leadership and support on a weekly basis. These suggestions might be applied to all educational organizations in a church.

(1) He can study records to determine whether each teaching unit is func-

tioning and where worker vacancies exist. (2) He can walk through the build-
ing(s), evaluating present use of space and location of possible new units. (3)
He can walk through the building on Sunday morning and observe in the various departments or he may visit Sunday School classes at different times. (4)
He can attend and participate in the Sunday School council and weekly workers' meetings. (5) He can recognize Sunday School workers during the worship hour. (6) He can preach on the mission of the church and relate the place
of the Sunday School to that mission. (7) He can attend various Sunday
School department activities, such as fellowships, banquets, and retreats. (8)
He can be involved in training Sunday School members in how to witness. (9)
He can participate and lead out in planned visitation and witnessing through
the Sunday School.[7]

THE PASTOR WITHOUT A STAFF

Each pastor must develop an approach suitable to the situation in light
of the needs and resources peculiar to a given church. Most churches have
only a pastor to give leadership from the perspective of the minister. They
do not have other vocational ministers. They look to the one person who
is their minister to lead them in the major ministries the church attempts to
carry out.

Many churches have a pastor who is bivocational or dual-professional
and earns part of the family's essential livelihood from a job other than the
pastorate. The number of such situations is increasing. Yet some of the
pastors who have no other ministers with whom to work are very effective
in their ministry.

How are they able to do it? There is no single formula for success for
the pastor without a staff, or for any other pastor, for that matter. It is possible, however, to identify some marks of the pastor who is effective.

The pastor without a staff must *live a disciplined life.* This usually includes developing a personally productive pattern for when to work and
when to do other things than work. It means the pastors should take reasonable care of themselves in terms of prayer, work, exercise, rest, eating,
family time, study and personal development, and other essentials for a
productive life. Such disciplined living becomes even more essential for
the pastor who is bivocational or dual-professional.

The pastor without a staff must *recognize his own humanity and limitations.* It is unrealistic to expect that a person will do each task as though it
were the only task for which one is responsible. A person does not have to
capitulate in order to acknowledge that there is a time for working and a
time to refrain from working.

Unwillingness on the part of some to acknowledge their human limitations, coupled with unreal expectations of some church members, can
make the things one does accomplish become devoid of joy. It can lead to
lowered productivity and on to "burnout." One must come to terms with

the fact that there can be more items on one's "to do list" at the end of a busy and productive day of ministry than there were at the beginning of the day, due to the many things that arise during some days of ministry.

One's workday must end at some reasonable time. The effective pastor seeks rest and restoration and saves the remaining tasks for another time. God does not expect the impossible from humans. God only expects the possible, and certainly knows our limits.

The pastor without a staff must *see and utilize the potential in other people*. This means that the effective pastor sees in others the capacities to grow and to share in ministering. The wise pastor develops a sensitivity to the gifts God has given to others and learns to envision what these gifts might mean if challenged, trained, and put to use in the work of the church.

The pastor without a staff must *develop volunteer leaders through whom the ministry can be multiplied*. Often this requires one-to-one relationships with individuals who have potential to render needed service to the cause. It includes helping individuals to see their own gifts and potential, and to become interested in relating to the worthy endeavors of the church in the expression of their gifts. It requires that ministers truly care about individuals, and not just about humanity in general. Individuals respond to this kind of leadership and will go to great lengths to help in their church's ministries with this kind of leadership. The pastor who relates well to individuals is likely to challenge a church's potential, with or without other ministers to help in the task.

The pastor without a staff must *learn to work with key volunteer leaders of church programs as though they were staff members*. It probably doesn't help to title them "staff," because in fact they are not staff. Still, these leaders should be a pastor's first level of relationship as together they lead in the church's ministries.

THE MINISTER OF EDUCATION
AND OTHER STAFF LEADERS

One phenomenon of churches in the twentieth century has been the growth of the number of churches who have ministers in addition to the pastor. While the concept of multiple ministers is as old as the New Testament churches, the vast majority of churches in history and at present have but one minister, the pastor. In churches cooperating with the Southern Baptist Convention, for example, approximately 62 percent have fewer than three hundred members. These churches have 24 percent of the members in that denomination. "The pastor is usually the only employed staff member in a church with fewer than three hundred members."[8]

Most of the churches with more than three hundred members have one or more people serving either part-time or full-time as ministers, in addition to the pastor. The total memberships of those churches with multiple ministers exceed considerably the total memberships of the churches with a pastor only. Several thousand churches have employed people to serve as ministers of education. Many others have additional people employed as educational specialists with age groups. Many churches also have employed people to serve as associate pastors, assistant pastors, ministers of music, ministers of recreation, and various other specialized ministries.

The pastor is the leader of the ministries team. The minister of education and other ministers should be seen as people who are called to minister in the same occupational sense as the pastor. Of particular concern to our subject is the minister of education, along with other educational ministers a church might have. What is the role of the minister of education in a church? What does this mean with regard to the pastoral role in education?

The pastor is the pastor of the educational ministries of a church. The pastor is the chief educational minister. The pastor should be seen as the "chief among equals." The minister of education and other educational ministers share the pastoral ministry responsibilities of a church. Those ministries are not the property of any one person. They belong to and are the responsibility of the church itself. The minister of education can and should render many specialized educational services to the church, in keeping with the overall leadership role of the pastor. The chart in Figure 5 is a sample of what a minister of education might do.[9]

It should be obvious that those things a minister of education does regarding the educational ministries of a church need not be duplicated by the pastor. They should be performed within the bounds of the pastor's guidance as prescribed by the church. The pastor with educational ministers with whom to work should take the initiative to keep informed about those essential parts of the educational ministry that will enable the pastor to be effective in maintaining the unique leadership role given by the church.

Part of the work of the educational minister is to keep the pastor informed, especially of the critical points regarding the educational ministries. These critical points can be determined by those involved in leadership roles. Minimally they should include information about possible new ministry plans, possible major adjustments or other changes affecting educational efforts, important organizational problems or changes, particular personnel needs or problems, major indicators of progress or of potential difficulties, and any other matters felt by either party to be of interest or concern to the pastor. It is important that this information for the pastor be communicated early enough to allow adequate time to exert appropriate pastoral influence on the situation.

The pastor and other ministers of a church should be a team, as contrasted with a loose collection of individual ministers concerned only with their personal concepts of their ministry as individuals. They are indeed

Figure 5

The Work of the Minister of Education: An Overview

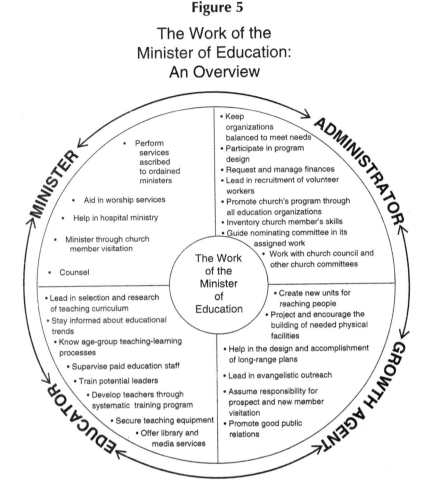

individuals. It is quite normal and natural that each would have personal concepts about ministry. The overriding consideration, however, is that a church has ministries to conduct, and its ministers are to be its servants in leading the church to fulfill its mission. When a church has several ministers to serve the church, fortunate are the church and the ministers when they work together, subordinating their individual differences for the good of the body, the church.

CONCLUSION

A church has needs that are to be met by people through leadership ministries. God has given some for this purpose. Pastors, other ministers, and volunteer leaders have responsibilities for leadership ministries in a church. The ministries of a church involve the mutually supportive assignments of guiding, proclaiming, leading, equipping, caring, and undergirding.

The pastor has a unique and vital role in the leadership ministries of a church. In addition to the singular kinds of ministries the pastor must personally perform, there are responsibilities and needs for the pastor to help others as they share in the ministries of a church. It is indispensable that the pastor develop the capacity to share with others the responsibilities which they can accept and perform.

In very small churches, this means sharing the load with volunteer workers, especially those who lead major ministry organizations of the church. In large churches it also means sharing the load with other ministers called of God and by the church to join with the pastor in serving the church to the end that the church can fulfill its mission.

The minister of education and other educational ministers work, with the pastor's guidance and support, to minister to the educational needs of the church. It is vital that the pastor keep informed regarding the educational ministries of the church, and that the pastor give appropriate leadership and support to these ministries. In case there are other educational ministers, a team concept in which all team members work together for the best interests of the church must be developed.

CONCERNS FOR FURTHER STUDY

Consider these questions as you continue to reflect on the pastoral role in education.

1. What do you see as some of the implications of viewing the basic tasks for church leadership ministries as interlocking and mutually supportive?

2. How can a pastor become an enabler of other people and give appropriate energies to other significant responsibilities of a pastorate?

3. Why should a pastor be concerned with the educational ministries of a church if there are other ministers on the staff who are called, trained, and employed by the church to lead in the educational ministries?

CHAPTER 12

Volunteer Leaders in Education

A church is an association of volunteers. In obedience to God's expectation, church members chose to come together in fellowship of their own free will. They have voluntarily responded to the call of God to discipleship. They have voluntarily and individually sought to identify with a body of believers of like faith commitment, and have been received into the fellowship of the body. They share in the privileges and in the responsibilities of church membership.

Among the privileges of belonging to a church fellowship are having a voice and a vote in the decision-making processes and the government of the church. Another privilege is being eligible to be considered for an elective office or a job, some place of responsibility in the life and work of a church. There are other privileges, and there are other responsibilities. This chapter is about the privilege and responsibility of serving in the educational ministries of the church.

THE CHURCH DEPENDS ON VOLUNTEERS

It is easy to observe that there are many things to be done in a church that attempts to establish and maintain a comprehensive plan for ministering to those in its fellowship. Add to these responsibilities those which are essential in the ministries to those people not yet reached for Christ and church membership, and the number of jobs is almost overwhelming.

There are Bible classes and departments that call for teachers and other leaders. There are discipleship groups or individuals who need guidance and training. There are mission study and mission action groups that require leaders. There are choirs and other music ministry groups that need leaders or advisors. The ministries to families, the stewardship ministry, the media library ministry, the recreation ministry, the deacons, the administrative service groups and individuals (church committees, church officers, and the Church Ministry Leadership Team—the Church Council or Council on Church Ministries), and other ministries a church might foster make it necessary to call on the members to accept responsibility for much of the work.

Sincere people sometimes suggest that the church should stop kidding itself about doing its work with volunteers and simply employ qualified people to do the teaching and educational ministries. These advocates usually cite the modern technological capabilities now available for education. One qualified teacher could teach many pupils. They speak of how hard it is to get people to agree to teach, to advise, or to lead. Some say that only the less capable are likely to be available to teach on a volunteer basis in the church. They envision great strides of progress in education in the church by way of a staff of employed, paid educators.

Their sincerity should not be mistaken for good judgment. Three reasons are enough to show that there is not the slightest possibility that a church could fulfill its educational mission with an all-paid staff of educators. First, few if any churches have enough money to employ enough qualified people to staff a well-organized educational ministry. Second, not enough qualified people are available to answer the invitation to such a monumental task. Third, the kind of teaching and learning that could be made to occur through a paid teaching corps would most likely be limited to the cognitive domain—learning the facts and figures, the names of people and places—to the neglect of the affective domain—changes in attitudes, appreciations, feelings, and commitments to act. Both domains are essential to quality education. Furthermore, there is no guarantee that paid teachers would be more effective than volunteers.

Yet using volunteer teachers and leaders has its problems. The very task of discovering, recruiting, and training a volunteer work force sufficient for the challenge is a continuing problem. Most women now are employed outside the home, and are no longer as available for volunteer service. Many men hold down two or more jobs. Families are feeling financial pressures that preoccupy their energies with the need to provide more income. Distractions accompanying the proliferation of media entertainment, spectator sports, individual mobility, and other contemporary realities make it harder than before to get the attention of people, much less their support. The age-old concern with how to motivate volunteers lingers.

Still, many of these very same problems are present (only slightly altered in some instances) with people who are paid. Churches can ill afford to put their hopes on a paid work force only to discover that there also are consuming problems with paid personnel. If there are difficulties to be overcome whether paid or nonpaid, it seems for the church that the choice is clear: *insofar as is possible and feasible, go with volunteer workers!*

A volunteer is one who enters into or offers himself for a service of his own free will. A freedom and spontaneity of choice or action without external compulsion is implied. This does not mean the volunteer always comes forward without solicitation or recruitment and begins working. Some do. But most are enlisted by someone. Usage has added the connotation that the volunteer receives no financial compensation. Except for the difference regarding compensation, the paid church staff member might have as much claim to being classified a volunteer as the worker who receives no financial compensation.

Certainly there are some differences between working with a volunteer and working with a paid professional. Still, in ministry there is the reality that one who performs the tasks *because* he is paid to minister is grossly overpaid at whatever the rate of pay; while one who performs ministry well and without monetary motivation could not be paid enough.

The church depends on volunteers. A church might compensate some so that they can give full energies to leading in ministry. For the most part, it is wise and right for the members to share meaningfully in the work of the church. Many think the survival of effective ministries in a church properly depends on volunteers.

TWO TRACKS OF EDUCATION IN A CHURCH

One of the best reasons for engaging large numbers of church members in leadership roles is that those who lead have opportunities and experiences that enable them to grow far more in the faith than they would if they were not in leadership roles. Who learns more: the teacher or the members of a Bible class? Normally, who works more in preparation for the teaching-learning session, the teacher or the members? Who feels more strongly the need to learn, the one who is the leader in the learning session or those who are taught? Who feels more keenly the need to improve teaching and learning skills: the teacher or the members?

Churches in which the organizational model for their educational groups calls for a small teacher–pupil ratio actually have the possibility for an advanced track of teaching and learning. The ministers and other leaders have the opportunity to focus on equipping the many teachers in a much higher level of growth and development than that which is possible for the study group members whom these volunteer teachers teach.

Given the choice, for instance, of organizing a hundred adults into one large Bible study group under the teaching of a masterful and interesting teacher or organizing the same people into five groups of twenty with five possibly less-qualified teachers, the choice might well be to go with the five groups. Then there are five teachers who might be challenged and led to train and work to become more effective teachers. These five would grow far more than if they were only class members. In addition, there would likely be far more meaningful individual participation among those who attended a given session. The important personal ties between the teachers and pupils would more likely develop. This is especially vital in teaching spiritual and moral truth. It is essential to learning in the affective domain. There also would likely be more interest in reaching out to recruit other students in order to expand the class membership.

In reality, one should find ways to choose both alternatives. The masterful, interesting teacher could be called on to help the five grow and develop; and from time to time this exceptional teacher could lead the entire group in special Bible study projects that would provide enrichment and additional study opportunities.

There should be two significant tracks of educational ministries in a church: *the leader track* and *the member track*. Each track is vital. But the leader track should claim the larger share of assistance from a church's ministers and organizational leaders, as together they work to provide more effective ministries for the maximum possible number of people who might take part in these ministries. Such a strategy offers hope for a much better mobilization of a church's resources and for the essential multiplication of the work force that must occur if the gospel is to be shared with the masses of the world. The harvest still is ready; pray that the Lord of the harvest will send forth laborers. Determine to be part of the answer to such praying.

MOTIVATING VOLUNTEER LEADERS IN EDUCATION

The problems that tend to obstruct or limit the use of volunteers in a church's educational ministries are more numerous and complex than they were in the first half of the twentieth century. In a time when people should have more discretionary time, many seem to be harder to interest in volunteer service. And not everyone has more discretionary time, especially women in the work force.

MOTIVATION FROM WITHIN
How can a church cope with these and other difficult problems? Part of the answer lies in more effective and realistic planning of the church's ministries—highlighting priority ministries, consolidating and coordinating schedules, and other reflections of sensitive leadership.

How to motivate people looms as one of the largest areas of concern in any age. How does a leader interest others to act or to react in relation to the church's educational ministries? How does one get another to serve, to give time and other resources on behalf of a church's work? Let us look briefly at the matter of motivation.

In another volume, this writer described motivation:

> Put simply, a motive is what causes a person to act or to react. Motivation is the act of unleashing that within the individual which incites him to act or to react. When the unleashing is stimulated from within a person we call it intrinsic motivation. When the stimulus is generated from without, as would be the case with the use of incentives, we call it extrinsic motivation. Intrinsic motivation, which many feel to be the purer kind, is like impulses or springs, often unrecognized or unconscious, providing impetus or driving power arising in oneself. Extrinsic motivation, considered by some to be less preferred in terms of ethics, is like an inducement, a spur, a goad, or an incentive, stimulating from outside oneself the internal impetus, causing one to act or react.[1]

In any case, motivation comes from within a person.

Leaders can try to create conditions that touch the follower's inner mechanism. The Christian leader must exercise special care and high ethical sensitivity in attempting to create these conditions. The one being motivated must be fully respected, and must not be led into that to which he could not give full, conscious assent. No person has the right to violate another. Each is made in God's image and is of ultimate value. It is right to inform of needs, to present challenge and opportunity, and to speak of legitimate compensations or benefits to all concerned. Undue coercion, appeals to fear, withholding of vital information, and other such actions are out of order for the Christian leader in attempting to get others to serve.

It is helpful to study the literature regarding motivation. Research is plentiful. One of the most interesting and useful books is *Keys to Effective Motivation* by Reginald M. McDonough (Nashville: Broadman Press, 1979). Another good source is *Christian Education Handbook,* compiled and edited by Bruce P. Powers (revised edition, Nashville: Broadman & Holman, 1996), especially the chapter by Jerry M. Stubblefield entitled "How to Staff and Motivate." Stubblefield has a very helpful chapter on motivating in his book *The Effective Minister of Education* (Nashville: Broadman & Holman, 1993). McDonough's volume, *Working with Volunteer Leaders in the Church* (Nashville: Broadman Press, 1976) is another worthy contribution. George T. Russ's article on "The Importance of Volunteers" (*Search,* [fall 1993]: 58ff.) offers a sensitive and helpful treatment that includes a section on motivating.

A classic in the field of motivation is the book by Abraham H. Maslow, *Motivation and Personality* (New York: Harper and Row, 1970). His "Hierarchy of Needs" has become a standard symbol in motivational references. He identified needs of people as physiological, safety (security), social (affiliation), esteem (recognition), and self-actualization. Beyond these are the need to know and understand, and aesthetic needs.

Maslow postulated that a person's behavior at a given moment is usually determined by these needs. Satisfied at that need level, one might move to a higher-level need.

It is useful to know the make-up of people and to work within the light of such knowledge. The motivator should be guided also by the concerns mentioned earlier with regard to respecting the personhood of the motivatee.

THE HIGHEST MOTIVATION

At some risk of oversimplifying an admittedly complex matter, we should like to suggest a simple basis for appealing to church members to serve as volunteers: biblical love. The encyclopedia to the *Master Study Bible* defines love: "An emotion, sentiment, or feeling of pleasurable attraction toward, or delight in, something, as a principle, a person, or a thing, which induces a desire for the presence, possession, well-being, or promotion of its object."[2] Biblical love has no equal in terms of strength or worthiness. Leaders and followers can come together in any worthy endeavor when such love characterizes the people involved.

There is a positive correlation between the worthiness of a cause and the willingness of people to give themselves and their resources to it. With the worthiest of all causes—the cause of Christ—one might wonder why multitudes don't come forward to volunteer their services and their resources. Could it be that many leaders have not communicated the worthy cause in authentic love that is concerned for the good of the volunteer as well as for what the volunteer might contribute?

FOUR DIMENSIONS OF LOVE

Consider the appeal to biblical love as the motivation for volunteer service. The appeal needs to be presented in balance. There are at least four dimensions that must be included. They are love for God, love for the church, love for other people, and love for self. These dimensions must not be placed against one another, but must be seen as compatible and mutually supportive. And remember: both the motivator and the motivatee must relate to each dimension.

Love for God is commanded in Scripture. It is expected. In the light of his great love for us, it is a natural and normal response to God. We are admonished by Jesus himself to love God with all our being (Mark 12:30). Our love for God takes priority over our love for family and self. We are in such debt to God that there is no way to repay with service, but it is through obedience and service that we express our love for God. It is valid to offer (not coerce) believers opportunities for meaningful service to God.

Love for the church is a worthy and right basis for appealing to people to serve. Christ, the head of the church, "loved the church and gave himself up for her" (Eph. 5:25). Followers of Christ are instructed repeatedly in the Scriptures to love one another. Such love is taken in the Scripture to be a sign of the genuineness of one's love for God, the mark of a true believer. Members of the fellowship of believers should enjoy one another's presence. They should feel that they belong to one another. They should be concerned for the well-being of one another. They should desire to advance the interests of one another. This adds up to love.

A member who says he loves the Lord of the church but who demonstrates no love for the others of the fellowship casts doubt on the validity of his professed love for the Lord of the church. It is possible for one to feign a love for others in the church but who does not in fact love or know the Lord of the church; it is not possible to love the Lord of the church and have no love for the Lord's body, the church. One way members can manifest the reality of their love for the Lord and for his church is to serve. One way to serve is to help others grow and develop through the educational ministries of a church. An appeal to love for the church is a valid part of the approach to motivating volunteers.

Love for other people is a sound basis for appealing to members of a church to serve voluntarily. Some of this dimension is related to the prior point, love for the church, since the church is made up of people. But in this love for other people is included all people in or out of a church. This dimension not only speaks to the love that members of the fellowship should have for one another, but to the love that any Christian should have for any other human being.

An unfortunate reflection on some church members is that sometimes people who make no claim to the love of God appear to demonstrate more of the "milk of human kindness" toward others than do some who claim to love God and the church. In terms of the alleviation of human misery and need, it is fortunate that there are people other than Christians who are willing to give of themselves on behalf of others. Many do this, and some to heroic proportions. How much more their service might mean if it could be done for the glory of God!

With respect to the self-interest of the one who serves others, the service should come more because of the need of the person being served than because of what the one being served might come to mean to the church. The goal should be unselfish service. If there is a response beneficial to the church, well and good. If no such response is forthcoming, the serving goes on, because we care—we love. Love for other people is a valid appeal for motivating volunteers.

Love for self is an essential dimension of appealing to people to serve as volunteers. This aspect of a balanced approach to getting people to serve has been neglected.

The apostle Paul wrote that one must not think too highly of oneself. Jesus said that the gauge for one's love for a neighbor is one's love for self. Jesus apparently assumed a normal self-esteem that would lead a person to want for others what one should want for self. It is imperative for one who serves best to have a genuine love for self, while avoiding the extreme about which Paul cautioned. In appealing for people to serve, it seems right to help the prospective workers realize some of the ways in which they themselves might benefit from serving.

Present a balanced appeal that touches all these dimensions. Show potential volunteers how what you are asking them to do is a way of serving God. Present the need as an opportunity to demonstrate their love for others of the fellowship of believers and for other people for whom the church, the body of Christ, is concerned. Point out that they themselves have opportunities for growth and development, education and training, self-improvement, and happy fellowship, while they experience the joy of meaningful service. Such a loving, sincere, and balanced appeal bears fruit in motivating people to volunteer.

Ministers and other leaders should be careful, however, not to imply that those who do not respond to this or any other appeal to serve are defaulting on their professed love for God, the church, other people, or self. There are other factors that are important in the dynamics of the situation. The individual needs to feel right and good about her or his own gifts and potential in relation to the service opportunity presented. Furthermore, there are times in people's lives when, due to prior commitments or other valid reasons such as health problems, the most "religious" response they could make would be to say, "Not now." When the response is negative, their choice to decline must be respected without categorizing them as uncooperative or unconcerned. Rather, they most likely will have other opportunities to consider serving in a place and at a time when they can happily give their consent. People should not work for long periods of time as volunteers or as staffers with a hesitant, grudging spirit due to having been overly persuaded or otherwise coerced into service for which they do not feel suited or called. There are plenty of kinds of service for almost everyone to be able to have a joyful work opportunity.

MINISTERS AND VOLUNTEER LEADERS WORKING TOGETHER

There are some differences and some common denominators that affect the work of ministers and volunteers. Some people are employed by the church, while others are not financially compensated. Some people are ordained to their function, while others are not. Some are occupied as full-time workers in the church, while others have other occupations. All need to work together in the service of the church. All are chosen by church-approved procedures to serve the church. All are committed to the lordship of Christ in the church. They are concerned with helping others in Christ's name because others need help.[3] How should they work together, in light of these similarities and differences?

Among the attitudes and understandings that tend to make for the best effect when paid and unpaid people are working together are these: (1) The particular tasks of ministry are indeed ministry without regard for the status or the terms of compensation of the person who does them. (2) All who serve must have some opportunity to do tasks that have meaning, not just the chores that others choose not to do. (3) All deserve respect since they serve of their own free will, based on the love commitments that represent their response to God, the church, others, and self. (4) Each desires and rejoices in the successes of the others, whether paid or unpaid. (5) The strategy of the paid staff people is to enable the volunteers to accomplish their tasks with a reasonable sense of fulfillment, growth, service, and joy.

Some of the unproductive and usually unhappy attitudes in working relations among paid and unpaid workers stem from violations of the above suggestions. Others stem from such negative or discriminatory attitudes as (1) people of either category presuming that others are there to serve by doing menial tasks that are beneath their own dignity; (2) people assuming that their own role is to determine what those in the other category should do, and then leave it to them to do it and, in some manner, be accountable to them; and (3) those who are paid being treated as if they were hirelings, working only because they are paid. These and other such reflections of low esteem for others need to be eliminated insofar as possible if ministers and volunteers are to work together happily and productively.

There are joys almost beyond description when there are useful and productive working relations among those in staff positions and volunteer workers in the educational ministries of a church. Bonds of love, friendship, and fellowship come into being. All of this is in addition to the joy of accomplishing the work that fulfills the purpose of a church in its educational ministries.

CONCLUSION

All who serve in a church's educational ministries are, in some sense, volunteers. The church depends upon volunteers in addition to its ministers. There are many jobs to be done for which volunteers can be discovered, recruited, and trained. There is no suitable way for paid people to do all that needs to be done, without the meaningful collaboration of many volunteer workers.

Those who work as volunteer leaders in a church's educational ministries comprise a very significant educational ministry opportunity themselves. They are at the "graduate student" level of local church education.

They learn and develop as a normal and natural part of their preparation and serving to help others learn and develop. This is a very good reason to make extensive use of their services, even in preference to an educational design in which only elite educators serve as instructors.

Ministers and other leaders should try to learn about motivating volunteer workers. A simple basis for motivating that could incorporate all the best that is known about motivational theory is to appeal to biblical love. Though there are some differences in paid and unpaid workers, there is far more that they hold in common. With thoughtful and considerate attitudes, they can work together happily and productively.

CONCERNS FOR FURTHER STUDY

Consider these questions as you continue to reflect on the use of volunteer leaders in education.

1. Do you agree or disagree with the idea that a church should employ and pay qualified people to do all the teaching and educational ministries? Why?

2. Do you think you could develop an appeal to people to serve based on the biblical love approach as suggested in this chapter? How would you apply such an approach in asking a specific person to consider teaching preschool children in Sunday school?

3. What is the biggest hindrance you have observed in the working together of paid and unpaid workers? What would you suggest to overcome this?

CHAPTER 13

Organizational Leadership
Teams in Education

A worthy and comprehensive educational ministry in a church requires the leadership efforts of more than one person. Every church, whether large or small, needs leadership and consultation among several people, preferably on a regular basis, regarding educational ministries. This leadership and consultation need to take place in all three tenses of ministry: (1) *before,* in order to plan and prepare adequately for ministering; (2) *during,* in order to assure the proper conducting, including essential adjustments, of ministry plans; and (3) *after,* in order to evaluate—to determine the extent to which goals were achieved, to learn the lessons that would contribute to improvement, and to celebrate appropriately the progress made.

Many churches do not use a consultative leadership approach to their educational ministries. In these churches, each leader does that which seems right in his own sight, within the limits of his own concepts of the church, of the needs, and of his own responsibilities. In these churches the results are often like one might expect of a team of athletes who never get together to work out their plays or strategies before the contest; who never huddle during a game to call the next play or plays; who never come back into the huddle to inform others of what is happening in their positions, and to suggest what might work better. These athletes seldom need any plans for celebrating after their games, because they seldom have anything to celebrate.

LEADERSHIP TEAMS IN A CHURCH

A leadership team is not an additional organization. It is a group of people working together as a team for consultation and leadership by virtue of their holding places of responsibility in related organizations or parts of organizations.

In the early days of this century, Sunday school leaders in some churches met together from time to time to discuss the needs and problems of their Sunday school and to make plans for improvement. Some of these groups in Baptist churches were called the Sunday School Superintendent's Cabinet. In the organization formerly called Training Union (now Discipleship Training in churches cooperating with the Southern Baptist Convention), a similar leadership group was called the Training Union Executive Committee. In Woman's Missionary Union the leadership group was the WMU Executive Board. In the Brotherhood organization (a missions organization for men and boys) it was the Brotherhood Planning Committee. The music ministry leaders called their leadership group the Music Council. Some groups used committee or board terminology to identify themselves.

Some pastors around the country began to meet with the leaders of ministry organizations in churches they served, and they called the group the Pastor's Cabinet, on the order of the President's Cabinet in our national government. Some called theirs a committee, a board, or a commission. In each instance the idea was to bring together the key leaders of each organization for consultation, advice, and planning.

Southern Baptists, as well as United Methodists and some others, later came to use the term *council* to identify some of the leadership groups within a congregation. The major ministry planning and leadership group in United Methodist congregations is the Council on Ministries. For Southern Baptists the title Church Council came into use; and each of the organizations for educational ministry within a church might have formed a similarly named group: the Sunday School council, the Discipleship Training council, the Woman's Missionary Union council, the Brotherhood council, and the music ministry council. For overall church ministry planning, coordination, leadership and evaluation, a church council was recommended to be made up of the leaders of each of the organizational councils, along with certain other leaders, usually under the direct leadership of the pastor. The result has been to improve considerably the effectiveness of the ministries churches perform.

In the 1990s a newer descriptive name for these kinds of leadership groups is coming to be widely used. The term "Leadership Team" is on the rise in organizational work, both secular and religious. Numerous educational ministry organizations are using this name. "Leadership Team" has been used by many to explain the character of those units called "councils." To some, the term "council" has a connotation of authoritarianism that is less acceptable than it once was. Hence the advocacy herein of the term "Leadership Team" where previously the term "council" was used.

The functions of the groups remain essentially the same regardless of the name.

THE CHURCH MINISTRY LEADERSHIP TEAM

A church needs leaders who will work together to lead the church in developing and implementing a comprehensive, coordinated, effective ministries plan. Churches look to the pastor more than to any other person for guidance in this arena. Wise pastors call on the key leaders of organizations and groups in the church to work together on this important and ongoing need. This is what a Church Ministry Leadership Team is all about. As Truman Brown, Jr., wrote: "The church council [Church Ministry Leadership Team] is the servant of the congregation. It exists not to make decisions for the congregation but to help the congregation make its decisions wisely."[1] He continued:

> The church council is the logical setting in which priority needs of the total church can be identified and plans made to reach them. The church council's duties include the basic steps needed to lead the church to catch a vision and implement a plan to achieve that vision. The basic duties of the council [Church Ministry Leadership Team] are to: (1) Help the church understand its mission and define its priorities. (2) Coordinate studies of church and community needs. (3) Recommend to the church coordinated plans for evangelism, missions, Christian development, worship, stewardship, and ministry. (4) Coordinate the church's schedule of activities, special events, and use of facilities. (5) Evaluate progress and the priority use of church resources.[2]

In performing these duties a Church Ministry Leadership Team leads the way in effective ministry planning, coordinating, and evaluating.

In almost all instances the pastor serves as chairman of the Church Ministry Leadership Team. Among the duties of the chair are these: (1) lead the Church Ministry Leadership Team to perform its tasks; (2) prepare and distribute an agenda for each team meeting; (3) notify team members of the time and place of each regular meeting; (4) preside during Church Ministry Leadership Team meetings; (5) present plans and action suggestions to the team; (6) call for recommendations from the team during regular church business meetings; (7) plan for training of Church Ministry Leadership Team members so they can perform their duties effectively; and (8) supervise the preparation and distribution of Church Ministry Leadership Team minutes, reports, and plans that are necessary to the proper operation of the group.

A church must decide who serves on the Church Ministry Leadership Team. Leaders of all of the base ministry organizations in a church should be members of the Church Ministry Leadership Team. This could include the Sunday School director, Discipleship Training director, Music

Ministry director, Woman's Missionary Union director, Brotherhood director, and the pastor. The deacon chairman, the director of Media Library, the director of Recreation, and the chairpeople of certain committees of the church (Family Enrichment, Stewardship, Evangelism, Missions Development, and others as their work might pertain), might be asked to serve. In addition, any church staff members who are responsible for assisting in the total development of one or more of the ministry organizations of a church should be members of the Church Ministry Leadership Team. A member of the Church Ministry Leadership Team may serve as secretary to the team.

It is possible for the Church Ministry Leadership Team to get too large and cumbersome. It is a good idea to limit the regular membership to those who really need to be part of the church's total planning by virtue of their leading a church ministry organization. Any other person, leader or member, could have free access to the meetings and to a place on the agenda should the need arise.

The pastor and other leaders of a church are expected to be fair in their use of whatever power comes with being on the Church Ministry Leadership Team. The field of responsibility is that of ministry planning, coordinating, and evaluating—not church discipline, church government, or some other area of concern. It does not require a large number of people. For example, rarely would the chairpeople of some committees of the church need to be in Church Ministry Leadership Team meetings. When they do need to be present, they certainly should be. But one of the dangers of a very large group is that the group might become too preoccupied with its own authority. So consider working with a relatively small Church Ministry Leadership Team.

The Church Ministry Leadership Team should plan well ahead of any of the other leadership teams or groups in a church, in order to make it possible for the other groups to coordinate their plans with those proposed for the church at large. The church objectives and goals that the Church Ministry Leadership Team develops and recommends become guidelines for the total ministry plan of a church. The organizational leadership teams and other church groups relate their specific tasks then to the objectives and goals of the church. In this way it is possible to coordinate the work so that all the parts fit together harmoniously into one design for ministry. There is no more significant work of its kind in the life of a church than that which an effective Church Ministry Leadership Team performs.[3]

ORGANIZATIONAL LEADERSHIP TEAMS
LEAD IN DETAILED PLANNING

Each of the educational ministry organizations in a church has a leadership group. In growing numbers of churches these leadership groups are called *teams*. The organizational team is made up of the director of the organization, whatever general officers the organization has, plus the leaders of the major units within the organization. For example, in a very small Sunday school the leadership team might consist of the Sunday school director, the pastor, possibly a general secretary, and the teacher of each of the departments (preschool and children) and classes (youth and adult).

In larger Sunday schools the leadership team would have department directors as members rather than teachers. Division directors are used in even larger Sunday schools, especially where there are three or more departments within an age division. Division directors should be on the Sunday School Leadership Team and, in most instances, the department directors should continue as team members. The *Sunday School Plan Book 1992–93*, Louie L. Wilkinson, compiler (Nashville: Convention Press, 1991), lists these Sunday school leaders as the Sunday school council (leadership team): Director, Assistant Director, Vacation Bible School Director, Director of Teaching Improvement and Training, Outreach-Evangelism Director, Bus Ministry Director, Secretary, Pastor, Minister of Education, and Age-Group Representatives. Figure 6 illustrates the idea of the organization recommended for the ministry organization leadership teams.

The work of each organizational leadership ministry team is to lead in planning, coordinating, and evaluating their organization's ministries. Each organization has certain tasks to perform on behalf of the church. Each organizational leadership team must see that plans are made that will enable their organization to fulfill their responsibilities in the life of the church.

Sometimes organizational ministry teams plan activities and projects that are not directly related to the overall church goals or action plans, but that are consistent with the roles of their organizations. These plans also need to be coordinated with the general church calendar proposed by the Church Ministry Leadership Team.[4]

The Church Ministry Leadership Team usually determines the major action plans that each organization is responsible for implementing through activities and projects. The tasks of each ministry organization guide the Church Ministry Leadership Team in its decisions regarding which group should be responsible for planning activities and projects for a given action plan. Ordinarily an organization should expect to plan the activities and projects for those action plans which obviously involve its distinctive tasks. Some activities and projects require that leaders of more than one organization plan together. The idea is to develop a coordinated church ministries plan in which each organization contributes and relates in light of its own tasks.

Figure 6
CHURCH MINISTRY ORGANIZATION
LEADERSHIP TEAM

Once the activities and projects of all ministry organizations have been proposed within the organizations, the leader of each group brings the plans to the Church Ministry Leadership Team for coordination into a unified annual ministry plan. Unnecessary duplication can be eliminated, conflicting requests for resources can be resolved together, and the church calendar can be developed with the best interests of the total church given priority.

Organizational leadership teams plan for the resources they will need to carry out the activities and projects their organizations will direct. Among the resources they anticipate needing and try to provide are organization, leaders, training, materials, equipment, space, and publicity. Needs and plans in these areas, as well as anticipated needs for funding, are shared with the Church Ministry Leadership Team as part of the planning process.

The following suggestions offer guidance to an organizational leadership team in resource planning:

(1) Plan additional organization or organizational adjustments needed to carry out ministry plans for the coming planning period—usually one year. The pastor and possibly other staff members can advise and suggest resource materials at this point.

Organizational changes usually indicate the need for more leaders and the areas where they are needed. Once the organizational changes are determined, the organizational leadership team prepares a list of additional workers needed, including any adjustments in the positions filled by present workers. The church nominating committee then coordinates and directs the enlistment of workers to be elected by the church.

(2) Plan for leader training. The leader training needs depend on the actions scheduled and the skills leaders already possess. The organizational leadership team needs to work closely with the Discipleship Training director and those who assist that director to determine the training needs of the people who are to receive training. Those responsible for leader training should develop specific training plans for the leaders who need it. Often a given ministry organization might plan for its own workers' training. These plans should include the type of training to be offered, the possible dates for the training, the materials that will be needed, and the person or group who should conduct the training. The Church Ministry Leadership Team should review these plans before they are presented to the church.

(3) Plan to secure materials, equipment, and space. The needs in these areas should be listed. Assignments should be made to secure or reserve these well in advance of their date to be used. This includes not only the needs for special, short-term projects or events, but also for the year-round needs.

Curriculum materials should be selected carefully. (See the Curriculum Selection Checklist on page 216.) Resource people, like those who work in the media library, should have opportunity to work closely with the planners in selecting materials and equipment for learning and teaching. Lists of items to be purchased should be made available for the Church Ministry Leadership Team and the budget planners in order to assure adequate funding in the planning stage.

Requests for available space can be worked out by the Church Ministry Leadership Team, based on the requests from the various organizational leadership teams. Occasionally certain actions might have to be delayed or deleted, pending the availability of adequate space. Increasingly churches are learning that by flexible and creative scheduling they can make better use of present facilities and other physical resources, with resultant savings that can be used in others ways. Churches can ill afford to continue expanding their buildings and coping with rampant utilities expenses without first making the optimum use of the buildings they already have.

(4) Plan to inform appropriate people of the ministry plans—the activities and projects, and other items that are included. The organizational leadership teams should identify the audiences, determine the kind and extent of information to be communicated, set up a schedule for the publicity, and consider the media that are most suited to promoting the work. In some

churches there are committees, officers, church staff members, or other people who can be called on to give major assistance in communicating the information to those who need to know.

There are other things the leadership teams do as they lead their organizations. Powers described their duties briefly in *Christian Education Handbook*: Help the program (ministry organization) understand its mission and define its priorities in the light of church priorities; conduct studies of church and community needs related to program (ministry organization) tasks; coordinate the ministry organization's activities and schedules; and evaluate progress, effectiveness, and the priority use of church resources.[5] Robert A. Orr listed an additional duty: report regularly to the church.[6]

As the Church Ministry Leadership Team and the organizational leadership teams go about their work, they are contributing significantly to the educational ministries of the church. Almost all of that which they plan, conduct, and evaluate has direct bearing on the effectiveness of the teaching and learning a church experiences. Many who otherwise might not have the opportunity for quality teaching and learning of the faith do have this opportunity because of the diligent work of church leaders through the leadership teams. In the process, the members of the leadership teams themselves have experiences that cause them to grow and to develop as Christians. A church needs some structured way for its leaders to lead. Leadership teams are proving to be a good way for many.

CONCLUSION

Churches need the leadership of more than one person. It seems folly to attempt to engage in a comprehensive educational ministry without drawing on the wisdom and energies of many.

Increasingly, churches are planning, conducting, and evaluating their ministries with the use of leadership teams. Many churches use a Church Ministry Leadership Team for leadership in their ministries. People who are already in places of responsible leadership in the church's organizations usually comprise this Church Ministry Leadership Team, under the leadership of the pastor. A relatively small Church Ministry Leadership Team can lead effectively in a church's ministries. Others who need to relate to the Church Ministry Leadership Team should be able to do so easily. It is not a closed group.

Each of the base ministry organizations of an educational nature in a church should have a leadership team of its own. The organizational director, any general officers, and the leaders of major organizational components should be included in an organizational leadership team. Following the lead of the Church Ministry Leadership Team, the organizational leadership teams plan, conduct, and evaluate their work in the light of their unique tasks. The Church Ministry Leadership Team determines objectives and goals to recommend for the entire church ministries plan.

By using such group processes of leadership, it is possible in many churches to have more effective educational and ministry experiences than would otherwise occur. In the process, too, the members of the leadership teams have unique experiences that help them to grow and develop in the faith.

CONCERNS FOR FURTHER STUDY

Consider these questions as you continue to reflect on a church's leadership teams and the educational ministry.

1. What would you suggest are the advantages of a Church Ministry Leadership Team to the church that has only one minister?

2. What reasons could you suggest for meaningful use of a Church Ministry Leadership Team in a very large church with multiple staff members in its educational ministries?

3. In keeping with the suggestions of this chapter, what would be the specific composition of the Church Ministry Leadership Team and the organizational leadership teams in the church of your membership?

PART FOUR

HOW LEADERS LEAD

Certain processes are essential to the effective life of the educational ministry of a church. Certain actions or series of actions must take place in order to realize the hopes and aspirations of a church. Thus far in this book we have presented and underscored the importance of the educational ministry of a church in several dimensions. *Why* an education ministry is necessary constituted the focus of Part 1. *What* comprises the basic components of an educational ministry was the concern of Part 2. *Who* are the personnel in the educational leadership of a church was described in Part 3.

Part 4 deals with *how* a church educates—the major kinds of things leaders and members do in order to move a church from where it is to where it wants and needs to be. Of course, a church never really arrives. Any church that arrives has in reality begun the return trip. It is vital that a church keep on advancing.

A church's planning is a vital process. Leaders must design actions to reach certain goals. They must plan to meet the needs, and perhaps some desires, of the members and others for whom they are concerned. They must plan and organize for quality and for quantity in the educational ministries. Organizing is also a vital process. How a church plans and organizes to perform its educational ministries is the concern of chapter 14.

Earlier sections of this book have stressed that the work of a church's educational ministry can best be accomplished by using the gifts and services of many people. For many people to be included in the work force of a church on a continuing basis there should be some procedures for discovering, recruiting, and training on a year-round basis. These procedures cannot be occasional interests; they must have almost constant attention. How a church does these is the focus of chapter 15.

An adequate educational ministry requires many resources, in addition to the personnel resource. Chapter 16 deals with providing such resources as a spirit and climate for educating, curriculum materials, supplies, equipment, furnishings, space, and financial support.

A church must implement and evaluate its educational ministries. Worthy and effective promotion, proper supervision, adequate recording and reporting, and comprehensive evaluation are needed. These are considered in chapter 17.

The objective of Part 4 is to help those who lead the educational ministry of a church to know some effective ways of planning, conducting, and evaluating this ministry, and how to relate resources to the effort.

CHAPTER 14

Planning and Organizing to Meet Needs

Planning and organizing are vital processes which are essential to the educational ministry of a church. Those who are in positions of leadership in a church's educational organizations need to give frequent attention to these processes. The purpose is to anticipate the needs of those for whom ministries are intended and design plans, including proper organization, for meeting those needs.

It is true that neither good planning nor good organization nor both together will guarantee success. It is also true, however, that without good planning and good organization, failure is a real possibility.

PLANNING EDUCATIONAL MINISTRIES

Leaders of a church's educational ministries do not have the option of choosing whether to plan. The needs are too great to leave to chance. The urgency of the needs calls for the best thinking, the best data gathering, the best analyzing, the most creativity, and the best decision-making leaders can give.

It is not only essential to plan; it is also right. It is a natural thing for a person to plan. God made humans with the capacity to think about the future. It is one of the ways we are made in the image of God. God himself has modeled the role as a planner. His plan of redemption is the plan of the ages. We must be good stewards of the God-given capacity to plan. Like all gifts, it was not given merely for our possession, but for our use according to his purposes.

SOME PRINCIPLES OF PLANNING

Here we shall suggest some principles that seem to be particularly appropriate in planning a church's educational ministry.

Lean on God. "Trust in the Lord with all your heart, and do not rely on your own insight" (Prov. 3:5). God knows what the future holds, and he can help us plan for the future. The foundational dimension of planning is to try to discern the will of God and to relate to his will. To learn of his nature and of his concerns for the needs of people and to counsel with others who are intent on the same approach are among the ways we learn to lean on God.

Include implementers in planning. Everyone may have access to God. None has exclusive rights or powers of access. Those people who are expected to have some part in helping to carry out plans should be included in the planning. Better plans usually result from group thinking. "The consensus of the faithful" is a historic Christian leadership concept that has great wisdom and merit, in contrast with models of authoritative individual leaders. Support for plans developed via authentic participation of group members comes more readily because the plans are perceived to be better, and they usually are. Participants in planning are more likely to identify personally with that which they had some part in planning. Communication of plans is more effective when implementers are included in the planning.

Plan from ends to means. Determine the purpose and objectives—the ultimate reason and the final outcomes that are the objects of the plans. Then, plan the ministries, the organization, human resources, physical resources, financial resources, and the administrative guidance needed. Avoid end-means inversion—planning the what, when, where, who, and how before determining the why. Avoid making ends of means.

Put the church first. In the event of conflict between the best interests of the total church and those of any individual, group, or organization, the interests of the church should prevail. Furthermore, there is an attendant responsibility for those who plan the overall church ministries to plan far enough in advance for others to have opportunity to coordinate their plans with those of the church. The right to priority on the part of the church should be used judiciously. The church is made up of the individuals, groups, and organizations collectively. This principle intends to avoid having the church plans preempted by any of its components or subordinated to them.

Plan to meet priority needs. Take the time to get valid data about who needs help and what kinds of help they need most. There are many good things a church might plan to do, but some are imperative. Determine these priority needs, and plan for them first. If anything is to be deleted, let it be the low priority item.

Be specific. Do not plan according to an indefinite generality like, "There are large numbers of youth in our community and in our church who need to be reached for Bible study." Instead, find out their names, addresses, phone numbers, school grades, relationship to Christ and the church, family circumstances, and other pertinent information that would possibly help those who will attempt to minister to the youth. Consider what approaches offer the most promise in reaching the youth (or whatever age you are planning for), and choose the best from these approaches.

Avoid letting planning degenerate into cataloging problems. One of the banes of some churches is that some find it easier to list the obstacles, the reasons why a thing cannot be achieved, than to work to find solutions. Someone has said, "An obstacle is what you see when you take your eyes off the goal." In order to be effective, it is important to keep your eyes on the goal and to develop solution-minded planners. Learn to counter the obstacle raisers with approaches like, "Yes, but now how can we find some ways to meet these needs? We have a new day and a new opportunity. What do you suggest?" Don't allow perpetual indulgence in looking back. Look to the present and to the future, and try to meet those needs.

Aim for the range of challenge. In setting goals, set them so as to suggest that success is possible with good effort. At the same time, set the goals high enough that success is not a foregone conclusion. Between these points is a range of challenge that requires good effort, with the promise of possible success. If goals are set so high that no one thinks they can reach them, people lose heart for the effort. If goals are too easy, people tend to lose interest or to be indifferent.

Allow for flexibility. Good plans are marked by their allowance for change. Changed conditions often require changed plans. For example, it is much more pleasant to planners when they are planning for growth and improvement than it is when they are planning to adjust to reductions, but there are times when each might be warranted. Unexpected changes of circumstances, good or bad, usually require flexibility in the plans. Expect them, and don't be defeated or unduly upset by them.

Provide resources for planning. This is a leadership responsibility. There are materials and information that help in planning. There are organizational principles and leadership skills that planners need to know. Reliance on the Holy Spirit for wisdom and strength is a vital resource in planning. Leaders help to keep these and other resources available to fellow planners in order to enable them to do their best possible work.

Keep plans reasonably simple. Even sophisticated people often respond best to uncomplicated plans when it comes to group activities and other such relationships. Many seem to have overestimated the sophistication of the masses of people. The majority of the American people have not flown in an airplane. Most own no stock in companies. More than half have never traveled outside the United States. A large percentage do not even use credit cards. Through the media many are aware of much of which prior generations were not aware; but there are many who have yet to experience

themselves some of the marks of sophistication that others take for granted. Plans do not have to be fancy to be good. They do have to be targeted
to meet bona fide needs; and it helps if the plans are fairly simple.

Put plans in writing. This is especially important should the need occur
to refer to plans as action progresses. It also provides a record for any future use, and helps in evaluating. It is possible, of course, to do some good
planning without writing the plans. The elaborate writing of plans need not
become a part of planning. Nevertheless, there are good reasons for writing the salient features and facts about plans.

KINDS OF PLANNING

Many possible kinds of planning call for the attention of leaders of a
church's educational ministry. It is not so important to know all the theories and the procedures about planning as it is to lead the people effectively
in doing good planning. It does help for leaders to have some knowledge
of planning theory and technology. A leader is more apt to lead well who
knows something of the possibilities.

One of the ways of viewing kinds of planning is to see planning as (1)
operational, (2) annual or short-range, and (3) long-range. The operational
planning is that which is closest in time to the day-by-day, week-in and
week-out, month-by-month, quarter-by-quarter happenings in a church.
Almost all churches do some operational planning, even if it is only the re-
active decision-making required to move from one event to another. Many
churches regularly do annual planning, producing a calendar of church activities for a year. Some churches have found long-range planning to be
not only helpful, but also essential. This is planning beyond next year to
three, four, or five years and more into the future.

In theory, every church should have a long-range plan first, then an annual plan. The long-range plan would be a concept the church hopes and
plans will materialize within a definite time span. Goals and strategies for
ministry are "painted with broad strokes." Then annual planning and operational planning place the long-range plan into specific allocations of resources—dates on the calendar, personnel, budget, and other resources—
and the actual initiating, adjusting, conducting, and evaluating of that
which was planned. Let us look briefly at these kinds of planning.

Long-range planning offers a church some specific benefits. Through
the careful and prayerful study of the nature and purpose of a church, and
the stating of these in terms that have meaning to the people of a congregation, a church can know more clearly where it is headed in the long term,
and the kinds of actions that are imperative. This helps the church have a
clear sense of its identity and direction.

Through the examination of the real and specific needs of the church
and the community in which it ministers, and with priority planning to

meet these needs, members may experience genuine relevancy to life that otherwise might elude them. What a church does should be relevant to life.

Through wise and sincere utilization of large numbers of members in the planning and the implementation of plans for ministry, a unity of concern develops that touches members and their resources in ways that are not likely to happen otherwise. The sense of belonging and of being engaged in most worthy ministries that are relevant and that help the church to be the church are significant values for a fellowship. These serve to increase the motivation among members to work more and more effectively to relate their resources as good stewards.

Through long-range planning, a church that initially has the potential for growth can have a means of continuing to grow intentionally, both in quantity and in quality. It is as though they were making a trip to a distant place. They determine where they wish to arrive, identify probable points along the route, and plan to provide the means required to move them from point to point in the direction of their ultimate destination. There is a sense of real partnership with the Master Planner. One of the by-products is that members will experience the joy that comes from such feelings of relationship to the work of the Lord and the church.

The church should have an overall long-range plan, a major part of which will be accomplished through the educational ministry. There is a natural sequence or flow of planning that a church long-range plan should follow. It includes certain stages, phases, and steps. They include the following:

I. ENVISIONING STAGE

 Step 1: Pastor must lead the congregation to discover a need for a new dream.

 Step 2: Pastoral leaders must make a commitment to visionary growth.

II. PLANNING STAGE

Phase 1: Getting Started

 Step 1: Lead the congregation to authorize long-range planning and elect a long-range planning committee.

 Step 2: Train the long-range planning committee.

 Step 3: Prepare the church for long-range planning.

 Step 4: Write a mission statement.

Phase 2: Launching a Study of Church and Community

 Step 1: Select and train church and community study groups.

 Step 2: Church study group should analyze present and future church needs.

Step 3: Community study group should analyze present and future community needs.

Step 4: Consolidate church and community analyses.

Phase 3: Setting Goals for the Growing Church

Step 1: Select and train goal-setting work groups.

Step 2: Set long-range visionary goals based on priority concerns.

Step 3: Correlate goals into one set of long-range visionary goals.

Phase 4: Selecting Visionary Long-Range Action Plans

Step 1: Select and train planning work groups.

Step 2: Develop action plans for each goal.

Step 3: Consolidate action plans into a comprehensive visionary plan.

Phase 5: Completing and Communicating Long-Range Plans

Step 1: Prepare report of the church and community concerns, goals, and action plans.

Step 2: Present the long-range plan for congregational discussion.

Step 3: Present the long-range plan for congregational approval.

III. IMPLEMENTING STAGE

Step 1: Clarify the roles of the long-range planning committee and the Church Ministry Leadership Team.

Step 2: Train the Church Ministry Leadership Team to function effectively as implementers.

Step 3: Schedule meetings of the Church Ministry Leadership Team and long-range planning committee to evaluate assignments.

Step 4: Prepare annual report for churchwide study indicating progress.

Step 5: Establish process for short-range planning.

Step 6: Revise the long-range plan as needed.

Step 7: Keep the Stewardship committee informed.

Step 8: Recommend development of a new long-range plan.[1]

A church long-range planning committee, working closely with the pastor and staff, should be responsible for the arduous assignment of developing and presenting to the church a plan that, on acceptance by the church, will guide the church for the years ahead.

In educational planning in a church, the plans can hardly be projected for more than five years, lest they be off target due to changing needs. Even these should be subject to revision as circumstances and needs change within that time frame. The Church Ministry Leadership Team has responsibility for adjusting and leading in implementing the church's ministry plans in ways compatible with the church-approved long-range plan.

The long-range plan is the general framework that guides the many components of a church. The long-range plan itself must be kept current. It must not become an inflexible design that inhibits the church in its responses to needs. Its purpose is to help make possible more relevant priority ministries, not to hinder them. A good plan, however, would rarely deserve to be scuttled completely. It must be revised and updated, at least on an annual basis. At this time it would ideally be extended by adding another year to the plan. Many prefer a five-year cycle such as the one presented above.

Annual or short-range planning is essential to effective ministry in a church. This planning is usually initiated by the Church Ministry Leadership Team. It extends to include the organizational leadership teams. It also involves church committees and their planning. Pastor, church staff, and the volunteer leaders of church organizations and committees work together and produce such annual guides as the church calendar of ministry events, the church budget to support the ministry plans, and other tools that enhance and support the various ministries through the year.

With the church long-range plan as a primary guide, the Church Ministry Leadership Team reviews and confirms priority needs. Other information should be considered, such as current denominational emphases, new data from the community and the church membership, and other significant factors related to circumstances and conditions at the time. Short-range goals, a coordinated calendar for the church year, and a proposed budget related to the ministry plans become the practical expressions that help transpose long-range plans into specific annual plans for a given year.

The Church Ministry Leadership Team becomes the planning forum through which leaders of church ministries, including church committees as needed, can develop a total plan for the church that relates all of the ministries and support systems appropriately. Leaders of church base ministries, such as the Sunday School director, the Discipleship Training director, the directors of Woman's Missionary Union, Brotherhood, and the Music Ministry, and chairmen of committees, lead their organizations to plan to contribute through their unique tasks and gifts to the church's overall plans.

The Church Ministry Leadership Team also provides a helpful forum for the organizations to share information, and to seek counsel if needed, about the actions and events unique to their responsibilities. This communication network leads to better understanding, more appreciation, higher trust, and better cooperation among the various interest groups and ministry organizations in a church.

A variety of materials, training events, and other helpful items are available to assist the annual planning process in a church. There are church development guides, achievement standards, resource kits, plan books for ministry organizations (such as the annual *Sunday School Plan Book* and others), ministry organization leadership magazines, denominational calendars, and other materials that leaders can secure. There are training events related to church annual planning that are offered at various locations, such as the judicatory offices (e.g., Baptist associations or state conventions), and conference centers. Annual planning is a vital cog in the wheels of effective planning for the educational ministries of a church.

Operational planning is that which is required as plans previously made come to the implementation stage. Many decisions and other planning actions remain as leaders fill in the final details and make the essential adjustments as prior plans approach reality. There will be unexpected developments that call for schedule changes and other responses as the time for action approaches.

The organizational leadership teams, as well as committees of the church, do the detailed operational planning related to their respective assignments. When it is helpful or needed, the leaders relate their operational planning to the Church Ministry Leadership Team. It is usually adequate for organizational leadership teams to meet on a monthly basis, at a regular time. In churches with a very full agenda of events, some organizational leadership teams, such as the Sunday School Leadership Team, might meet briefly on a weekly basis for exchange of information, clarification of plans, problem solving, or other good reasons. Even these groups, though, probably need an extended session on a regular monthly basis for planning. Some groups, such as the Church Ministry Leadership Team or organizational leadership teams, have planning retreats during which they work on plans of several types related to their assignments.

Illustrative of other operational planning meetings is the weekly workers meeting that many Sunday school leaders consider to be indispensable to an effective Bible teaching ministry. Kenneth M. Dean, an experienced teaching improvement consultant, wrote, "In order for a church to provide and maintain a challenging Bible teaching program that is reaching prospects and adding new members to its Sunday School, it must have a well-planned weekly workers' meeting."[2] This meeting can help Sunday school workers accomplish planning, promoting, problem solving, preparation, personal support, and prayer for one another, for the members, for department activities, for church concerns, and for other objects.

Some of the most effective weekly workers meetings are in small churches with small Sunday schools that are not departmentalized. One agenda for such a meeting in a small Sunday school suggests a general period when all workers are together for about twenty minutes to handle the school's administrative concerns, to plan for reaching, witnessing, and ministering, and to pray together. There follows a teaching-learning period with all workers together for directed planning of age-group units and lessons (about thirty minutes). The meeting concludes with about ten minutes for special age-group time to prepare the room or area of the building for Sunday's session.

In larger, departmentalized Sunday schools, a better plan would be a three-part meeting, with about fifteen minutes for department directors to meet together, followed by a very brief time (five to eight minutes) for all workers together for general concerns to be cared for, and concluding with each department meeting separately for the agenda like that of the entire meeting of the small Sunday school. This latter segment requires about fifty to sixty minutes to be most effective. Each Sunday school should determine the best format to meet its needs. Going on the assumption that Sunday school workers are committed to doing the best possible job, such a meeting each week is an economy of their time and can result in many good accomplishments.

Sunday school leaders, including department directors, need training that will equip them to lead successful meetings with their workers. There are denominational materials to help with this important meeting. When recruited, Sunday school workers need to understand that the weekly workers meeting is part of the responsibility they are being asked to accept. The meeting must have priority scheduling in a church, and other organizations need to avoid duplication of leaders and schedules that would weaken this meeting. Many churches find that a time before or after the mid-week prayer meeting of the church is the prime time for a good weekly workers meeting.

There are numerous other planning needs. Committees, classes, task forces, leadership teams, and other groups need to function well in planning in order to provide effective ministries in education. There are meetings to preview and to select curriculum materials, usually on a quarterly or an annual basis, or both.

ORGANIZING FOR GROWTH

There is ample biblical and historical evidence to support the thesis that a church should desire to grow. Almost all churches do wish to experience growth. They want to experience "the divine-human process of adding to a church those who are saved through Jesus Christ, equipping them for responsible discipleship resulting in witnessing, ministering, and establishing new fellowships of believers."[3]

Few ideas in the field of practical (or applied) theology have received the attention of theoreticians and practitioners alike during recent years as has the idea of growing churches. Studies have been made to discover what makes churches grow. Seminaries and other institutions have established centers for the study of the subject. Many churches and some entire denominations have given growth a priority place in their ministries. It is a vital concern for those who would lead a church in its educational ministries.

In 1990, leaders of the Baptist Sunday School Board and the Southern Baptist Home Mission Board endorsed this definition of church growth: "Church growth is God at work through His redeemed people in adding to a church those who are saved by grace through faith in Jesus Christ and helping inactive believers come to renewed commitment. It is new believers added to existing churches and equipped to become responsible church members who minister and witness as personal soul-winners to others. It is strengthening the churches in fellowship, organization, and in world missions commitment."

For many years the Southern Baptist Convention has been interested in and knowledgeable of how to grow churches. The more recent interest of others has helped churches of this denomination to sharpen their thinking and to expand their understanding of important additional factors that contribute to growing churches. Others have helped Southern Baptists place more emphasis, for example, on acquiring and using more thorough demographic data in planning and providing for churches to grow. Likewise, others have drawn heavily from Southern Baptists in their knowledge of what makes churches grow.

Two rather fundamental conditions must precede any effective methodological approach for a church to grow. First, there must be people potentially available to be reached by a church. Even in a world of burgeoning population, some churches are not located among pockets of people, and they are not likely to experience great numerical growth, regardless of their desire for it. Such churches must focus on other vital dimensions of growth. None should make them feel they are untrue to the Great Commission if they do not have large numerical growth. A church can be a great church and not be a great big church.

Second, there must be a willingness to grow. This sometimes is a subtle factor. Few active members of a church would admit to not being willing for their church to grow. But the real truth behind this willingness to grow is the willingness to change. Growth requires change. Many who would nod in apparent assent to the pastor's preaching about reaching out to others balk at the suggestion of possible changes that must precede or accompany growth. Unless there are people potentially available to a church, and unless there is a willingness to grow (and to work at it), there is no formula that will produce growth. Wise church leaders who wish to lead their church to grow must be aware of and deal with these two conditions.

MARKS OF A GROWING CHURCH

What are some major characteristics of a growing church? An ad hoc growth study committee from the Sunday School Board and the Home Mission Board of the Southern Baptist Convention studied this question for a period of two years. They observed several common marks in growing churches of various denominations. These characteristics are not listed in a particular order, and they are emphasized in different ways in different growing churches.

1. Pastor and staff leaders are committed to and involved in growth.
2. Lay people are committed to and involved in growth.
3. There is a priority commitment to winning lost people to faith in Jesus Christ.
4. New believers and other members are equipped for personal growth, witness, and ministry.
5. They regularly experience worship, including music and preaching that are dynamic, challenging, joyful, and expectant.
6. They are a fellowship that expresses acceptance, concern, and love.
7. The Bible is central in preaching and study.
8. They use the Sunday school as the major growth outreach arm of the church.
9. They have a caring concern for meeting the needs of all people.
10. They make specific plans to grow in the context of their setting.
11. They express a world concern through Scriptural giving and individual participation.
12. There is a prayerful sensitivity to the leadership of the Holy Spirit.[4]

A study of these marks of a growing church would reveal numerous implications for the educational ministry of a church, along with other ministries. Subsequent lists of such characteristics published by other writers have been remarkably similar to those listed above.

GROWING THROUGH THE SUNDAY SCHOOL

Each of the educational ministries of a church is the most important ministry in the church in the area of its responsibilities. All of a church's educational ministries contribute to a growing church. But the Sunday school has been found to be the most effective growth outreach arm of the church. There are good reasons why this is true.

The Sunday school is the best organization for growth of a church. The Bible is the principal textbook of Sunday school. Curriculum materials are not the text, but are helps in understanding and teaching the text, the Bible.

The Bible has a unique appeal to students, both in and out of the church. It is the Sunday school's task to lead in the church's Bible teaching.

Reaching people for Bible study, witnessing to them about Christ, and leading them into church membership are major tasks of the Sunday school. It is natural that the organization with these tasks should be the leader of a church's efforts in these growth activities.

The Sunday school has the largest organization and the largest number of workers of the organizations in a church. Typically it has more small groups and more leaders than all the other organizations combined. Its workers can most readily lead in the outreach activities to prospective new members. In so doing they are simply putting their teachings into practice.

The Sunday school has the greatest potential constituency of all church organizations. Its members range from the youngest infants, even before they are brought to the church building, to the oldest people, even if they are unable to attend. People in almost all conditions or age groups are potential members of a Sunday school.

The Sunday school meets fifty-two weeks per year. Someone is present, teaching people the Bible, as surely as Sundays come and go. This fact is important. No organization in a church can do so well as can the organization that has no cancellations of schedule. Other church ministry organizations might do well to follow this example.

The Sunday school in America is the most readily recognized organization of the church to those outside the church. Even the least knowledgeable person outside the church has some degree of awareness of Sunday school, however vague it might be. This recognition can be an asset in outreach.

Sunday school has the prime time in most churches for attracting unreached people—Sunday morning. Most meet just prior to the major worship service on Sunday morning. Some meet just after the worship service, or between morning worship services, in some churches that have grown to need more than one morning worship service. Some churches have multiple Sunday schools each Sunday morning, meeting in a variety of patterns. Almost any of these Sunday morning times is better than any other time of the week for a Sunday school approach to Bible study, although some churches offer effective study times in addition to Sunday.

One person out of three enrolled in a Southern Baptist Sunday school has been reached for Christian conversion. This ratio has remained constant for decades. Only one person in approximately 240 has made a profession of faith in one of these churches without having been enrolled in its Sunday school. It seems clear that the major strategy for a church to reach the unreached would be to enroll them and engage them in Bible study through the Sunday school.

ACTIONS FOR SUNDAY SCHOOL GROWTH

There are some proven essential actions that tend to produce Sunday school growth. Through decades of church growth by growing Sunday schools, knowledge about how to use the Sunday school to grow churches has developed.

The Flake Formula. Shortly after the turn of the century, an energetic layman, Arthur Flake, led Southern Baptist Sunday school work. He developed a five-step procedure for growing a Sunday school now known as the Flake Formula:

> Know the possibilities.
>
> Enlarge the organization.
>
> Provide the space.
>
> Enlist and train the workers.
>
> Go after the people.

Thousands of churches followed these five steps to reach millions of unreached people.[5]

Barnette's Seven Laws of Sunday School Growth. J. N. Barnette, Flake's successor, developed *Seven Laws of Sunday School Growth.*

1. The law relating to number of workers: Enrollment in Sunday School increases in proportion to workers at the ratio of ten to one. One way to take a growth stance is to increase the number of workers in keeping with the ratio. There is a natural tendency among some to prefer to combine classes or departments in order to have larger groups in attendance. Rather, enlisting more workers who will minister to the members and potential members should build attendance.

2. The law relating to size of units: Units (classes, especially) normally reach their maximum growth within a few months after they are started. Classes should begin the church year with a healthy nucleus but with room to grow before reaching the optimum size. A class of youth should begin the year with eight to twelve members, with some known potential members. During the year, the class will probably grow to reach its optimum size, which is fifteen members. But this growth will occur only if planners allow for growth when the organization is begun.

3. The law relating to new units: New units grow faster and win more people to Christ and provide more workers. Generally the first year is the most productive growth year for a Sunday school class. Hence, a measure of newness can be arranged each year by reorganizing the classes and departments, allowing room for growth.

4. The law relating to grading: Grading by ages provides the logical basis for adding new units. While there are other ways to group, age

is the most common denominator for a continuing organization. Age-grading is best suited to teaching directed to the life needs of members.

5. The law relating to promotion: Promotion on the age basis follows the natural laws of growth and development. Annual promotion (advancing to newly created groupings based on age of members) is necessary in a growing Sunday school. To get away from annual promotion is to invite limits in the growth rate.

6. The law relating to visitation: Enrollment and attendance increase in proportion to visitation (the number of personal visits). Cards, letters, and phone calls are useful, but none of these can be as effective as visits to absentees and to potential members.

7. The law relating to the building: The building sets the pattern for Sunday school growth. A Sunday school cannot successfully grow beyond the capacity of its building. Some have learned to use the buildings more efficiently through multiple scheduling (having Sunday school during more than one period, or otherwise getting multiple use of the space). But the law holds: we shape our buildings, then the buildings shape us. A church will never need the room it does not provide and use wisely.

Coupled with the compatible use of the Flake Formula and the Seven Laws of Sunday School Growth, the Southern Baptist Convention more than doubled in church membership in the ten-year period between 1945–55, a feat that had taken a hundred years before 1945 to accomplish. The contributions of Flake and Barnette can scarcely be measured. Many growing churches of a variety of denominations continue to use these concepts effectively.

Anderson's Caveat. More recently, Andy Anderson, and many others who use the "Sunday School Growth Spiral" he developed to implement the Flake and Barnette concepts, advocate a ratio of only eight students to one worker, rather than ten-to-one to achieve maximum rates of growth.

Piland's Nine Basic Actions for Sunday School Growth. Harry Piland, successor to Flake, Barnette, and A. V. Washburn as the national Sunday School leader for Southern Baptists, identified Nine Basic Actions for Sunday School Growth:

Make a commitment to growth.

Identify and enroll prospects.

Start new classes and departments.

Enlist workers.

Train workers.

Provide space and equipment.

Conduct weekly workers' meetings.

Conduct weekly visitation.

Teach the Bible to win the lost and develop the saved.

These basic actions have remained the focus for good Sunday school work in many churches. You will notice that the Flake Formula and Barnette's Seven Laws resemble Piland's Nine Basic Actions.

Church planters and planners have identified three physical factors that might limit growth of a church: the number of people who can be accommodated in worship services, in Sunday school, and the parking lot. The smallest capacity item of these three will be the most influential growth limiting physical factor for a church.

A close examination of almost all growing Sunday schools would reveal some evidences of Flake's formula and of Barnette's laws. They are foundational to growing Sunday schools. There are new ways of saying some of the truths they embody, but the truths endure. Given the potential people to reach, and a willingness to grow (including a willingness to change and to work), these concepts can guide a church to grow.

Doing the Basics with a Flair

The brief history of Prestonwood Church reflects what many have considered a very dynamic and creative congregation. Unique ministries such as the monthly concert series, "Saturday Nights in Dallas," the annual "5K Run," the citywide mission outreach, "To Dallas with Love," are but a few of the various ideas that have found permanency within the life of the church.

The early years were characterized by a most effective mail program to the emerging community that lifted church promotion to a new level. One of the finest contributions Prestonwood made to church growth was the use of off-site Bible study locations, which enabled the young church to grow at a very rapid pace even though space was not available and would not be available for several years.

Today, Prestonwood continues in its creative style with innovative ministries such as "Metro Bible Study," which reaches 600 single adults every Monday evening, and the "Tuesday Power Lunch," which ministers to 500–1200 business people weekly.

This creative bent, however, masks a very important ingredient concerning Prestonwood Church. This exciting congregation that reached 10,000 members within a ten-year period was not built on the latest technique or clever idea. It was established on the proven basics of church growth that are magnificently expressed in what Southern Baptists have traditionally referred to as the Church Organized . . . the basic, age-graded Sunday School, which utilizes the formula created over fifty years ago by a Mississippi layman named Arthur Flake.

This formula, which states that one must know the possibilities, enlarge the organization, enlist and train leaders, provide space and evangelize, has proven to be a most creative tool for reaching boomers, busters, and whatever people may be called in the 21st century.

Prestonwood is going to be enthusiastic and creative in the years ahead and will always be open to new approaches, whether it be in small groups or Saturday night services, but one thing will be sure about the future: the leadership will not abandon that which is serving well for new ideas until those ideas have been tested and proven by time and results.

The best way to be on the cutting edge of creativity is to build on the basics with a flair.

SOME SPECIAL TOOLS FOR SUNDAY SCHOOL GROWTH

There are many other approaches and devices that are potentially useful to a church in planning and organizing for growth. Here we shall mention but a few.

Cultivation Evangelism. The approach offered by a veteran education leader in growing churches, R. Othal Feather, is the plan described in his book, *Outreach Evangelism Through the Sunday School* (Nashville: Convention Press, 1972). The concept is still valid. Essentially a detailed plan for cultivation evangelism through the Sunday school, the genius of the concept (in addition to accurate information about those who are prospective Christians) is the careful matching of prospective members with witnesses. Sunday school workers who know the person about whom there is a concern for reaching and winning to Christ try to identify the person in all the church (in or out of the Sunday school work force) who would be most likely to relate to the prospective member effectively. This person is asked to accept the assignment for an extended relationship with the prospective member and, through a continuing thoughtful cultivation of genuine interest and friendship, to try to reach the prospective member for enrollment in Sunday school for Bible study. Once enrolled, the possibilities of winning the person to Christ are greatly enhanced.

The Action Plan. A unique approach to enrolling people in Bible study through the Sunday school was developed by Andy Anderson, a pastor in Florida and later a national worker in Sunday school growth. The approach, called "Action Plan," is both a short-term campaign/blitz of a community and a long-term basic-enrollment technique that operates on the strategy of enrolling in Sunday school Bible study "anyone, anywhere, anytime, so long as they give their consent." Historically, people have come to the church to be enrolled in Sunday school. The uniqueness of this plan is that members may enroll people in their homes, at work, at school, in shopping centers, or wherever they desire, as long as the enrollee consents. Statistics indicate that, with appropriate follow-up, the attendance percentages of people so enrolled is scarcely different from the attendance percentages of those already on Sunday school rolls by the more traditional methods of enrolling members. Some churches have used the campaign/blitz Action Plan with phenomenal increases in their enrollment. Some churches have enrolled as many in a few weeks with this strategy as they had in a previous decade or more.

The Sunday School Growth Spiral. One of the planning tools that has grown out of the recent emphasis on growth through the Sunday school is the "Sunday School Growth Spiral." A copy of the spiral is shown in Figure 7B. This tool for planning for growth is based on traditional growth principles and procedures and is compatible with contemporary growth approaches. It offers a way of planning a systematic pattern of outreach and growth for a Sunday school and a church. Using the spiral, Sunday school leaders quarterly plan for year-round growth at a steady pace, in all the items listed on the spiral. They then work to reach their goals, and monitor their progress with the spiral.[6]

CONCLUSION

Good planning and organization are essential to a church's educational ministries if they are to be most effective. Leaders must lead in planning. They should study planning and learn to do it well. There are many helpful principles and procedures which they need to know and use.

There are various kinds of planning. We briefly considered three kinds: operational, annual (short-range), and long-range. Ideally a church should develop a long-range plan, and work back through the other two kinds, with the long-range plan as the guide. A church long-range planning committee, the Church Ministry Leadership Team, the leadership teams of

Figure 7A—Guide to the Use of Sunday School Growth Spiral

The Growth Spiral is a Sunday school growth plan based on quarterly enrollment goals.

Notice that the chart is made up of rows of blocks and lines. Each row of blocks represents the information printed in the center box (enrollment, units, and workers). Each line lettered A to E represents one quarter of a year. Line E, however, is the current figure in each case. Starting with line E, dated 10/1/94, record the figures your Sunday school had (or expects to have) on 10/1/94 for all blocks on line E.

Enrollment—Line A, block numbered 1, dated 9/30/95. Record here the school's enrollment goal.

Prospects—Line A, block numbered 2. Record the goal for the number of valid prospects for enrollment. Include resident church members who are not enrolled. A minimum goal is a prospect list equal to the Sunday school enrollment.

Units—Line A, block numbered 3. Record the number of units needed to help reach the enrollment goal by September 30, 1995. Use the Sunday School Organization Planning Chart (p. 90) to determine this figure.

Workers—Line A, block numbered 4. Enter the total number of workers needed to help reach the enrollment goal by September 30, 1995. Use the Sunday School Organization Planning Chart (p. 90) to determine this figure.

Workers Meeting Attendance —Line A, block numbered 5, The minimum goal for attendance at weekly workers meeting is 75 percent of the workers.

Training Awards—Line A, block numbered 6. The number of Sunday school training awards each quarter should equal one-half of the number of workers.

Space—Line A, block numbered 7. Use the same number for space as shown for units above.

Contacts—Line A, block numbered 8. The number of weekly contacts should equal one-half the enrollment goal. Record one-half the number in line A, block 1.

Outreachers—Line A, block numbered 9. The number of outreachers each week should equal at least the number of units (line A, block 3).

Sunday School Attendance—Line A, block numbered 10. Assuming that the same quality of work prevails as growth occurs, the same percentage of members would attend. Determine your percentage by your present Sunday school enrollment. Take that percent of the enrollment goal on line A, block 1, and enter it on line A, block 10.

Worship Service Attendance—Line A, block numbered 11. Determine your present attendance percentage between Sunday school and morning worship and, using this percentage, enter your projections for worship service attendance.

Offerings—Line A, block numbered 12. The present per capita giving normally will hold as the Sunday school grows. Show here your new total, based on your projected Sunday school attendance.

Baptisms—Line A, block numbered 13. It is difficult to predict baptisms, but assume that under the Growth Spiral you will baptize at least the same portion of new members as in the past. Estimate how many unsaved will be enrolled during the year and apply the appropriate percentage to this figure. Then add the result to your current average number of baptisms to get the total for block 13.

Now that the goals are recorded, you are ready to complete the Spiral.

Subtract each "E" figure from the corresponding "A" figure to get the net increase for the year. Next, divide each resulting figure by four to determine the quarterly increase. List the cumulative totals by quarters in lines D, C, and B. For example: If line E shows 12 units at present and line A indicated a goal of 19, the difference would be 7, or a gain of 2 (fraction rounded off upward) each quarter. Thus, line D would show 15 units; line C, 16; and line B, 18. Keep in mind that special emphasis during one quarter could make the number in that quarter greater than the numbers in other quarters.

In planning for growth, remember to order literature in advance for the people you plan to enroll.

For additional help, see *Keys to Growth: A Sunday School Growth Spiral Approach*.

Figure 7B

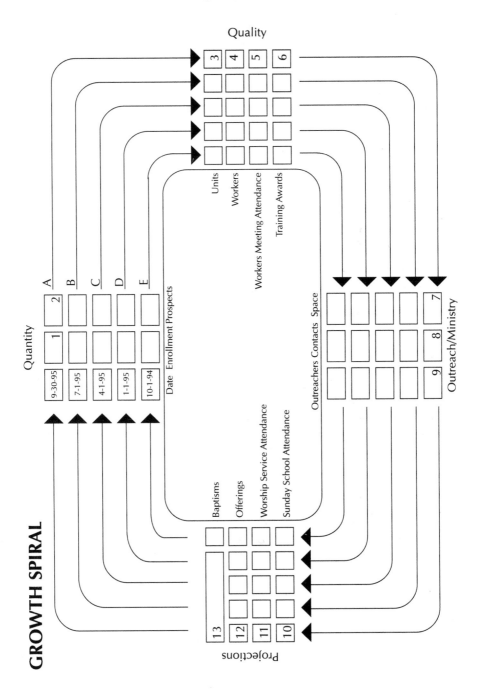

various church ministries, church committees, pastor and staff, and other church leaders and groups engage in planning.

A church needs to plan and organize for growth. With people to be reached and with a genuine willingness to grow, there are some effective ways by which a church can experience growth. The marks of growing churches are now well known, as are a variety of methodologies for growing. For many, the most effective organization a church could use for growth is its Sunday school. All of a church's educational ministries contribute to good church growth, but the Sunday school offers the most promise for initially reaching the unreached. The leaders of a church's educational ministries should give careful thought and leadership to this significant dimension of their responsibility.

CONCERNS FOR FURTHER STUDY

Consider these questions as you continue to reflect on a church planning and organizing to meet needs.

1. What would you offer as a brief rationale for planning a church's educational ministries?

2. In your reflection, what are two of the most important principles of planning you would offer?

3. Apart from the Sunday school, what would you suggest as a viable approach to reaching large numbers of people who would be added to a church? What if you used your suggestion in conjunction with the Sunday school for growth?

CHAPTER 15

Discovering, Recruiting, and Training Workers

The work of a church is the work of God, performed through his people who make up the church. A church's work of teaching and learning requires the efforts of many of its members if the work is to be done well. Many veteran church educators and pastors conclude that a church has potentially available to it the workers needed for what God wants that church to do.

True, the workers do not just appear and begin to teach, to disciple, to minister, or to lead. Some in a church must lead in discovering, recruiting, and training workers. That responsibility is the focus of this chapter.

DISCOVERING THE GIFTS OF THE MEMBERS

People differ from one another in many ways. This is both fortunate and interesting. One of the significant ways people of a church differ is in their abilities and gifts. They have varied talents and aptitudes, endowed by God. Each has some gift or gifts.

There are enough tasks to be performed in a church's educational ministries to make good use of almost any gift a person has received. A person who is gifted of God has a responsibility to develop that gift and to offer it back to him in obedient service. A church has a responsibility to be a means of helping individuals discover their gifts and of helping them use their gifts to relate with meaning to the work of God. The ministries of education in a church call for many gifted workers.

One of the most rewarding areas of ministry is the ministry of helping people to discover, identify, and affirm their gifts, and to find ways to develop and use them. Church leaders need to give almost constant attention to the various ways they can help members in this discovery.

There are many ways to discover people's gifts and their potential for meaningful service. Almost all of the ways, methodologically speaking, depend on the leaders' being sensitive, caring, and observant. Yet most leaders, however sensitive, caring, and observant, can benefit from using some proven ways of finding the gifts and the gifted people. Here we shall suggest some possibilities.

PERSONAL OBSERVATION

One way to discover people who might be appropriate for consideration and guidance regarding their place in the work force of a church is to observe personally their participation pattern in regular and special church activities. Notice their responses. Look for indications of interest on their part in what is going on in the ministries of the church. Confirm their interest through conversations about their opinions and feelings regarding experiences in which they are involved. A simple question such as, "How did you like that . . . ?" or "What did you think of that . . . ?" can open the door for a leader to get an impression of the interest and readiness of a member. Don't pounce with an immediate recruitment appeal. Observe over some period of time, and remember what you are learning about each person. Make notes and keep a file on individuals, if necessary. If you go to this extent, date the notes and put down the gist of the conversation or their remarks. Later reflect on these impressions as you prepare to become more definite with individuals about their interest in serving.

INTEREST/TALENT/EXPERIENCE INVENTORY

Another way that is widely used by effective church leaders is to maintain an interest/talent/experience inventory on church members. There are forms available at denominational book stores and in other places. Many leaders make up their own questionnaires that they use to secure information about members for possible use in worker recruitment and development. There are forms to use in conducting a survey of members for this inventory, ranging from hand-tabulated cards, to pick cards, to computer forms. Keep the questionnaire as simple as possible, asking only the questions about which you might do something if members responded with the requested information.

Some leaders gather information for this inventory by surveying the membership periodically. Others call on new members of the church and secure information as part of the overall plan of assimilating new members. Some obtain the information during the new member orientation sessions. Some conduct mail surveys of the membership. Some find it useful to establish a data bank as part of the church's master membership profile and to keep the information updated rather than repeatedly asking veteran church members to fill out another questionnaire each year or two.

DEVELOP SENSITIVITY

A wise and useful way that allows for a valuable personal touch in the discovery of people with worker potential is continually to develop among all the present work force—teachers, leaders, directors, coordinators, church staff, and other workers in the church—a sensitivity to the service potential and interests of members in their classes, departments, and groups of various kinds. Make it a mark of desirable achievement among present workers to alert the general leaders of the progress individuals are making in their growth and readiness for service.

Lead all teachers of adult Sunday school classes to set one goal each year in the area of identifying people who might "graduate" into the work force of the church's educational ministries. Leaders of adult groups in other educational organizations could use the same approach. Periodically, perhaps twice a year or once a quarter at most, ask each of these teachers of adults to forward the names of those in their classes who might be ready for consideration. Use a form such as the one in Figure 8 for this systematic discovery of prospective workers who might be candidates for a preservice training experience.[1] Of course, keep the channels open at all times of the year for teachers and others to recommend prospective workers.

Keep track of the productivity of present workers in helping to discover other potential workers. Commend them, and recognize them appropriately in private and in public. In this and in other ways, the entire present work force becomes a network for discovering the gifts of others. Most teachers and other leaders experience unique joy when they are successful in helping to discover the gifts of their pupils. A great teacher is known by the pupils who go on into more mature experiences than would be possible by staying forever in a class. Graduating into a service opportunity is such an experience.

GET-ACQUAINTED TIMES

There are other ways to help discover gifts. During get-acquainted times, ask people to present one another to the group instead of introducing themselves. These presentations to acquaint people with one another could follow structured questions about each individual—including information about their special interests, talents, and experience in church service. Such sharing should be treated as normal and desirable, as one way to express the interest of groups in the individuals who comprise their membership.

Figure 8

PROSPECTIVE STUDENT FOR SUNDAY SCHOOL WORKER TRAINING COURSE

(Teacher of Adults: Complete the card. Return the card via the record collection system, or give directly to the course director, who will make all recruitment contacts.)

One mark of a productive adult class in Sunday school is the preparation of people who are ready and willing to consider serving in the general work force of the Sunday school. Teachers and members should rejoice when a member moves into service beyond the class.

A new course to train potential workers for our Sunday school is about to begin. Please suggest confidentially one of your members you consider ready for such training. If you wish to recommend more than one, use a separate card for each.

Member's name _____   Phone_____

Your name_____   Date _____

Comment_____

_____

_____

_____

PASTORAL ENCOURAGEMENT

An important way to undergird the discovery efforts is for the pastor to speak forthrightly about the church's ministries and the opportunities they afford for members to serve. Such occasions should not be the generally futile appeals that almost beg people to volunteer to serve. They must be on a higher level, citing the privileged nature, the growth experience, and the obedient offering of self that are represented in serving.

Rarely should there be public appeals for volunteers for specific jobs in the educational ministries of a church. Too often some who respond to such appeals tend to be the least qualified for the need. Such response could possibly create a very awkward situation. The work deserves more prayerful and thoughtful selectivity than dependence on public appeals allows.

It is important appropriately to discover and match the abilities, gifts, and aptitudes of members with the needs of the church. Too often the need of the church is the only factor considered. Better service, lower worker turnover, more job satisfaction, and other benefits can come from giving major attention to associating gifts and interests of individuals with the needs of the church for workers.

RECRUITING CAREFULLY AND SYSTEMATICALLY

Organization is only an idea until there are people in places required by the organization. People "make" an organization. A church might have a very well designed concept for a Sunday school organization, but the concept is only a good beginning. People must be selected, recruited, and confirmed by church action to fill each place of responsibility. The pastor and/or minister of education should work with the various ministry leadership teams to determine what positions each ministry will have for the coming church year. Once these are determined, the recruitment process begins.

SELECTING PROSPECTIVE WORKERS

Many churches depend on a church committee to lead in the selection and coordination of the actual recruitment of workers for the church ministries. This worker nominating committee is the primary method used. The nominating committee is selected by approved church procedure and accountable to the church for leading in staffing its ministries. In some churches the pastor appoints this committee and submits the names to the church for approval, subject to changes the church might make. In other churches the members of this important committee are chosen by ballot in a church business session. Each church should select its committee and determine the length of service according to approved procedures.

Many churches have a nominating committee of three or five people who are from the general church membership (not necessarily elected workers already serving in certain positions in the church). This committee nominates directors of ministries, who, on election, relate to the nominating committee in an ex officio relationship. These committee members and ministry directors work together to coordinate the recruitment of all others who serve in the respective ministries.

The church nominating committee should serve as the clearing house for potential nominees for all church-elected positions in the volunteer organizations (not the church staff positions). This committee leads the work of selecting and recruiting, and should call on many other people to assist in the process.

An early matter for the nominating committee is to determine or review the qualifications required by the church for people to be eligible for consideration for elected service. In some instances, the church itself might be asked to approve the qualifications on the recommendation of the nominating committee.

There are many possible ways to state qualifications for selection. In addition to being a Christian and a member of the church in consideration, one very simple but profound statement is of the threefold criteria of (1) faithful, (2) willing, and (3) capable. These simple labels should be expanded to fit the needs of each church.

A prospective worker should be faithful in obvious ways to the Lord. He or she should be faithful to the church, perhaps as demonstrated by reasonable regularity in attendance, positive attitudes toward the church and its ministries, and being supportive of its chosen leaders. The prospective worker should be faithful to commitments that the accepted responsibility requires. A person considered should be faithful to himself and truthful, keep promises, and have a wholesome self-esteem and genuine integrity.

Willingness should include a determination to work diligently to accomplish what the job requires. This might include visiting, attending planning meetings, and other specific activities. It should include willingness to work cooperatively with others and to consider fairly those changes that might be necessary to improve the work. It should include a willingness to work toward personal growth and improvement of skills.

Being capable might mean capable of learning and growing to be an effective worker. A worker prospect who is faithful, willing, and capable of learning and growing to be an effective worker is to be preferred over one who has "all kinds of abilities," but who is not faithful or willing to perform a job responsibly. The former can be helped to become capable by good training and supervision. The latter is hard to help because of a lack of faithfulness and willingness. Of course, it is a delight to find a very capable person with abilities already well developed who is also faithful and willing.

Another concern of the nominating committee is to oversee the formulation of specific job descriptions for the positions that people are to be asked to consider. The committee members need some awareness of what the jobs require. Those who are to make the recruitment contact need to be able to present the job clearly and briefly to the prospective worker. Most of the general church ministries have available in their leadership materials some model job descriptions for the usual positions the ministries require. Often these will be adequate.

With the job qualifications and the job descriptions in hand, the committee can then consider the information available regarding the gifts, abilities, and interests of the prospective worker. Prayerfully they can relate the needs for workers with these other bodies of information and requirements and seek to match the right people with the right jobs. Once there is agreement as to which people should be asked to consider which jobs, the nominating committee should make the assignment for the recruitment contact.

Often in this selection stage, a ministry leader might present to the committee a request for clearance to contact someone whom the leader has already discovered to be a possibility as a worker in some position in the ministry he or she represents. In many instances it would be wise to approve such requests. Among other reasons, it is a suitable way of commending the leader for the effective scouting done. But there is a concern here that is of critical importance: if the nominating committee is to be effective in coordinating the overall worker selection, recruitment, and confirmation processes, the committee must have the prerogative of determining in what positions certain ones will be asked to serve. Violate this fundamental principle, and the committee might as well be dismissed, for it cannot fulfill such a responsibility without the authority commensurate to the assignment.

Sometimes an aggressive and concerned leader will get ahead of the nominating committee and recruit a worker, and then come to ask the committee to endorse such action. In such instances it could be best to let the recruitment stand, but definitely reaffirm the committee's requirement that in all future instances clearance needs to be obtained prior to recruitment. Continual violation of this understanding undermines the entire concept of a church committee trying to help match the best potential workers with the service position that most needs their gifts.

RECRUITING THE WORKERS

The nominating committee, at times assisted by the pastor or the minister of education, recruits the heads of ministries. From that point, the one who would be the new worker's supervisor in the event that the recruitment is successful should be the one to make the recruitment contact. This person should be in the best position to talk realistically with the potential worker about exactly what the job requires and how they might work together.

The *enlistment interview* should be the beginning of a bond between the parties involved that results in a mutual commitment to try to do the work as it deserves to be done. The enlister should find a time and place to visit with the prospective worker when they can have an unhurried private conversation about the invitation to serve.

The enlister should discuss with the prospective worker the need, the challenge, the requirements, the potential problems, the training opportunities, the curriculum materials and basic approaches to their use, the present and possible membership of the group, the essential activities the job requires, the resources available, and whatever other information pertains to a realistic understanding of the position. Allow time for the prospective worker to think and to pray about the decision before giving an answer. Before concluding the initial interview the enlister should ask when the prospective worker thinks the decision can be made. He should invite the prospective worker to contact him with any questions that might arise pertinent to the decision. A contact from the enlister to offer to clarify any matter would sometimes be in order. The person making the enlistment contact should report the outcome of the enlistment effort promptly to the nominating committee.

CONFIRMING THE WORKERS

The church should have opportunity to approve those recruited to teach and lead in its ministries. This approval should include the leaders of the units of ministry organization, such as the teachers and outreach leaders of Sunday school classes, the leaders of training groups, the chairpeople of committees, and possibly others. Generally classes, committees, and other groups can choose the internal leaders of their own subgroups. Church election or approval of workers serves to establish the church's oversight of its ministries, and is an appropriate and needed relationship. Furthermore, it is a way of affirming those chosen to serve.

Some churches ask their elected workers to make a commitment to a *covenant statement* related to their service. Samples of this type of statement are in some of the leadership magazines and manuals. These covenants vary from a kind of contractual agreement that the worker will follow, to a body of worthy goals of work and conduct toward which the worker promises to strive faithfully.

Still another way of confirming workers is through a *commissioning service*. A sample taken from a printed Sunday morning worship bulletin follows.

COMMISSIONING SERVICE FOR WORKERS OF THE CHURCH

Minister: And I heard the voice of the Lord saying, "Whom shall I send, and who will go for us?"

Workers: Then I said, "Here am I! Send me."

Minister: Because thou hast called us to salvation and to Christian living,

Workers: We consecrate ourselves to thee.

Minister: Because thou has commanded us to witness to the gospel of saving grace,

Workers: We consecrate our lips to thee.

Minister: Because thou hast commanded us to teach the unsearchable riches of thy word,

Workers: We consecrate our minds to thee.

Minister:	Because thou hast called us to minister to people wherever we find them in need,
Workers:	We dedicate our hands in thy service.
Minister:	Because we have been called of God, what can we give in service to him?
Workers:	Take our lives and let them be consecrated Lord to thee.
Minister:	And what else can we give thee?
Workers:	Take our lips and let them be filled with messages from thee.
Minister:	Because of thy love to us,
Workers:	Take our wills and make them thine.
Minister:	Because we are so often limited in our understanding,
Workers:	We plead the direction of thy Holy Spirit, O Lord.
Minister:	Because the work we face is often unpleasant and difficult,
Workers:	Make us constant in our work.
Minister:	Because our sins of selfishness often lead to misunderstanding and wrong attitudes,
Workers:	Keep our hearts pure, O Lord.
Minister:	Because of the magnitude of the opportunity to challenge and mold the lives of others,
Workers:	Help us to reflect the character of Christ in our living and service.
All:	O Jesus, I have promised to serve thee to the end; be thou forever near me, my master and my friend.
	We beseech thee, O Lord, to use the ministry of our works for the edifying of the body of Christ, the church, until we all come in the unity of the faith, and of the knowledge of Jesus Christ thy son, unto mature Christian workers, unto the measure of the stature of the fullness of Christ.

PRAYER OF CONSECRATION

All:	Let the words of our mouths and the meditations of our hearts be acceptable in thy sight, O Lord, our strength and our redeemer.

A job well done in the careful and systematic recruitment of workers for the educational ministries of a church pays dividends in many ways. The fellowship in service among well-functioning groups of workers in church ministries is some of the richest and best in all the life of the church. Ministers who concentrate on helping to create and maintain the leader groups in a church multiply their own ministries through these good leaders.

TRAINING WORKERS

To multiply the teaching and learning in a church it is necessary to multiply the teachers and leaders. As indicated earlier, improving the teacher and leader level in a church represents an educational ministry in itself. A church must provide and arrange for the growth and development of its teachers and leaders in educational ministries. A church which fails to train its teachers and leaders cannot expect to do well the teaching and learning tasks for its members.

Readers might refer to the chapter "Training Teachers and Leaders" in *Christian Education Handbook,* edited and compiled by Bruce Powers (rev. ed., Broadman & Holman, 1996). Also, a very helpful publication for Sunday school leader training needs is the *Sunday School Leader Training Handbook* by Wayne A. Poling (Nashville: Convention Press, 1991). For our purposes here we shall mention major kinds of teacher and worker training and indicate the kinds of resources a church can use in its teacher and leader training.

KINDS OF TRAINING

One way to examine the kinds of training a church might use for teachers and leaders is to view training as (1) preservice training and (2) inservice training. Both dimensions are vital to doing the best work.

Preservice training is timed to equip those who are just about to go on duty in a place of service. Sometimes this training is made available before one has actually been recruited for a specific place of service. In some instances the trainee might have been suggested as a prospective worker by the class teacher where the trainee attends Sunday school. This is one good way to select candidates for preservice training.

Preservice training might range from a single conference session to orient people to the particular work they have agreed to do, to a rather intensive series of training sessions such as those outlined in *Training Potential Sunday School Workers* (Revised); or the more recent *Conducting Potential Sunday School Worker Training.* One of these resources offers guidance in detail for conducting either a thirty-two session series over a sixteen-week period or a twenty-four session series over an eight-week period for people selected as potential workers in Sunday school. The other offers both a quarter-length plan schedule and a month-length plan. (See note 1 at the end of this chapter).

The single conference session could be profitable if that is all that can be done, though it is extremely limited. There are leadership materials, especially periodicals for the leaders of specific ministries of a church, that could contribute immensely to the effectiveness of a one-session conference. Such materials could be presented to the prospective worker with instructions to examine the contents and then come for a follow-up session to discuss the contents in detail. A creative leader can develop other formats and find resources for preservice training.

Inservice training possibilities are as varied as schedule options allow. For example, the following schedule options for training sessions are adapted from "Using the Sunday School Leadership Diploma to Train Workers" by Joseph M. Haynes.[2]

Times to Accomplish Training

1. Friday night and Saturday morning workshops
2. All-day workshops
3. Consecutive night sessions or a week of study
4. Weekend training sessions, using Saturday morning and afternoon
5. Training retreat
6. Associational training school
7. Sunday night training time
8. Individual study, using "personal learning activities"
9. Combination of reading book and joining others for write-up session
10. Courses offered one night or day a week until completed
11. Duplicate sessions offered one day and night until completed
12. State and/or regional training endeavors
13. Leadership conferences at Glorieta and Ridgecrest Conference Centers
14. Sunday morning for potential workers
15. One night for three weeks with covered-dish supper in homes
16. One-night training blitz from about 6:00 to 11:30
17. Two nights (Monday and Tuesday) each week for two weeks
18. Wednesday afternoon or evening
19. Weekly workers meeting time
20. Make copies of questions for individual study
21. Job descriptions, directed reading/listening programs, directed observation/evaluation

THE CHURCH STUDY COURSE

Possibly the most productive and most promising approach to leader and member training is known as the "Church Study Course." It is a system consisting of short courses for adults and youth combined with a credit and recognition system. Also available in the system are noncredit short courses for children and preschoolers. These short courses are for use in addition to the ongoing study and training curricula in churches. The

courses range from two and a half to ten hours in length, and may be studied individually or in groups. In 1995 there were more than 600 courses in
24 subject areas, leading to 107 specialized leadership diplomas and numerous other certificates for other studies. The Church Study Course system is primarily for leadership training, but many courses are designed
also for all members.

The Church Study Course was developed and is maintained by the Baptist Sunday School Board, in cooperation with other agencies of the Southern Baptist Convention. It is used predominantly by Southern Baptists,
although the system is flexible to include any people or church groups who
wish to participate.

The records are computer-kept, at no cost to participants. People from
more than 106 countries were participating in the system in 1993. Periodic,
free printouts of individual records are sent to churches, enabling leaders
to keep track of the accomplishments and to assist in planning for the training needs of their members. An annual *Church Study Course* catalog gives
full details about the system and lists each of the courses.[3]

This truly remarkable system has the potential of long-term usefulness
in training, especially for training teachers and leaders in the church organizations.

SEMINARY EXTENSION

Many significant training opportunities are available to ministers and
laymen through extension education. One of the most successful of these
is the Seminary Extension of the Southern Baptist Convention, which operates under the joint direction of the seminaries of that denomination.

Leaders in a church should locate the nearest center for Seminary Extension courses, and examine the offerings there with a view to encouraging teachers and leaders to make use of any suitable training opportunities.
These courses afford a rich variety from which to choose in helping teachers and leaders train for their work in a church's educational ministries.

CONCLUSION

Some of the most educational work of a church is that which goes on in
discovering, recruiting, and training the workers who will teach and lead
in the educational ministries. It is vitally important for a church to have effective ways of accomplishing each of these responsibilities. Church leaders must be sensitive, caring, and observant as they seek to select, recruit,
confirm, and train workers.

Systematic approaches such as the use of interest/talent/ experience in-
ventories, the church nominating committee, planned training events and
courses, the Church Study Course, Seminary Extension courses, and other
approaches should be designed or selected and used to do a thorough and

comprehensive job with the work force in a church. A church that trains its educational work force has some hope of doing the job that is needed in educating its members.

CONCERNS FOR FURTHER STUDY

Consider these questions as you continue to reflect on a church discovering, recruiting, and training workers.

1. Why shouldn't a church just concern itself with getting whoever will agree to work in a given job, without going to all the trouble of trying to match gifts of individuals with job needs?

2. Why shouldn't the pastor and other church staff members do the worker recruitment for all the church ministries?

3. What kinds of plans would you make if it were your responsibility to develop training plans for all the Sunday school workers in your church?

CHAPTER 16

Providing Adequate Resources

Those who work in a church's educational ministries need certain resources to do their tasks effectively. It is possible to do the work without all the desired material resources. It is usually impossible to wait until all the desired resources are available before beginning to work. Sometimes the ministries must be performed with inadequate resources. A church has some responsibility to try to provide the resources to enable teachers and leaders to do their best possible work. In this chapter we shall look at some of the resources that are essential for the educational ministries.

PROVIDING A SPIRIT AND CLIMATE FOR EDUCATION

The chief resources for those who teach and lead are not material but spiritual. The chief spiritual resource is the Holy Spirit. The Great Commission, itself a mandate to teach and to observe all of God's commands, concludes with the assurance of the very presence of God. Christians know that the Holy Spirit dwells in them to instruct, to guide, to convict, and to comfort. Reliance on the promised Holy Spirit is the first requirement as a resource for an effective teacher in the realm of spiritual and moral teaching. No other resource can substitute for his presence and power.

The presence and power of the Holy Spirit are not such that anyone or any group can acquire, store, or dispense as needed. Each child of God has equal opportunity of access to his presence and power. Each has the privilege and the capacity and the responsibility to communicate with God and to seek his help through the Holy Spirit. What leaders can and should do is to keep before the teachers and leaders the necessity of reliance on the Holy Spirit and of each one seeking to be aware of his presence and asking for his power to help them in their work. A genuine sense of partnership between God through the Holy Spirit and devoted believers who are faithful, willing, and becoming capable is a powerful force for the good work of a church, which is indeed the work of God.

A climate conducive to teaching and learning is also a major resource for an effective church educational ministry. This climate is greatly influenced by the attitudes of leaders and members toward learning and knowledge.

On the one hand, it is important to have a sense of knowing some things for certain, and knowing them well. For example, the sure desire of God for mankind's redemption needs to be well known among leaders and teachers, in keeping with biblical teachings such as 2 Peter 3:9, "The Lord is not slow about his promise as some count slowness, but is forbearing toward you, not wishing that any should perish, but that all should reach repentance."

On the other hand, it is also important to be aware and to acknowledge that there are some things that are not yet known, some of which are not likely to be known. For example, "But of that day and hour no one knows, not even the angels of heaven, nor the Son, but the Father only" (Matt. 24:36). It is usually a detriment to the best teaching and learning in a church for some teachers to claim to know the unknowable and to imply some spiritual caste system that exalts themselves and belittles others. Cults are the result of such know-it-all leadership. There is little room for genuine teaching and learning in such a setting.

A good climate for teaching and learning is one in which there is a sense that there are some things we know with certainty and there are some things that, try though we might, we cannot know; but there are many, many things that are knowable with our effort and the Holy Spirit's help. Knowing these things could make life more what it should be. These knowables add richness, perspective, and other meaning to life in Christ. They add the kind of freedom to living that was intended when the Lord said, "If you continue in my word, you are truly my disciples, and you will know the truth, and the truth will make you free" (John 8:31–32).

Leaders in a church's educational ministries should try to provide such a climate for teaching and learning. They can do this by continually manifesting an attitude of being learners themselves, as they help make it possible for others to learn. Also, they must continue to participate in learning opportunities, such as training events, study programs, and other activities that help assure that they are growing people. Creative leaders will find other ways to provide a climate and spirit for educating.

PROVIDING CURRICULUM MATERIALS

We have attempted to make it clear that the Bible is the principal text of the educational ministries of a church. In Part 2 we have already seen some of the essentials about choosing curriculum materials and about the relationship of the extrabiblical materials to the Bible. Here we shall briefly present some of the processes related to providing the materials.

A church has the responsibility and the right to determine what its members will study under the sponsorship or in the name of the church. In order to help assure that the church fulfills this responsibility and reserves this right, there should be a procedure for selecting and approving curriculum materials. Consider these suggested items as a possible procedure:

(1) The Church Ministry Leadership Team shall recommend to the church the line or lines of curriculum materials for use in the teaching and learning organizations.

(2) Parties advocating a variation from the approved lines of curriculum materials shall first present their proposal to the respective ministry leadership team for consideration, well in advance of the anticipated use of the materials. If the ministry leadership team joins in advocating the variation, the ministry director (who also is the director of the ministry leadership team for that organization) shall present the proposal to the Church Ministry Leadership Team. After approval by the Church Ministry Leadership Team, the variation shall come as a recommendation of the Church Ministry Leadership Team to the church. If the Church Ministry Leadership Team should not approve, the leadership team of the particular ministry involved shall determine whether to recommend the variation to the church for consideration.

(3) In the event that a church ministry group contradicts the church-approved policy and procedure for curriculum selection, the leadership team for that ministry and/or the Church Ministry Leadership Team shall instruct the teacher or leader regarding the due process. From that point the process shall be followed as stated above. Teachers or leaders who persist in violating the church's position on curriculum selection shall forfeit their positions as teachers or leaders.

A church that is affiliated with a denomination having a publishing house for curriculum materials is wise to give full and fair consideration to its products first. Such consideration should include keeping abreast of what is offered by the publishing house through catalogs, pamphlets, brochures, and other means. From time to time these leaders should examine carefully selected publications their church is using, and compare them item for item with other lines of similar materials. Use the "Curriculum Selection Checklist"[1] in Figure 9 to help determine the curriculum line most suited to the needs of the particular organizations.

The regularly used curriculum materials should be provided for in the church budget, with allowances for the current enrollment, new members, special projects, and new items that might be available during the year.[2]

Figure 9

CURRICULUM SELECTION CHECKLIST

Use this checklist to compare lines of curriculum you might consider for use with a given age group. Secure samples of each line you wish to consider. Examine the materials carefully. Check each item on the list below. Write a check beside the line that is best on each factor. Compare the basic pieces of each line: the pupil's material; the teacher's material. Choose and use the curriculum that best meets your needs.

Factors to Consider	Curriculum Lines		
	A	B	C
1. There is ample, appropriate use of the Bible.	___	___	___
2. The teachings are doctrinally sound.	___	___	___
3. Doctrinal emphases are balanced.	___	___	___
4. Coverage of the Bible is comprehensive.	___	___	___
5. The educational philosophy is valid.	___	___	___
6. Concepts presented are suited to the age group.	___	___	___
7. Content addresses life needs appropriately.	___	___	___
8. Teachings encourage appropriate responses.	___	___	___
9. Methodology is properly related to content.	___	___	___
10. Methods are suited to our worker's skills	___	___	___
11. Training materials are available to develop worker's skills.	___	___	___
12. Learning activities are right for the age group.	___	___	___
13. The materials support the church program.	___	___	___
14. Materials advance purposes of this organization.	___	___	___
15. Quality teaching/learning aids are readily available.	___	___	___
16. Supplementary commentaries are available.	___	___	___
17. Art use is in good taste.	___	___	___
18. The layout is attractive to the user.	___	___	___
19. The binding is sufficiently durable.	___	___	___
20. The paper quality is adequate.	___	___	___
21. The print size is right.	___	___	___
22. The print is clear and easy to read.	___	___	___
23. Use of color in materials is attractive.	___	___	___
24. Service for ordering, receiving, paying is good.	___	___	___
25. Consultation in use of materials is available.	___	___	___
26. Volume (number of pages) in each piece is adequate.	___	___	___
27. The cost in relation to the benefits is suitable.	___	___	___
28. The cost per comparable items is best.	___	___	___
29. _____.	___	___	___
(Other factor we consider important)			
30. _____.	___	___	___
(Other factor we consider important)			

Based on this comparison, curriculum line ____ seems best for us. It is available at the following address:

_____
_____
_____

The curriculum materials should be used principally in preparation for the teaching and learning sessions. They should not be prominent in the actual session, unless they are contributing to the teaching method as a visual aid or in some similar way. In other words, it is not the periodical or other material that should be taught, but the biblical truth related to the needs of the group. It is important that the Bible be brought, seen, and properly used during teaching and learning sessions. Members of a Sunday school class, for example, are not appropriately impressed about the importance of studying the Bible if their teacher teaches them from something other than the Bible itself. The use of a good teaching plan or outline and selected teaching and learning aids in the session should be all a well-prepared teacher needs in addition to the Bible.

In most churches the pastor must take the initiative to lead in the selection and use of curriculum materials, working with the Church Ministry Leadership Team and others. In churches with a minister of education, that person should have primary responsibility for this leadership area. In some instances a church with no educational staff might have a gifted and trained lay member who could be the principal leader in curriculum matters.[3]

Media Library personnel can render valuable service to the educational ministries in the selection, distribution, and use of curriculum materials. Leaders should consult and plan with the Media Library staff to assure that materials are placed where they will be used. This is especially helpful regarding materials to be used across organizational lines, such as materials for the family.

The choices and decisions made regarding a church's curriculum plan and the materials that support it are some of the most vital in a church's life. There is far more to the matter than just filling out the order forms. It is with the help of curriculum materials that the real curriculum—what happens to help people learn and develop—is experienced. Curriculum materials that are based on the Bible, designed to meet the needs of people, penetrate and undergird the total church program, and appropriately relate method to content, in addition to other criteria, are essential to help a church reach its educational objective: to help people become aware of God as revealed in Jesus Christ, respond to him in a personal commitment of faith, live in conscious recognition of the guidance and power of the Holy Spirit, and grow toward Christian maturity.

PROVIDING OTHER ESSENTIAL RESOURCES

A church must provide other essential resources in order to be most effective in its educational ministries. Among these resources are adequate space (usually one or more buildings), equipment, furnishings, supplies, and funding.

SPACE

Just as there are known ratios for teachers or leaders to members, there are optimum space requirements for each age group. Contrary to some opinions, preschoolers and children require more space for education than do youth or adults. This is true because of their need to move around, their inability to sit still for long periods, and because of the more fundamentally physical ways in which they learn. Consult Figure 10 for recommended space provisions for the various ages for educational purposes.

More and more churches are learning to get multiple use of educational space by varied schedule arrangements. Some have more than one "shift" of Sunday school in the same space, for example. This can be done in several ways. One way is to have one Sunday school meet while an early worship service is in session, followed by another Sunday school and worship service. This means that there is full occupancy of both educational and worship space for two consecutive periods.

Another schedule possibility is to have one Sunday school meet early, followed by a single worship service, and then by a second Sunday School. This involves three consecutive periods.

Another schedule is to have one Sunday school at the traditional time prior to the single morning worship service, and then have a second Sunday school during the worship service. This involves only two consecutive periods, and has the flaw of having the second Sunday school participants regularly absent from the worship service.

Still another variation that normally uses only two consecutive periods calls for those age divisions using a department and class format (usually youth and adults only) to have about half of the classes conduct their sessions first in class-size rooms, while the others are in the department room, and then at the mid-point of the period change places. This fully occupies both class and department spaces simultaneously during one period, followed by the church worship service.

There are other possible ways to get multiple use of space. Concern about these possibilities is likely to become more and more of interest to churches with the increasing costs of building materials, interest rates on money for building, and the rapidly escalating costs of energy to heat and cool. Still another factor is the cost to individuals and families in making multiple trips to the meeting place of the church.

Church leaders must search diligently for new ways to get more of the ministries of the church accomplished with less consumption, proportionately, of the church's financial resources. Otherwise, churches face the prospect of reduced ministries locally and in missions, staff reductions, and reduced attendance for the educational, worship, and other activities in the church buildings. There is an urgent need for mature, responsible, effective experimentation regarding space use, energy efficiency, and

Figure 10

Determining Space in Age-Division Rooms

Organization and Space Needs for Division Grouping and Grading

		For Each Department			For Each Class			Suggested Floor Space Per Person				
								Department		Assembly	Classroom	
Division	Age	Maximum Enrollment	Average Attendance[a]	Capacity of Spaces[b]	Max. Enrol.	Aver.[a] Attend.	Cap. of Space	Min.[c]	Recommended	Recommended	Min.[c]	Recommended
Preschool	B-1	12	5-8	7-10								
	2-3	20	9-13	12-16	NA			20 sq. ft.		25+	None	None
	4-5	25	11-16	15-20								
Children	6-8	30	14-20	18-24	NA			20 sq. ft.		25+	None	None
	9-11[d]											
Youth	12-14	50	23-33	30-40	10	5-7	6-8					
	15-17	60	27-39	36-48	15	8-10	9-12	8 sq. ft.		10	10 sq. ft	12
Adult	18 up	125	56-81	75-100	25	12-16	15-20	8 sq. ft		10	8 sq. ft	12

Space is provided for each person expected to be in the rooms of the building. Determining the number for which to plan this space is a result of a careful analysis of projected enrollment, organization, and attendance. In determining the total number of square feet of educational space required, the church should add to the floor space mentioned above enough space for offices, corridors, stairways, rest rooms, storage, service space, and other accessory areas. This will require a total square footage from 35 square feet to 45 square feet per person in the educational building. Many churches provide even more space.

a Average attendance in churches ranges from 45% to 65% of enrollment.

b Capacity space to provide is figured at 60 to 80 percent of enrollment to be adequate for high expected attendance. Percentage to be used should be determined by the individual church's record of enrollment and attendance.

c Minimum square footage may sometimes be necessary in smaller churches and mission buildings.

d Existing assemblies with classrooms may be used by departments in the Children's Division. Provide additional tables, chairs, and chalkboards as needed.

Church Architecture Department, The Sunday School Board of the Southern Baptist Convention, Nashville, Tennessee ministry scheduling to help churches continue and grow in their effectiveness.[4]

Church leaders should seek counsel from proven advisers regarding building plans and possible variations in their use of buildings already existing. Denominational educational and building consultants are readily available to many churches, and should be consulted. Other experienced pastors and educational ministers can offer helpful counsel. Their counsel might also help in scheduling and in acquiring equipment and furnishings for good teaching and learning.

EQUIPMENT, FURNISHINGS, AND SUPPLIES

Equipment and furnishings are important provisions for a church's educational ministries. The numerous possibilities might seem overwhelming to the inexperienced educator, if considered all together.

The space for the smallest babies and one-year-olds, for example, might need all of the following: cribs, diaper bag shelf, diaper rinsing with flush bowl, tape or disc player, adult rocking chair, safety chair, sink-refrigerator combination, utility tables, wall supply cabinet, clear glass windows with low sills, an adult toilet, and a playpen.

Toddler space should be furnished and equipped with the following: an area for cardboard blocks, book rack with slanting shelves, diaper bag shelf, doll bed, child-size toilet, open shelves with closed back, tape or disc player, child-size rocking chair, rocking boat and steps, wall supply cabinets, and clear glass windows with low sills.

Two- and three-year-olds need space equipped and furnished as follows: chairs with ten-inch seat height, cabinet sink, book rack with slanting shelves, child-size toilet, clothes drying rack, coatrack for adults and one for children, doll bed, open shelves with closed back, painting easel, puzzle rack, tape or disc player, child-size rocking chair, play stove, small table, wall supply cabinet, and clear windows with low sills.

Space for four- and five-year-olds needs equipment and furnishing including these: clear glass windows with low sills, toilet with child-size fixtures, wall supply cabinet units, picture file desk, children's coatrack, picture rail, tackboard, block shelves, nature shelves, art shelves, book rack with slanting shelves, painting easel, clothes drying rack, tape or disc player, studio-type piano, cabinet-sink, play stove, doll bed, chest of drawers, child's rocking chair, small table, art table, puzzle table, puzzle rack, picture file desk, rack for adults and for children's wraps, and one chair with either ten- or twelve-inch seat height for each child as well as an adult-sized chair for each teacher.

Children have these equipment and furnishing needs in their educational space: one chair with twelve- or fourteen-inch seat height per child, one table for each six children, portable shelves with closed back, studio-size piano, book rack with slanted shelves, portable coatracks for children and adults, storage cabinets, combination chalkboard, tackboard, and picture rail, cabinet for pictures and posters, tape or disc player, toilets on the hall, and sink.

Youth and adult space should have: stacking or folding chairs with eighteen-inch seat height, small table or lectern in the department area, secretarial table, studio-size piano, movable coat and hat rack, chairs (possibly with tablet arms), small teaching table, folding tables available, freestanding chalkboard, chalkboard-tackboard fixed to the wall, shelves, easel, and wastebasket.

Those who plan for new buildings should make a list of equipment and furnishings for each age group, and include the cost estimates for these as they plan. Some items are more essential than others and should be the first secured in the event the space cannot be fully equipped and furnished from the beginning. A planned schedule for adding needed furnishings and equipment is advisable, in order to bring the facilities up to recommended quality. These additions should be included in the annual church budgeting process.

There are many other items of equipment and furnishings, when the ministries are considered which cross organizational and age-group lines. Media library, recreation, music, and all other ministries need the best equipment and furnishings a church can justifiably provide. Leaders of these and other ministries should have opportunity annually to request budget funding for their needs.

Supply items, such as chalk, art supplies, teaching aids, paper, scissors, paste, and numerous other supplies are recommended and are useful in the educational experiences. A church should have a simple procedure for coordinating the purchasing, storage, and distribution of these kinds of items. Some churches use a simple request form that the intended user completes and submits to the church office. One person usually secures the items and informs the requester of their availability. In addition, the items that are commonly used in many areas can be secured and stored conveniently for the workers to use as needed, without a special request.

These essential resources require funding. They should be considered integral parts of a church's funding processes. All ministry activities and the resources needed to support them should be funded in keeping with the church's approved financial plans. For most churches, small and large, this would mean that plans should be made to include funds in the church budget.

BUDGETING FOR EDUCATIONAL RESOURCES

Plans for each ministry should be made in advance of the budget planning. The Church Ministry Leadership Council, the various ministry leadership teams, church committees whose work requires expenditures, and other groups that are considered a part of the church's ministries need to determine their proposed activities for the coming year, rank them in priority order, and place a realistic cost estimate on the ministries. Respective leaders present these to the church budget committee in the order of their priority.

In the likely event that the budget planners cannot anticipate sufficient funds for all of the requests, the requesters of funds should have opportunity to determine which of their requests shall be deleted or modified. It is the function of budget planners to (1) anticipate income from all sources, (2) recommend categoric limits for the various ministry areas in keeping with the church's budgeting experience as modified by expected ministry adjustments, (3) compile the allocation requests into a unified budget as fairly and openly as possible, (4) secure church approval of the budget, and (5) oversee the financial operation of the church budget during the year, making adjustments as directed by church action and policies.

It is not the proper function of the budget committee to be expected to recommend which ministries to delete or modify, whose salaries to raise, cut, or leave the same, and other such specific decisions that should be dealt with by other church groups. To expect such decisions of the budget committee is an unfair imposition on them and on the other planning groups in a church. Lead each group to do its own work, and to relate that to the work of other groups in the light of each group's proper responsibilities. Such a process shows due respect to all leaders and provides religious growth and development for those involved. Further, it sets a good example of a church working together with a minimum of concern for power and manipulation.

One other word of caution might be useful regarding funding church ministries and the activities related to them. Many consider it questionable ethically and legally for groups in a church, or for the church as a whole, to engage in on-site services and sales activities to raise money for church functions. Ethically, if the services rendered are indeed services, they probably compete to some extent with regular business enterprises that depend on their service for a livelihood. Legally, few churches are certified or have been examined to qualify to serve food to the public or to engage in other sales or services to the public. Also, the proceeds from such services or sales probably are not properly reported for tax purposes. A church should be a good neighbor and a good corporate citizen.

Find other appropriate ways to fund church activities. Call upon members to increase their gifts. Charge actual cost for participation in certain events and possibly help underwrite such costs from the budget receipts. Probably no ethic or law would be jeopardized if the names of youth or others interested in earning from their services were made known to the members, who then could use their services at their homes for baby-sitting, lawn care, car washing, or other such help. It seems out of character to have the church gathered at the church property to engage in business for a profit.

CONCLUSION

A church needs certain resources for ministry. Chief among these essential resources is a spirit and climate for education. Reliance on the Holy Spirit is foundational. A good attitude toward teaching and learning is also necessary. Suitable curriculum materials are vital. The curriculum materials selected and used in a church should be clearly under church guidance and control.

A church also needs such resources as space (buildings), equipment, furnishings, supplies, and money to make all these and other resources available as needed. Church planning groups, such as the Church Ministry Leadership Team, the various ministry leadership teams, certain church committees, and other groups need to plan and work together to try to provide the best resources they can justify to support the ministries and their activities.

The ministry needs should be determined, and costs estimated, and funds secured in a manner that manifests that a church is a family of God's children. Then even the "mundane" areas of administering resources become experiences for growth and development of those involved.

CONCERNS FOR FURTHER STUDY

Consider these questions as you continue to reflect on a church providing adequate resources.

1. What suggestions would you make regarding providing a spirit and climate in a church that encourages education?

2. Secure a set of Sunday school teacher's materials for one of the age divisions from one line from your denomination and compare it with either another line from your denomination or that of another source. Follow the "Curriculum Selection Checklist" in this chapter. What are your conclusions?

3. How do the space provisions and the equipment and furnishings in your church compare with those suggested in this chapter? What would you recommend to improve the provisions in your church?

CHAPTER 17

Implementing and Evaluating

The potential of an effective educational ministry in a church is mammoth. It can encompass almost all that a church does. People are taught. They study, learn, and develop in Christian character. They are discipled, and they go about their lives and do the work of a church. In order to help in all of these and other aspects of a church's life and work, leaders must lead. They must lead in determining what the nature and purpose of a church is, what are needs of people a church should attempt to meet and how a church might meet those needs, and then in how the work should be done.

The emphasis of this chapter is on how to do what needs to be done. To implement a church's ministry plans means to accomplish them, to complete them with appropriate action, to carry them out, to fulfill their intentions.

Several kinds of activity are required for implementing a church's ministry plans. The plans must be promoted. Teachers and leaders must be guided, supervised, and helped to succeed. Those involved need to know specifically what is happening and to whom through records and reports. They must know how well the work is going, to how many, and what might be done to improve.

ESSENTIALS OF GOOD PROMOTION

The ministry plans of a church deserve and need to be promoted. Promotion is what is done to advance something, to further it, to move it forward. Who could be opposed in a church to good promotion of the church's essential ministries? Wise leaders will not knowingly irritate the sensitivities of those whose support and participation they are trying to secure. They will ponder their own motivation and be ethical about avoiding manipulation. But surely wise leaders will promote, if anything is to happen!

Promotion in a church can be seen in at least two types of activity: (1) publicity and (2) enlistment. Publicity in this context is making known to people the information designed to advance the interests of a cause. The people are those in and out of the church to whom a church is trying to minister. The cause is the activity to which the church wishes those people to relate. The information includes the facts and truths about the activity that will convey to people what they need to know in order to decide about their participation.

Publicity is accomplished in many forms. In many churches, oral announcements at meetings are perhaps the most common way. Numerous—sometimes too many—announcements are made in classes, departments, and worship services. On the other hand, some have deleted announcements entirely from worship services. However, this seems to be an extremely negative reaction. Few other occasions in the life of a church find as many of its congregation together at one time and place as do the worship services. An approach and a time for announcements in that setting (in good taste and effectively) can be accomplished. In some churches this is done in the worship services at the beginning of the period, after all have arrived in the room. Perhaps a better time is at the end of the worship period, just prior to dismissal. This would seem most often to be an opportune time to focus attention on further activities of ministry, when the real expression of service is just beginning.

Announce only a very few items, three or four at most, in a session. Limit them to those that are of general interest to the particular group. For example, the announcement to the entire congregation of a committee meeting would rarely be warranted, unless the purpose is to inform the congregation of a vital meeting of general interest. If the concern is to get committee members to attend, contact them individually, not by general announcement. Furthermore, leaders should not be expected to announce to the congregation just any note someone hands or whispers to them as they are on the way to the platform.

Posters, church bulletin articles, bulletin boards, advertising in the media, dramatic skits, and other means can be useful in publicizing a church's ministries. Apply to announcements and to other means of publicity the suggestions that follow in this section.

Enlistment often can be more effective when preceded and accompanied by good publicity. Enlistment is securing the participation, support, or help of people. A church enlists teachers and leaders. It enlists members to attend and to support and to participate. It enlists people outside the church membership in activities in keeping with the church's purposes. It begins with some presentation of the cause, moves to a decision or commitment of people to participate, and is actually realized when the people follow through on their decision or commitment.

Enlistment sometimes is accomplished through appeals to groups, with a response called for at the time of the appeal. Some enlistment is best done by one-to-one contact. The nature of the cause and the time available for enlisting are among the factors that help to determine whether the appeal should be to groups of people or to individuals by one-to-one contact. Sometimes people are asked to register their decision or commitment on a card or other form. There are times when such an active response is helpful both to firm up the decision and for follow-up purposes.

These *suggestions about promotion,* whether publicity or enlistment, should be the kinds of considerations leaders would use in trying to be effective as promoters:

(1) Determine the basic facts about the activity: why it is offered (focus on needs and benefits), what it is, for whom it is, when it is (date, day, and time), where it is, who will lead it, costs (if any direct cost to participants), how a person should respond if interested (either in more information or in making a commitment—sign a card or roster, buy a ticket, tell their teacher), preparation a person might need to make (if any), and the deadline for deciding and committing (if needed).

(2) Identify the target audience for whom the promotion should proceed.

(3) Decide what means of publicity will be used and who will do each part. Make clear assignments to those who will do the publicizing. Consider using the leaders who are responsible for leading the activity in the publicity. Too often one person attempts to do all the public announcements, and one result is that the announcer loses impact on the audience over a period of time. Inject a variety of promotional personnel.

(4) Plan for the best ways to enlist people and for those who will do this best. Make clear assignments to these people. In events or activities that involve a series of sessions, consider seeking commitment from people for the entire series in one decision. This could help the people avoid having to decide whether to participate in each session. Make it clear how people indicate their commitment to participate.

One of the major concerns of many churches is how to attract people, both irregular attenders who are members and nonmembers, to basic educational activities such as Bible study (Sunday school) and discipleship training. There are many on the membership rolls of these organizations and others who are as unreached in terms of participation as those who have not been reached for enrollment. They could hardly be driven away, because they are already away. Then there are the multitudes for whom a church is concerned who have never been members. Good publicity can get through effectively to only a few of these hard-to-reach people. Special

enlistment techniques can help to attract some. Some might never participate as hoped; still, a church must try.

For those difficult-to-attract people, the first approach recommended is
to use the regular organizational structure in efforts to reach them. In Sunday school this is the teacher, along with the outreach leader and group
leaders. They should plan and carry out a systematic approach to contact-
ing the nonattenders who are members or nonmembers. In the course of a
quarter they can make some contact weekly, such as a visit by the teacher
to deliver a Sunday school lesson periodical, a phone call, a visit by the
outreach leader, a letter, a visit by the group leader, a church worship service bulletin in the mail with a personal note, a visit again by the teacher
and a class member, another phone call, a visit by the group leader, a second letter, another visit by the outreach leader, and another visit to deliver
the next quarter's lesson periodical.

Still another sometimes-productive plan is to determine who in all of
the church has some possibility of building a bridge of friendship over an
extended period of contacts with the unreached or irregularly attending
person. Ask a person who lives in the same neighborhood, works at the
same location, has a mutual acquaintance, or has some other point of contact with the person about whom you are concerned to spend six months
getting to know and to relate to that person. They could visit their homes,
share a work break, go shopping together, celebrate birthdays or other special occasions, attend some community activities or church activities together, or other good occasions, that would allow a genuine bond to be
established and a concern to be expressed. Some will respond and be
blessed by such an effort. Of course, the interest should not disappear after
the person is reached, lest it reflect a superficiality that should not exist.

Sometimes members who have not been attending for a long period
might be invited to a meeting with the pastor. It could be a fellowship-
dinner meeting, either at a home or at the church. At this gathering with a
small number of people at a time, the pastor could explore with them what
kinds of Bible study or other organizational activities they might desire.
Consider planning to arrange for what they would like, if possible. This approach has been especially effective with husband-wife nonparticipating
members in activating their interest in Bible study or in discipleship training.

In any event, it is important that the people of the church not give up in
seeking ways to promote the cause of the church, to reach people for Christ
for the sake of all concerned. In the words of Paul, "Love never ends" (1
Cor. 13:8). It is not always acknowledged, but it remains. If love is demonstrated even after all the methods have failed, some will respond. Ours
is not the burden of winning, but of being faithful to witness. God does the
winning. We try to be useful to him in the process.

SUPERVISION

It is the work of some to lead others in the work, to the end that the total work is accomplished and the workers are supported in terms of personal growth and development. This is the meaning of supervision.

Some confuse supervisory responsibility with quality of personhood. They mistake assignment to certain tasks to be primarily an indication of personal status, and are hindered by feelings of superiority-inferiority in personal terms. They do not understand the body analogies of the Scriptures. This is unfortunate when it happens in any setting; it is out of place in a church.

Of all places and institutions, a church should be one in which people are treated equally as people. This was a chief delight of the early church. When this principle has been violated, the church has assumed a character different from a church, though it retains the name. There are different levels of responsibility due to the nature of different tasks, but the people are no more or no less people because of the different tasks they have. The church body gives the responsibility and the freedom to act (the authority, if you please) commensurate with the responsibility. Still, the assignment is task-related, and not indicative of personal power or status over others.

Supervision is a biblical concept. "Supervisor" is an English word that came directly from Latin *super,* meaning over, and *visor,* meaning one who sees. The Latin word matches the Greek word of the New Testament, *episcopas,* a combination of *epi,* meaning over, and *scopas,* meaning seer. *Episcopas* is the term from which the word *bishop* is derived. The educational ministries of a church need many *episcopoi!* They are the pastor, heads of organizations, division leaders, department leaders, teachers of classes, and leaders of groups of many kinds. Each has as part of his or her work assignment the responsibility of leading others in performing their work as it relates to the total work of a church. This requires supervision.

The supervisor works as an enabler of others. In church ministries, a supervisor leads those who work together in an assignment area to determine how they should do their work. He or she tries to see that workers have what they need in the way of encouragement, information, directions, feedback opportunities, organization, training, time, materials, money, space, equipment, furnishings, planning, preparation, evaluation, and other resources essential to getting the job done well. Followers have some responsibilities for these resources, too, but the supervisor has primary responsibility for taking the initiative.

RECORDING AND REPORTING

The work of the educational ministries of a church requires records and reports in order to keep leaders and members adequately informed of the activities and progress of the ministries. Recording and reporting also have historical value. Through records˜and reports, trends and needs appear which inform leaders and others so that they can know better how to proceed and what adjustments might be made to help improve the work. Each unit and each organization should keep certain records of their activities and report regularly to the next larger unit in the church's organization.

TEN COMMANDMENTS OF SUPERVISION

1. Thou shalt establish and maintain adequate communication.

2. Thou shalt set clear and reasonable deadlines.

3. Thou shalt check appropriately on progress.

4. Thou shalt make needed help available.

5. Thou shalt encourage workers to seek help.

6. Thou shalt develop solution-minded workers.

7. Thou shalt attack problems, not people.

8. Thou shalt time guidance for optimum good.

9. Thou shalt avoid trivia.

10. Thou shalt learn from mistakes.[a]

---

a. Adapted from Charles A. Tidwell, "Be a Better Supervisor," *Church Administration*, April 1977.

All church ministries should report regularly to the church itself. The reports of a church's major ministries usually come in monthly or quarterly business meetings, with a summary report on an annual basis.

Many records systems have already been established, and the materials for them are easily available. The catalogs of denominational suppliers and others in the business should give church leaders the choices of record and reporting materials they need. A rapidly growing number of churches have found computer services useful for assistance in various areas of record keeping and reporting. Many churches still rely on handwritten record systems. Leaders should choose and/or design the records they feel they need, and diligently advocate their proper use.

There are some well-designed, denominationally supplied record systems for the various educational ministries of a church. They help to focus not only on quantity—how many are in attendance or on the roll—but also on quality—who made certain preparation for the sessions or who rendered certain ministries to others. The information from such records should cause leaders to respond to certain needs the records reflect, and to try to improve or otherwise modify their efforts and the results.

It is helpful to train those who secure the records to help insure that full and adequate information is obtained. Annual training sessions of the records keepers, often called secretaries (of classes, departments, or other groups), are recommended.

It is usually wise to keep all church ministry organization records in the church office when they are not in use during meetings at the church. It is also important to have systematic ways of modifying the records, such as adding to the roll, transferring members, or dropping them from the roll. For example, a single multiple-use form can serve all of these purposes. Such a form should be completed in the class or elsewhere and returned through the regular channels to the person who is authorized, in keeping with approved procedures, to record the information on the official records. To do otherwise is to have records that are inaccurate and that do not help consistently to implement the purposes for which records are needed.

EVALUATING QUALITY AND QUANTITY

Evaluation involves several specific activities including:

- accurately analyzing what is occurring or what has occurred;
- comparing that with the intent or hope (the goal);
- observing the reasons for any differences between happenings and intentions;
- learning from the experience what might be done to improve or to increase (or both) the victories in the future;
- celebrating victories.

There are many degrees of intensity in evaluation, ranging from an informal "Wasn't that great!" to a detailed accounting and analysis of facts and figures, their meanings, suggested changes, and how to get the changes into the system.

Evaluating a church's educational activities often deserves more than the informal appraisal suggested by a passing comment. A form such as that in figure 11 might be useful to the Church Ministry Leadership Team and to respective ministry leadership teams in evaluating each of the major tasks and the activities related to them.

It is important to evaluate quality and quantity. A church cannot afford to neglect one in pursuit of the other. It is possible to have poor quality with small numbers, or any other combination of these elements. The

Figure 11
Evaluation Form

Use this form in the Church Ministry Leadership Team and/or organizational leadership teams to evaluate *tasks* and related *activities* either at termination of each activity or at year's end. Use this rating scale: (1) *excellent;* very adequate; (2) *good,* but needs a few improvements; (3) *fair,* but needs major improvements; (4) *poor;* not at all adequate.

TASK: EQUIP CHURCH MEMBERS FOR DISCIPLESHIP AND PERSONAL MINISTRY

Activity List	Organizational Adequacy	Leaders		Resources		Funds	Promotion (Publicity, Enlistment)	Overall Effectiveness	Other
		Number	Effectiveness	Materials, Supplies	Space, Equipment				
1.									
2.									
3.									
4.									
5.									
6.									
7.									
8.									
9.									
10.									

absence or presence of one does not automatically assure the other. It is a worthy ambition for a church to want to do as well as it can with as many as it can.

Other aspects of the educational ministries should be evaluated. Teacher training and preparation and experiences of learners are illustrative of other areas that need to be appraised from time to time. Standards of excellence for classes, departments, and entire ministry organizations can be useful tools for comprehensively evaluating the work of each of those units.

There are many possible principles of evaluating that might help church leaders. Several of these were identified in a much earlier book entitled, *Working Together Through the Church Council.*[1] They apply particularly to the evaluating work of a Church Ministry Leadership Team: (1) planners and implementers evaluate; (2) develop evaluation criteria before implementing plans; (3) evaluate qualitatively and quantitatively; (4) time evaluation to get maximum benefit; (5) evaluate processes and results, not personalities; (6) evaluate objectively and subjectively; and (7) communicate evaluation findings. These and other guidelines can help to improve and to increase the effectiveness of the educational ministries of a church.

CONCLUSION

A church has a mission to accomplish. It engages in educational and other ministries to accomplish that mission. Leaders must lead in this implementation. There are numerous elements involved. Among them is *promotion*—the publicity and the enlistment required to bring people and ministry plans together. There is *supervision*—directing the work of others to accomplish the work and to support the workers and those whom they serve.

Records and reports are also important parts of implementation. They serve to keep leaders, members, and others informed so that the ministries can be improved and increased.

Evaluation is also an essential part of effective leadership. It is important to know what was accomplished, how well, for how many, and what the lessons of the past experiences can teach for the present and the future.

CONCERNS FOR FURTHER STUDY

Consider these questions as you continue to reflect on a church implementing and evaluating its educational ministries.

1. Think of the most effectively promoted event or activity you have observed in a church's educational ministry. What were the key elements in the promotion? What might have been done even better?

2. Can you distinguish for yourself the quality of personhood from tasks to be performed (1) with you as the supervisor; and (2) with you as the supervisee?

3. Do you agree that both quality and quantity are essential in the ministries of a church? Why or why not?

APPENDIX ONE

Growth and Human Needs

It is important to observe human needs with an eye to individual growth and development. While all people may share the same categories of needs for Christian teaching and learning, the ways of meeting these needs and the immediate outcomes of the educational efforts vary according to the readiness of the individual. This readiness can be fairly closely ascertained by the age of the individual. Few would try to evoke from a child in the younger preschool (birth through three years) a profession of Christian conversion. However, foundations laid at this age have the potential for fulfillment when the child is consciously ready to receive Christ of his or her own volition.

These needs will be described according to one of the frequently used patterns of age-grouping:

- Preschoolers—birth through three years, younger preschool, and older preschool (ages four and five)

- Children—younger children (ages six through eight or grades one through three) and older children (ages nine through eleven or grades four through six)

- Youth—ages twelve through seventeen or grades seven through high school

- Adults—age eighteen or high school graduation through age twenty-nine; young adult; and adult (thirty and older).

NEEDS FOR CHRISTIAN CONVERSION

PRESCHOOLERS
Younger preschool children need:

1. to begin to associate God and Jesus with feelings of love and happiness;

2. to think of the Bible as a special book that tells about God and Jesus;

3. to feel that the church is a place to learn more about God and Jesus.

Older preschoolers need:

1. to feel that God loves them at all times;

2. to realize that there are some things that please God;

3. to love God and want to please him;

4. to learn that the Bible is a special book that helps us know how to please God;

5. to think of Jesus as their friend and helper.

CHILDREN

Younger children need:

1. to feel love and reverence for God and to know that God loves them;

2. to develop a desire to do things that please God and to grow in their understanding of ways to please God;

3. to learn to love and trust Jesus as their friend and to have a growing awareness that Jesus is God's Son;

4. to grow in their understanding of what it means to forgive and to know that God wants to forgive them when they do wrong;

5. to develop a consciousness of personal need for God's help in doing right things;

6. to feel free to approach Christian adults for understanding guidance.

Older children need:

1. to understand that all people do wrong and that all wrongdoing displeases God;

2. to face the fact that the wrong things they do are sins against God;

3. to realize that Christ's death for our sins makes possible forgiveness and new life for every person who repents of sin and trusts Jesus Christ;

4. to understand that a person becomes a Christian by trusting Jesus as Savior—not by being baptized and joining the church or simply trying to be good;

5. to realize that they need God's forgiveness for their own sins;

6. to turn from sin to simple trust in Christ as their personal Savior and Lord when the Holy Spirit has made them ready for such response and commitment.

YOUTH

Youth need:

1. to recognize their failure and inability to live up to God's standard of righteousness and their consequent need of a Savior;

2. to turn from sin and commit themselves personally to Jesus Christ, trusting him to give complete and continuous salvation;

3. to gain, after conversion, a growing sense of assurance of the reality of that experience and its implications for the lordship of Jesus.

ADULTS

Young adults need:

1. to become aware of the nature and prevalence of sin and to recognize God's judgment upon it;

2. to realize their own sin and consequent need of the salvation that God has provided in Christ;

3. to turn from sin and commit themselves to Jesus Christ, the Son of God, who gives complete salvation to all who trust him;

4. to gain, after conversion, a growing sense of assurance of the reality of that experience and its implications for the lordship of Jesus.

Adults need:

1. to become aware of God's judgment concerning sin and of his mercy; to realize their own failure and inability to measure up to God's standard of righteousness and their consequent need of the salvation that God has provided in Christ;

2. to recognize the all-sufficiency of Jesus Christ, working through the Holy Spirit, to give complete salvation to all who trust him; to turn from sin and commit themselves wholeheartedly to Jesus Christ as personal Lord and Savior;

3. to gain, after conversion, a growing assurance of the reality of that experience and its implications for the lordship of Jesus.

NEEDS FOR CHURCH MEMBERSHIP

PRESCHOOLERS

Younger preschoolers need:

1. to have happy experiences with friendly people at church;

2. to feel that the church is a special place where all members of the family may go to learn more about God and Jesus.

Older preschoolers need:

1. to think of their church as a place where they have happy experiences;
2. to grow in their ability to participate in church worship services with their families;
3. to feel that they are a part of the church life.

CHILDREN

Younger children need:

1. to like to attend church and to participate in the worship services with their families;
2. to grow in understanding that members of the church are a special group of Jesus' friends who have had the experiences of conversion and baptism;
3. to begin to understand that joining the church is a serious matter, always to be preceded by conversion, and that it involves responsibilities as well as privileges.

Older children need:

1. to form the habit of regular church attendance and of participating with understanding and joy in church services and activities;
2. to understand that a New Testament church is composed of people who have already become Christians and who have been baptized in obedience to Christ;
3. to understand that a person joins the church only after trusting Jesus as Savior, with a conviction that he or she is a Christian and should be baptized in obedience to Christ.

YOUTH

Youth need:

1. to unite with a church by baptism upon public profession of faith in Christ as Savior and Lord (if they have not already done so);
2. to grow in understanding and appreciation of the nature, mission, practices, and leadership of their church;
3. to grow in loyalty to their church and to endeavor to render faithful service to Christ and other people through the church;
4. to develop the habit of attending services regularly and of participating in the fellowship and program of the church with understanding and appreciation;
5. to give regularly and proportionately for the support of their church and its worldwide program;

6. to transfer their church membership promptly when changing place of residence.

ADULTS

Young adults need:

1. to unite with a church by baptism upon a personal profession of faith in Christ (if they have not already done so);

2. to grow in understanding and appreciation of the meaning, purpose, faith, and practices of their church;

3. to grow in loyalty to their church and the world program of Christ;

4. to participate wholeheartedly in Christian service in and through the channels of their church;

5. to transfer their church membership promptly when changing place of residence.

Adults need:

1. to unite with a church by baptism upon a personal profession of faith in the Lord Jesus Christ (if they have not already done so);

2. to grow in understanding and appreciation of the meaning, purpose, faith, and practices of their church;

3. to participate in and actively cultivate the fellowship of their church;

4. to participate wholeheartedly in constructive Christian service in and through the channels of their church;

5. to grow in loyalty to their church and the world program of Christ;

6. to have their membership in a church in the community where they reside.

NEEDS FOR CHRISTIAN WORSHIP

PRESCHOOLERS

Younger preschoolers need:

1. to feel that they can talk to God at any time;

2. to want to say thank you to God;

3. to grow in their enjoyment of beauty, music, and meaningful Bible stories.

Older preschoolers need:

1. to know that they can talk to God at any time and anywhere;

2. to have satisfying experiences in talking to God;

3. to grow in their ability to participate in worship with children of their own age;

4. to develop a growing appreciation of beautiful surroundings, music, Bible passages that are read aloud, prayer, the offering, and the preacher's message.

CHILDREN

Younger children need:

1. to feel and demonstrate loving respect for God;

2. to talk to God spontaneously and naturally at any time they feel a sense of wonder, worship, or need;

3. to have meaningful experiences in private worship and to worship with members of their own age group;

4. to participate regularly in public worship and to find satisfaction in doing so.

Older children need:

1. to understand that worship is an experience of reverent communion with God and that people may engage in worship alone, with their families, with friends, and with groups at church;

2. to cultivate the practice of regular private worship, including daily Bible reading and prayer;

3. to do their part to maintain and to participate in family worship;

4. to attend regularly the worship services of their church and to participate meaningfully and reverently in praying, singing, Bible reading, and listening.

YOUTH

Youth need:

1. to understand further the meaning of worship and to desire to engage in worship;

2. to grow in appreciation of all elements that make worship meaningful, both in worship services and in personal devotions;

3. to grow in ability to participate meaningfully in worship experiences with people of their own age group and with the church congregation;

4. to practice daily individual worship, including devotional Bible reading and prayer for self and others;

5. to encourage participation in family worship experiences.

ADULTS

Young adults and adults need:

1. to develop a deepening understanding of the meaning and values of worship;
2. to develop a growing appreciation of all the elements that make for meaningful worship, whether in private or in the group;
3. to develop and maintain the practice of daily individual worship, including the devotional Bible reading, meditation, and prayer;
4. to develop the habit of regular attendance at the worship services of their church and the ability to participate with understanding and appreciation;
5. to encourage, provide, and participate in experiences of family worship.

GROWTH AND NEEDS FOR CHRISTIAN KNOWLEDGE AND CONVICTIONS

People have many needs for Christian knowledge and convictions. They need to know and have convictions about a number of things with respect to the Bible, the great realities of the Christian faith, the Christian movement, and their church and denomination.

PRESCHOOLERS

Younger Preschoolers. With respect to the Bible, younger preschoolers need:

1. to grow in awareness that what the Bible says is more important than what other books have to say;
2. to gain some acquaintance with meaningful Bible stories and verses.

With respect to the great realities of the Christian faith, younger preschoolers need:

1. to begin to think of God as the one who made them;
2. to begin to think of God as the one who helps them to have good things;
3. to begin to think of God as the one who cares for them;
4. to begin to think of Jesus as the one who loves them.

With respect to their church, younger preschoolers need:

1. to begin to think of their church as a place where people love Jesus and help others;
2. to begin to be aware that there are many churches.

Older preschoolers. With respect to the Bible, older preschoolers need:

1. to begin to understand that God helped authors know what to write in the Bible;

2. to become familiar with some of the surroundings and customs of the people the Bible tells about;

3. to enjoy hearing Bible stories and verses in their understanding of Bible truths and learn to relate them to their own experiences;

4. to grow in the realization that the Bible is God's way of telling us how to live happily with others;

5. to know that the Bible was meant for all people.

With respect to the great realities of the Christian faith, older preschoolers need:

1. to know that God made the world and everything in it;

2. to know that Jesus can do things that no one else can do because he is God's Son.

With respect to their church, denomination, and the larger Christian movement, older preschoolers need:

1. to know that there have been churches for a long, long time;

2. to know that their church is one of many churches all over the world;

3. to know ways their church and other churches help people to know about Jesus;

4. to know that the money brought to church is used to help others know about Jesus.

CHILDREN

Younger children. With respect to the Bible, younger children need:

1. to develop love and appreciation for the Bible as a unique book and to feel that it is true and deserves respect and obedience;

2. to develop an elementary understanding of its structure, how it came to be written, and how it has been preserved;

3. to become acquainted with customs, geography, and other facts concerning Bible backgrounds;

4. to enjoy hearing, reading, and learning Bible stories and truths;

5. to grow in understanding ways the Bible can help them in everyday life;

6. to commit to memory many Bible verses.

With respect to the great realities of the Christian faith, younger children need:

1. to have a growing understanding of what the Bible teaches about God, about Jesus, and about right and wrong;

2. to realize that the friends of Jesus should believe and do what the Bible teaches.

With respect to the Christian movement, younger children need:

1. to realize that the church they attend is one of many such groups of Jesus' friends in many parts of the world;

2. to recognize that people of other Christian groups also help in Jesus' work.

With respect to their church and denomination, younger children need:

1. to know why we have churches and some of the things churches do;

2. to find answers to their questions about church ordinances and church membership.

Older children. With respect to the Bible, older children need:

1. to recognize that the Bible is an inspired message from God and that its teachings are to be accepted and followed in all that we believe and do;

2. to develop an increasing understanding of the origin, structure, and transmission of the Bible;

3. to learn about the customs and geography of Bible lands in order to understand better many of the teachings of the Bible;

4. to develop a growing knowledge of basic stories and truths;

5. to gain from individual and group Bible study increasing guidance and motivation for daily living;

6. to grow in skill in using the Bible;

7. to memorize appropriate Bible passages.

With respect to the great realities of the Christian faith, older children need:

1. to recognize increasingly that God is real and that a vital relationship with him through faith in Christ is the most important factor in one's life;

2. to begin to understand that the Christian faith includes many doctrines that are important for one's belief and conduct;

3. to gain increasing knowledge of basic Christian doctrines.

With respect to the Christian movement, older children need:

1. to grow familiar with the lives and work of some of the early leaders in the growth of the Christian movement;

2. to become acquainted with the names and work of some of the great leaders of their denomination;

3. to gain some acquaintance with the history and beliefs of other Christian groups;

4. to learn some ways in which our beliefs are like those of other groups and some ways in which they are different.

With respect to their church and denomination, older children need:

1. to grow in understanding and appreciation of beliefs and practices of their denomination;

2. to grow in knowledge of their denomination's life and work and to develop increasing loyalty to their denomination.

YOUTH

With respect to the Bible, youth need:

1. to accept the Bible as a way by which God speaks to them and as the final authority in all matters of faith and conduct;

2. to understand something of the origin of the Bible and of God's use of people in writing, preserving, and translating it;

3. to grow in understanding of the contents of the Bible and of the customs, geography, and history out of which the Bible came;

4. to acquire a growing comprehension of how Bible truths apply to personal daily living and to community and world problems;

5. to commit choice passages to memory.

With respect to the great realities of the Christian faith, youth need:

1. to grow in their concept of the reality and nature of God as a personal, loving Father;

2. to grow in their understanding of God and humankind, sin and salvation, and the Christian's life and work;

3. to develop a growing conviction about the truth and finality of the Christian faith.

With respect to the Christian movement, youth need:

1. to learn some of the outstanding facts of Christian history;

2. to become acquainted with some of the outstanding facts about other Christian groups and our common heritage with them;

3. to become aware of present-day trends and issues in the Christian movement and to realize that these hold meaning for their own lives as well as for the cause of Christ.

With respect to their church and denomination, youth need:

1. to grow in understanding distinctive features of their denomination's doctrine and polity and to develop growing convictions as to the soundness of both;

2. to add to their knowledge of the history, organization, programs, problems, and needs of their denomination and to develop an increasing sense of responsibility for the work of their denomination.

ADULTS

Young Adults.

With respect to the Bible, young adults need:

1. to recognize the Bible as a unique revelation from God and to accept its authority as supreme in matters of faith and conduct;

2. to gain fuller understanding of the origins of the Bible, the history of its preservation, and the significance of the many translations and versions;

3. to achieve an increasing knowledge of the content of the Bible and a growing understanding of the customs, geography, and history out of which the Bible came;

4. to acquire a growing comprehension of how Bible truths apply to personal daily living, to family life, and to community and world problems;

5. to commit choice passages to memory.

With respect to the great realities of the Christian faith, young adults need:

1. to grow in understanding of the nature, attributes, and disposition of God;

2. to grow in understanding of the nature of people, of sin and salvation, and of the varied elements of Christian experience;

3. to grow in understanding of the Christian concepts of personal righteousness and social responsibility;

4. to develop a growing conviction about the truth and finality of the Christian faith.

With respect to the Christian movement, young adults need:

1. to know something of the general outline of Christian history;

2. to learn some of the outstanding facts about other Christian groups and our common heritage;

3. to grow in understanding of present-day trends and issues in the Christian movement and to develop ability to evaluate the significance of those trends and issues for their own lives, their own church, and the cause of Christ throughout the world.

With respect to church and denomination, young adults need:

1. to understand something of the history of their denomination;

2. to understand the distinctive features of the doctrine and polity of their denomination;

3. to grow in their understanding of the program, missionary outreach, problems, and needs of their church and denomination; to develop worthy convictions about the doctrines and mission of their denomination and about their personal responsibility to their denomination.

Adults

With respect to the Bible, adults need:

1. to recognize the Bible as a unique revelation and message from God and to accept it as authoritative in all matters of faith and conduct;

2. to understand the origin of the Bible and its history, preservation, and translation;

3. to understand the customs, geography, and historical backgrounds out of which the Bible came;

4. to gain an orderly and increasingly comprehensive grasp of the content of the Bible;

5. to acquire a growing comprehension of how Bible truths apply to personal daily living, family life, and community and world problems;

6. to commit choice passages to memory.

With respect to the great realities of the Christian faith, adults need:

1. to grow in understanding of the nature, attributes, and disposition of God;

2. to grow in understanding of the nature of people, of sin and salvation, and of the varied elements of Christian experience;

3. to grow in understanding of the Christian concepts of personal righteousness and social responsibility;

4. to develop a growing conviction about the truth and finality of the Christian faith.

With respect to the Christian movement, adults need:

1. to learn some of the outstanding facts of Christian history;
2. to learn some of the outstanding facts about other Christian groups and our common heritage with them;
3. to understand significant present-day trends in the Christian movement and to evaluate the meaning of those trends for their own lives and the cause of Christ.

With respect to their church and denomination, adults need:

1. to learn some of the outstanding facts about the history of their own denomination;
2. to understand the distinctive features of the doctrine and polity of their denomination and to have solid convictions as to the soundness of both;
3. to know the organization, program, missionary outreach, problems, and needs of their denomination and to understand their personal relationships to the whole of the denomination enterprise.

NEEDS FOR CHRISTIAN ATTITUDES AND APPRECIATIONS

Individuals need to develop Christian attitudes and appreciations regarding God, the meaning of existence, self, others, the Bible and divine institutions, and the present world.

PRESCHOOLERS

Regarding God and the meaning of existence, the younger preschool child needs:

1. to begin to associate feelings of happiness with God;
2. to want to thank God for good things;
3. to begin to be aware of the difference between fantasy and reality.

Regarding self, the younger preschool child needs:

1. to begin to realize that he or she is a person;
2. to feel loved and wanted;
3. to begin to realize that there are certain things he or she can and cannot do.

Regarding others, the younger preschool child needs:

1. to begin to be aware of the feelings of others;
2. to begin to adjust to the needs and interests of others;
3. to experience some feelings of wanting to help others;
4. to begin to be aware of what others do to help him or her.

Regarding the Bible and divine institutions, the younger pre-schooler needs:

1. to enjoy the Bible as a special book;
2. to enjoy church as a special place;
3. to enjoy Sunday as an especially happy day;
4. to begin to feel that God wants families to be happy.

Regarding the present world, the younger preschool child needs:

1. to begin to feel that the world God made is good;
2. to begin to be aware of life and death processes of plants and animals.

Older Preschoolers. Regarding God and the meaning of existence, the older preschool child needs:

1. to experience a deepening reverence for God's power and greatness; to accept the fact that God made the world; to have a growing appreciation of ways God cares for things in it;
2. to love God and to want to do the things that please him;
3. to trust God as the one who loves and cares for all people; to feel that God is near and that one can talk to God any time, anywhere; to want to talk to God;
4. to feel thankful for the many ways God helps him or her;
5. to grow in awareness of the difference between fantasy and reality.

Regarding self, the older preschool child needs:

1. to feel secure in God's world, because he or she is an important part of God's plan;
2. to begin to realize that God made him or her and gave the ability to think, to make choices and decisions, and to be creative; to begin to realize that people are more important than anything else God made;
3. to realize that God wants people to have strong, healthy bodies and to use them in ways pleasing to God;
4. to realize that God can help a person in ways that no one else can;
5. to want to do things in ways pleasing to Jesus and to want to grow in the ways in which Jesus grew.

Regarding others, the older preschool child needs:

1. to realize that it is a part of God's plan for people to be friendly and to help one another;
2. to grow in appreciation of others and what they do for him or her;
3. to develop in ability to share, to work, and to play happily with others;

4. to accept the fact that God made and loves all people and to have kind attitudes toward them;

5. to want others to know about Jesus.

Regarding the Bible and divine institutions, the older preschool child needs:

1. to develop a growing love for the Bible and a growing appreciation for ways it can help in everyday life;

2. to grow in understanding of the importance of the church;

3. to think of Sunday as a special day of worship and activities pleasing to God;

4. to think of happy homes as a part of God's plan;

5. to grow in his appreciation of people in authority and in willingness to cooperate with them.

Regarding the present world, the older preschool child needs:

1. to feel that the world God made is good and that nature, work, and the ability to do many things are gifts of God;

2. to want to help others in making the child's world a better place.

CHILDREN

Younger Children. Regarding God and the meaning of existence, the younger child needs:

1. to experience deepening reverence and respect for God and his work in the world;

2. to trust God as the one who created, loves, and makes provision for the needs of all people and other creatures;

3. to feel assured that God listens when people pray to him and answers in the way that is best;

4. to feel sorry when he or she disappoints God, but to know that God loves him or her and wants to forgive;

5. to feel a sense of gratitude to God for all of his good gifts;

6. to feel that Jesus loves and helps him or her, to love and trust Jesus as a personal friend, and to desire to please him.

Regarding self, the younger child needs:

1. to develop wholesome appreciation of his or her own value as an individual whom God loves and who can make important contributions to the group at home, at school, at church, and at play;

2. to think of his or her body as something good and something to be cared for and used in ways pleasing to God;

3. to grow in ability to self-evaluate and to recognize his or her respon-
    sibilities;

4. to grow in understanding of the values of cooperative work and in
    ability to be a good member of the group;

5. to recognize all his or her talents and abilities as gifts from God and
    to want to develop and use them in worthwhile ways.

Regarding others, the younger child needs:

1. to feel kindly toward all people everywhere, regardless of their dif-
    ferences;

2. to respect the feelings, the rights, and the property of others;

3. to grow in willingness to share work, play, and possessions with
    others;

4. to recognize that others make real contributions to his or her life and
    to want to make some friendly return;

5. to want to help others to know about Jesus.

**Regarding the Bible and divine institutions, the younger child
needs:**

1. to grow in love for the Bible and in desire to use it in everyday living;

2. to love and show respect for the church building as a special place of
    worship;

3. to begin to appreciate the elements of public worship;

4. to think of Sunday as a special day to be spent in worship and other
    activities that honor God;

5. to recognize the home as part of God's loving plan for people and to
    develop an attitude of love and respect and consideration for all in his
    or her home;

6. to continue to grow in his or her appreciation for authority and in
    willingness to cooperate with people in authority.

Regarding the present world, the younger child needs:

1. to feel secure in the knowledge that God's plan for the world pro-
    vides for each person's needs;

2. to begin to realize that although he or she sees others doing wrong
    and is often tempted personally, Jesus can help to choose the right
    way;

3. to realize that work is part of God's plan for everyone and to want to
    do what he or she can to help.

Older Children. Regarding God, the older child needs:

1. to reverence God and to want to know and to obey his commandments;

2. to love and trust God as the all-wise and all-good Heavenly Father, who loved us and gave his Son to be the Savior of the world;

3. to feel secure in God's care and grateful for his goodness.

Regarding the meaning of existence, the older child needs:

1. to think of the beauties and wonders of the world and of science as expressions of God's greatness and goodness;

2. to feel secure in the world because God made it and controls it and cares what happens to people;

3. to believe that God has a purpose for our lives and to want to use his or her life for God's glory and for the good of others.

Regarding self, the older child needs:

1. to realize that because God made us, our mind, body, and life are important;

2. to realize that he or she needs God's forgiveness, love, and help;

3. to understand that the mind and body are gifts from God to be cared for and developed;

4. to want to use the mind and body in Jesus' service.

Regarding others, the older child needs:

1. to begin to appreciate the worth of all people, regardless of their race or other differences;

2. to feel responsible for the way he or she treats people of all groups, races, and nationalities;

3. to grow in ability to love other people and to treat others as Jesus would have her or him treat them;

4. to feel responsible for telling others about Jesus.

Regarding the Bible and divine institutions, the older child needs:

1. to develop a growing love for the Bible and a deeper desire to govern everyday actions by its teaching;

2. to grow in love for and loyalty to the church;

3. to develop increasing respect and appreciation for baptism and the Lord's Supper;

4. to respect Sunday as the Lord's Day and to enjoy doing on Sunday things that honor Jesus;

5. to appreciate the home as part of God's plan of caring for people and to desire to do his or her part to make the home a happy place;

6. to feel that rules and laws are a necessary part of God's plan for living and to want to obey the laws of home, school, and community.

Regarding the present world, the older child needs:

1. to feel secure in the knowledge that God made and cares for the world and gave us the ability to discover and use the secrets of nature;

2. to feel that, though there is sin and wrongdoing in the world, she or he can have the strength through Christ to choose the right way;

3. to want to do his or her part to make home, school, and neighborhood better.

YOUTH

Regarding God, youth need:

1. to love and trust the Heavenly Father, Jesus Christ as Lord and Savior, and the Holy Spirit as ever-present counselor and source of power;

2. to reverence God, respect his commands, and seek to know and do his will;

3. to develop a sense of gratitude to God for all his goodness.

Regarding the meaning of existence, youth need:

1. to regard all existence as the expression of God's creative power, wisdom, and goodness;

2. to feel secure in the knowledge that this is God's world and that God's purposes are being worked out in it;

3. to realize that a person created in the image of God is of infinite worth, has marvelous possibilities, and possesses spiritual needs that only God can supply.

Regarding self, youth need:

1. to recognize the body, mind, and total personality as gifts from God to be cared for, developed, and used for God's glory and the good of others;

2. to have as their personal ideal the attainment of a mature Christian personality;

3. to evaluate their talents as they consider a future vocation;

4. to realize that they stand in constant need of God's forgiveness and help.

Regarding others, youth need:

1. to acquire a sense of kinship with every person in the world and to cultivate an attitude of unselfish devotion to the welfare of people of all cultures, races, and social levels;

2. to cultivate the desire to apply Christian principles in relationships within the family, at church, at school, and in the community;

3. to feel a concern for the salvation of others and to accept the obligation to help give the gospel to the world;

4. to develop wholesome attitudes toward people of the opposite sex in their peer group.

Regarding the Bible and divine institutions, youth need:

1. to develop a growing love for the Bible and appreciation of the purpose for which Christ founded the church and an increasing concern for its life and work;

2. to develop an increasing love and appreciation for their home and feel a growing obligation to contribute to the happiness and well-being of their family;

3. to develop increasing loyalty to the ideal of personal purity, looking toward marriage and family life;

4. to regard Sunday as the Lord's Day to be used to honor the risen Christ;

5. to respect the ordinances of baptism and the Lord's Supper as means of honoring Christ;

6. to respect civil government and to feel the obligations of good citizenship as set forth in principle in the New Testament.

Regarding the present world, youth need:

1. to feel that the world as God made it is good and that all the resources of nature and the necessity to work are gifts of God designed for the enrichment of life;

2. to recognize the many manifestations of evil in the world and to resolve to live a life dedicated to God, to resist the appeal of evil, and to be a positive force for morality and justice;

3. to feel a deepening sense of responsibility for the improvement of moral and social conditions in his community.

YOUNG ADULTS

Regarding God, young adults need:

1. to reverence God, respect his commandments, and seek to know and do his will as the supreme good;

2. to love and trust the Heavenly Father, Jesus Christ as Lord and Savior, and the Holy Spirit as ever-present counselor and source of power;

3. to develop a sense of gratitude to God for all his goodness.

Regarding the meaning of existence, young adults need:

1. to regard all existence as the expression of God's creative power, wisdom, and goodness;

2. to see themselves in relation to all existence in such a way as to feel secure in the purpose and sovereignty of God;

3. to regard life as a trust from God to be used for his glory and the good of others;

4. to believe with confidence that the Bible and the Holy Spirit are their guides in making the best use of this life;

5. to believe that the main purposes of God for mankind are redemption and development in righteousness.

Regarding self, young adults need:

1. to realize that, as people created in the image of God, they are of infinite worth and have marvelous possibilities;

2. to realize that they stand in continuing need of forgiveness and strength from God;

3. to recognize that they possess spiritual needs and capacities that only God can supply;

4. to acknowledge that their bodies are a divine trust to be cared for, to be protected from abuse, to be disciplined in habit, and to be employed in honest labor, unselfish service, and healthful recreation;

5. to dedicate all of their God-given abilities to the pursuit and achievement of worthy aims and to test their worthiness by the teachings of Jesus;

6. to have as their personal ideal the attainment of a mature, well-balanced Christian personality.

Regarding others, young adults need:

1. to cultivate an attitude of Christian love, the willingness to practice forgiveness, and the determination to apply Christian principles in all relationships;

2. to accept responsibility for the influence of their lives on all people whom their lives touch;

3. to feel and manifest wholesome attitudes toward people of the opposite sex;

4. to cultivate a sense of belonging to the human race as a whole;

5. to develop an attitude of Christian concern for the welfare of people of all cultures, social levels, and races;

6. to feel a concern for the salvation of all people everywhere and to accept the obligation to share the gospel and blessings of the Christian faith;

7. to feel a responsibility to pass on to future generations the good in our social heritage enriched by their own contribution to it.

Regarding the Bible and divine institutions, young adults need:

1. to develop a growing love for the Bible and an appreciation of the relevance of Bible teaching to daily life;

2. to respect the divine nature and purpose of the church and to give it a place of sacred preeminence over all institutions of human origin;

3. to respect the ordinances of baptism and the Lord's Supper and to seek through the right observance of them to honor Christ;

4. to regard the Lord's Day as the Christian sabbath to be used to the honor of the risen Christ;

5. to accept the standards set by Christ and the New Testament for marriage and family life;

6. to respect the institution of civil government as being divinely appointed and to accept the responsibilities of good citizenship.

Regarding the present world, young adults need:

1. to feel that the world as God made it is good and that the resources of nature and the necessity to work are gifts of God designed for the enrichment of life;

2. to recognize that evil is a dominant force in the world order and that while the Christian must live in this world, he or she is not to share its spirit nor indulge in its sins but is to resist evil and be a positive force for morality and justice;

3. to develop a deepening consciousness of responsibility for the social order and a courageous purpose to work for its improvement.

NEEDS FOR CHRISTIAN LIVING

PRESCHOOLERS

The younger preschool child needs:

1. to begin to associate some simple Bible truths with daily living;

2. to begin to recognize the rights and feelings of others.

The older preschooler needs:

1. to begin to accept the Bible as a guide for conduct in everyday life;

2. to grow in understanding of prayer and in ability to pray;

3. to want to do things in ways pleasing to Jesus;

4. to grow in ability to make right choices;

5. to develop in the ability to help make his or her home happy;

6. to have an increasing love for all people which will be expressed in friendliness and cooperation.

CHILDREN

The younger child needs:

1. to grow in ability to relate Bible truths to daily problems and needs;

2. to continue growing in understanding of prayer and in ability to pray;

3. to make sincere efforts to be more like Jesus;

4. to develop growing skill in self-control, self-direction, worthy self-expression, and ability to make right choices;

5. to develop habits of friendliness, helpfulness, cooperation, kindness, and courtesy toward all with whom he or she comes in contact, in work and in play.

The older child needs:

1. to depend on Jesus each day to help her or him choose the right way;

2. to learn how to use his or her own Bible and to gain from it direction for daily living;

3. to make progress in developing Christian character that will express itself in all areas of experience;

4. to gain strength for Christian living through private and group prayer;

5. to try to grow as Jesus grew—in mind and body, and in relationships with God and with other people;

6. to do her or his part to make the home happy by obeying parents and accepting cheerfully a personal share in the work at home.

YOUTH

Youth need:

1. to grow in consciousness of the living Christ as the Lord of their life;

2. to accept with confidence the Bible and the Holy Spirit as guides in making the best use of their lives;

3. to grow in understanding of why and how to pray;

4. to seek to pattern all personal conduct in accordance with the teachings, spirit, and example of Jesus;

5. to strive to be Christlike in attitudes toward and relationships with parents and other members of their family;

6. to continue to make progress in developing Christian character that will express itself in all relationships.

ADULT

The young adult and the adult need:

1. to live daily in vital fellowship with Jesus Christ, seeking always to bring the whole life under the direction of the Holy Spirit;

2. to engage regularly in serious Bible study and to use the Bible as a guide for life;

3. to learn the spirit, art, and values of prayer and to practice prayer in daily experience;

4. to pattern all personal conduct in accordance with the teachings, spirit, and example of Jesus Christ;

5. to do all possible to make the family life Christian;

6. to refuse to enter into relations and participate in activities which compromise or violate New Testament principles;

7. to seek to apply Christian principles and standards of conduct to all social relationships.

NEEDS FOR CHRISTIAN SERVICE

PRESCHOOLERS

The younger preschool child needs:

1. to begin to help at home and at church;

2. to begin to learn to play happily with others.

The older preschool child needs:

1. to tell others about Jesus;

2. to be a helper at home and at church;

3. to be happy when giving money to help others know about Jesus;

4. to do helpful things for others;

5. to begin to accept his or her limited abilities and to help as best he or she can;

6. to receive satisfaction from doing things with others;

7. to participate in group activities that make others happy.

CHILDREN

The younger child needs:

1. to tell others about Jesus;

2. to participate and cooperate in all the church activities in which he or she may have a part;

3. to enjoy giving money and other possessions that he or she can share;

4. to begin to discover personal talents and to have opportunities to develop and use them in worthy self-expression;

5. to accept personal limitations and to use his or her abilities to achieve;

6. to participate in group activities that make others happy.

The older child needs:

1. to show love for Jesus by telling family and friends about him and inviting them to church;

2. to serve in his or her church through the organizations, through attendance at regular church services, and through giving money for the work of the church;

3. to try day by day at home, at school, and elsewhere to treat others with kindness and fairness as Jesus would;

4. to begin to develop a sense of citizenship responsibility by participating in group and community service projects that contribute to fair play, justice, law enforcement, general health, relief of distress, and other worthy causes.

YOUTH

Youth need:

1. to dedicate their talents to God and to develop skills in Christian service;

2. to seek God's will for their lives and to begin to prepare for a vocation in keeping with that will;

3. to witness faithfully to their Christian faith and to seek to win others to Jesus Christ;

4. to appreciate and take advantage of the training and service opportunities offered in their church program;

5. to learn to work unselfishly on a team by filling well the places of service in their church suited to their ability and stage of development;

6. to be good stewards of money as an expression of their gratitude to God and as a means of supporting their church in its world missions program;

7. to show compassion for people in need;

8. to participate in group and community service projects that contribute to social welfare;

9. to accept the ideal of self-giving service as the true goal of life.

ADULTS

Young adults need:

1. to seek and use opportunities to invest their talents and skills in Christian service;

2. to witness consistently to the truth and power of the Christian faith and to seek to win others to Jesus Christ;

3. to work faithfully for the building up of their church and to serve sacrificially in and through their church;

4. to give money from worthy motives and according to biblical teaching for the support of their church and its work;

5. to show compassion for people in need and to do deeds of helpfulness in daily life;

6. to find God's will for their lives, to prepare adequately for the vocation to which they are called, and to enter that vocation with a sense of dedication to Christian service;

7. to serve effectively as a member of a team and to serve without desire for self-glory;

8. to dedicate their total personality and resources to world missions as the means of carrying forward the redemptive undertaking of Jesus Christ;

9. to join with others in cooperative action for the improvement of social conditions, the creation of a more Christian society, and the realization of God's purpose for mankind.

Adults need:

1. to witness consistently to the truth and power of the Christian faith and to seek to win others to Jesus Christ;

2. to work faithfully for the building up of their church and to serve sacrificially in and through the church;

3. to give money from worthy motives and according to biblical teaching for the support of their church and its work;

4. to show compassion for people in need and to do deeds of helpfulness in those people's lives;

5. to find God's will for their lives and to fulfill that will in their vocation;

6. to engage in those phases of Christian service that are best suited to their individual capacities, environment, occupation, and social group;

7. to serve effectively as a member of a team and to serve without desire for self-glory;

8. to take a worthy part as a Christian in community service projects;

9. to dedicate their total personality and resources to world missions as the means of carrying forward the redemptive undertaking of Jesus Christ;

10. to join with others in cooperative action for the improvement of social conditions, the creation of a more Christian society, and the realization of God's purpose for mankind.

The Twelve Apostles—Organized

These are the lists of Jesus' chosen apostles as given in Matthew, Mark, Luke, and Acts.

	Mark 3:16ff.	Matthew 10:2ff	Luke 6:14ff.	Acts 1:13ff
1	**Simon Peter**	**Simon Peter**	**Simon Peter**	**Simon Peter**
2	James	Andrew ———— Andrew		James
3	John	James ———— James		John
4	Andrew	John ———— John		Andrew
5	**Philip**	**Philip**	**Philip**	**Philip**
6	Bartholomew (Nathanael)	Bartholomew — Bartholomew		Thomas (Didymus)
7	Matthew (Levi)	Thomas	Matthew	Bartholomew
8	Thomas	Matthew	Thomas	Matthew
9	**James the son of Alpheus**	**James the son of Alpheus**	**James the son of Alpheus**	**James the son of Alpheus**
10	Thaddeus (Judas the brother of James; Lebbeus)	Thaddeus	Simon the Zealot (the Cananean)	Simon the Zealot
11	Simon the Cananean	Simon the Cananean	Judas the brother of James	Judas the brother of James
12	Judas Iscariot — Judas Iscariot — Judas Iscariot			————

"Observe the three groups of four, headed by Simon Peter, Philip, and James the son of Alpheus, respectively. *The great variety in the arrangement of the other names makes this uniformity significant.* (italics mine) It seems clear that there are three recognized groups among the apostles. (Bengel, Broadus, Clark)"[a]

Prepared by Charles A. Tidwell

a. A. T. Robertson, *A Harmony of the Gospels for Students of the Life of Christ* (New York: Harper and Bros., 1950), pp. 271–72.

APPENDIX THREE

Sunday School Worker's Covenant

Believing that the privilege of guiding people in the Christian way of life is worthy of my best, I covenant, as a worker in the Sunday school of my church, to . . .

- Order my conduct in keeping with the principles of the New Testament, and seek the help of the Holy Spirit that I may be faithful and efficient in my work (Eph. 4:1).

- Be regular and punctual in attendance; and, in case of unavoidable absence, give notice thereof as far in advance as possible (1 Cor. 4:2).

- Make thorough preparation of the lesson and for my other duties each week (2 Tim. 2:15).

- Use the Bible with my group on Sunday morning, or other meeting times, and help them to understand and love it (Ps. 119:16).

- Contribute my tithe to my church's budget (Mal. 3:10).

- Attend the regular planning meetings (Luke 14:28–30).

- Visit prospects frequently and make a special effort to contact absentees each week (Acts 2:46).

- Study one or more books from the Church Study Course each year (Prov. 15:28a).

- Cooperate wholeheartedly in the plans and activities of the church and school (1 Cor. 3:9).

- Be loyal to the program of the church, striving to attend all worship services (Heb. 10:25).

- Make witnessing a major endeavor (Prov. 11:30).

- Seek to discover and meet the needs of those with whom I come into contact, especially fellow church members and prospects for my church (Gal. 6:2).

- Pray regularly for the church, the Sunday school, the officers and teachers, and for the pupils and the homes from which they come (1 Thess. 5:17).

- Apply the teachings of Christ in moral and social issues of my everyday life (James 1:22).

With the help of God, I will do my utmost to keep this covenant.

Signed _____   Date _____

APPENDIX FOUR

Weekly Workers Meetings

PLAN 1 (FOR SMALL SUNDAY SCHOOLS)

GENERAL PERIOD (ALL WORKERS TOGETHER). . . . 15 MINUTES

- Administering School Concerns
- Planning for . . . Reaching, Witnessing, Ministering
- Praying together

TEACHING–LEARNING PLANNING PERIOD . . . . . . 45 MINUTES

- All workers together for directed planning of age-group units and lessons (about 30 minutes).
- Special age-group preparation time to prepare room or area of building for Sunday's session (about 10 minutes)

PLAN 2

DEPARTMENT DIRECTOR'S PERIOD. . . . . 15 MINUTES

(meeting in separate room from the supper)

GENERAL PERIOD . . . . 5 MINUTES

(all workers around supper table)

DEPARTMENT PERIOD . . . . 55 MINUTES

- Administering Department Concerns

- Planning for . . . Reaching, Witnessing, Ministering
- Planning for Teaching-Learning (30 minutes)
- Praying Together

PLAN 3

GENERAL PERIOD .... 10 MINUTES
(all workers together)

DEPARTMENT PERIOD .... 50 MINUTES
- Administering Department Concerns
- Planning for . . . Reaching, Witnessing, Ministering
- Planning for Teaching-Learning (30 minutes)
- Praying Together

For further details on weekly workers meetings, see *BREAK-THROUGH: Sunday School Work* and *BREAKTHROUGH: Small Sunday School Work*. Also refer to each issue of *The Sunday School Leader*.

OUR WEEKLY WORKERS MEETING SCHEDULE

AGENDA/ACTIVITIES	TIME	LOCATION
(List items on your schedule: general period, department/ division periods, teaching-learning period, supper)		
_____	_____	_____
_____	_____	_____
_____	_____	_____
_____	_____	_____
_____	_____	_____
_____	_____	_____
_____	_____	_____
_____	_____	_____

See the suggested Plan 1, Plan 2, and Plan 3 for a possible agenda/ schedule for your Sunday school. Write in the plan that you will be following for your meetings.

Selected Bibliography

Anderson, Andy. *The Growth Spiral*. Nashville: Broadman and Holman, 1993.

Autry, James A. *Love and Profit: The Art of Caring Leadership*. New York: William Morrow and Company, Inc., 1991.

Batten, Joe D. *Tough-Minded Leadership*. New York: American Management Association—AMA-COM Division, 1989. (See also the video by the same title, American Media Incorporated, 1454 30th Street, West Des Moines, Iowa 50265.)

Bennis, Warren, and Burt Nanus. *Leaders*. New York: Harper and Row, 1985.

Benson, Clarence H. *A Popular History of Christian Education*. Chicago: Moody Press, 1943.

Black, Wesley O. *Introduction to Youth Ministry*. Nashville: Broadman & Holman, 1991.

Blanchard, Kenneth, and Norman Vincent Peale. *The Power of Ethical Management*. New York: Fawcett Crest, by Ballantine Books, 1988.

Brown, J. Truman, Jr., comp. *Visionary Leadership*. Nashville: Convention Press, 1991.

Bryan, C. Doug. *Learning to Teach, Teaching to Learn*. Nashville: Broadman and Holman, 1993.

Coleman, Lucien E., Jr. *Why the Church Must Teach*. Nashville: Broadman Press, 1984.

Covey, Stephen R. *The 7 Habits of Highly Effective People*. New York: Simon and Schuster, Inc., 1990.

DePree, Max. *Leadership Is an Art*. New York: Bantam Doubleday Dell Publishing Group, Inc., 1989.

Ford, LeRoy. *Design for Teaching and Training*. Nashville: Broadman Press, 1978.

Gangel, Kenneth O. *Feeding and Leading: A Practical Handbook on Administration in Churches and Christian Organizations*. Wheaton: Victor Books, 1989.

Grubbs, Bruce, ed. *Helping a Small Church Grow*. Nashville: Convention Press, 1980.

Hadaway, C. Kirk. *Church Growth Principles: Separating Fact from Fiction*. Nashville: Broadman Press, 1991.

Hauk, Gary H. *Family Enrichment in Your Church*. Nashville: Convention Press, 1988.

Hendricks, William L. *A Theology for Children*. Nashville: Broadman Press, 1980.

Hinkle, Joseph W., and Melva Cook. *How to Minister to Families in Your Church*. Nashville: Broadman Press, 1978.

Holcomb, Tim J. *Personnel Administration Guide for Southern Baptist Churches*. Nashville: Convention Press, 1988.

McDonough, Reginald M., comp. *A Church on Mission*. Nashville: Convention Press, 1980.

Mims, Gene. *Kingdom Principles for Church Growth*. Nashville: Convention Press, 1994.

Mosley, Ernest E. *Priorities in Ministry*. Nashville: Convention Press, 1978.

Orr, Robert. *Being God's People*. Nashville: Convention Press, 1987.

Piland, Harry, and Ernest Adams. *BREAKTHROUGH: Sunday School Work*. Nashville: Convention Press, 1990.

Poling, Wayne. *Conducting Potential Sunday School Worker Training.* Nashville: Convention Press, 1992.

Powers, Bruce P., ed./comp. *Christian Education Handbook.* Rev. ed. Nashville: Broadman and Holman, 1996.

Powers, Bruce P., ed./comp. *Church Administration Handbook.* Nashville: Broadman Press, 1985.

Raus, Robert P. *Ministry Through Camping.* Nashville: Convention Press, 1987.

Reed, James E., and Ronnie Prevost. *A History of Christian Education.* Nashville: Broadman and Holman, 1993.

Reynolds, William J., comp. *Building an Effective Music Ministry.* Nashville: Abingdon Press, 1975.

Schaller, Lyle E., and Charles A. Tidwell. *Creative Church Administration.* Nashville: Abingdon Press, 1975.

Sherrill, Lewis Joseph. *The Rise of Christian Education.* New York: The Macmillan Company, 1994.

Sisemore, John T., comp. *The Ministry of Religious Education.* Nashville: Broadman Press, 1978.

Smart, James. *The Teaching Ministry of the Church.* Philadelphia: Westminster Press, 1954.

Stubblefield, Jerry M. *The Effective Minister of Education.* Nashville: Broadman and Holman, 1993.

Taylor, Marvin, J., ed. *An Introduction to Christian Education.* Nashville: Abingdon Press, 1966.

Tidwell, Charles A. *Church Administration: Effective Leadership for Ministry.* Nashville: Broadman Press, 1985.

Tidwell, Charles A. *Training Potential Sunday School Workers.* Rev. ed. Nashville: Convention Press, 1985.

Tidwell, Charles A. *Working Together Through the Church Council.* Nashville: Convention Press, 1968.

Towns, Elmer L. *An Inside Look at 10 of Today's Most Innovative Churches.* Ventura, Calif.: Regal Books, 1990.

Westerhoff, John. *Will Our Children Have Faith?* New York: Seabury Press, 1976.

White, Ernest O. *Becoming a Christian Leader.* Nashville: Convention Press, 1985.

Wyckoff, D. Campbell. *How to Evaluate Your Christian Education Program.* Philadelphia: Westminster Press, 1962.

Notes

CHAPTER ONE

1. James D. Smart, *The Teaching Ministry of the Church* (Philadelphia: Westminster Press, 1954), 13.
2. Lewis Joseph Sherrill, *The Rise of Christian Education* (New York: Macmillan, 1944), 21.
3. Ibid.
4. Ibid., 6.
5. Clarence H. Benson, *A Popular History of Christian Education* (Chicago: Moody Press, 1943), 16.
6. Sherrill, *Rise of Christian Education*, 18–20.
7. Ibid., 13.
8. Ibid., 14.
9. H. I. Hester, *The Heart of Hebrew History* (Nashville: Broadman, 1962), 169.
10. Smart, *Teaching Ministry*, 15, 16.
11. Sherrill, *Rise of Christian Education*, 16.
12. Howard P. Colson, "The Biblical Precedent," *The Ministry of Religious Education*, ed. John Sisemore (Nashville: Broadman, 1978), 16.
13. Sherrill, *Rise of Christian Education*, 17.
14. Hester, *Heart of Hebrew History*, 301.
15. Sherrill, *Rise of Christian Education*, 33.
16. Hester, *Heart of Hebrew History*, 256 ff.
17. Benson, *History of Christian Education*, 24.
18. Sherrill, *Rise of Christian Education*, 45.
19. Ibid.
20. Ibid., 47.
21. Benson, *History of Christian Education*, 25.
22. Ibid., 31. For a more detailed explanation, see Sherrill, *Rise of Christian Education*, 83–89.
23. Howard P. Colson and Raymond M. Rigdon, *Understanding Your Church's Curriculum*, rev. ed. (Nashville: Broadman, 1981), 17.

CHAPTER TWO

1. H. Clay Trumbull, *Yale Lectures on the Sunday School* (New York: Charles Scribner's Sons, 1904), 66–67.

2. Benson, *History of Christian Education*, 13–14.

3. Colson and Rigdon, *Understanding Your Church's Curriculum*, 17.

4. Ibid.

5. Colson, "Bible Precedent," 22–23.

6. Sherrill, *Rise of Christian Education*, 140.

7. Ibid., 142.

8. See ibid., 142–53, for a fuller discussion of these five kinds of teaching.

9. Ibid., 186.

10. Ibid., 153.

11. Benson, *History of Christian Education*, 44.

12. Sherrill, *Rise of Christian Education*, 159.

13. See ibid., 183–97, for a fuller discussion of education in early Christian worship services.

14. Ibid., 201–207.

15. Ibid., 173.

16. Ibid.

17. Ibid., 174.

18. Ibid., 175.

19. Benson, *History of Christian Education*, 64.

20. William Bean Kennedy, "Christian Education Through History," *An Introduction to Christian Education*, ed. Marvin J. Taylor (Nashville: Abingdon, 1966), 23.

21. Sherrill, *Rise of Christian Education*, 207.

22. Benson, *History of Christian Education*, 64.

23. Ibid., 69.

24. Ibid., 78.

25. Ibid.

26. Ibid., 80.

27. Ibid.

28. Ibid., 81.

29. Ibid.

30. Ibid., 82.

31. Ibid., 83.

32. Ibid., 83–84.

33. Ibid., 93.

34. Ibid., 95.

35. Ibid., 100.

36. Ibid., 109.

37. James E. Reed and Ronnie Prevost, *A History of Christian Education* (Nashville: Broadman & Holman, 1993), 255.

38. Benson, *A History of Christian Education*, 123.

39. Ibid., 236.

CHAPTER THREE

1. The author has drawn heavily in the remainder of this chapter and in the related appendix material on ideas and materials found in *The Curriculum Guide*, edited by Clifton J. Allen and W. L. Howse (Nashville: Convention Press, 1963), 6–35.

2. LeRoy Ford, *A Primer for Teachers and Leaders* (Nashville: Broadman Press, 1963), 138–39.

3. Ibid., 139.

4. Figure 1 is from Ford, *Primer for Teachers and Leaders,* 32–33.

5. For a discussion of these needs of persons, see Reginald M. McDonough, compiler, *A Church on Mission* (Nashville: Convention Press, 1980), chap. 2; and Robert A. Orr, *Being God's People* (Nashville: Convention Press, 1987), chap. 2.

6. Adapted from the educational objective as stated by designers of Southern Baptist curriculum materials, quoted in Colson and Rigdon, *Understanding Your Church's Curriculum*, 46.

CHAPTER FOUR

1. Daniel Aleshire, "Christian Education and Theology," *Christian Education Handbook*, Bruce P. Powers, editor/compiler (Nashville: Broadman Press, 1981), 27.

2. Ibid.

3. Herschel H. Hobbs, *The Baptist Faith and Message* (Nashville: Convention Press, 1971), 75.

4. Ibid.

5. Ibid.

6. Ibid., 74.

7. Ibid., 79.

8. Ibid., 80.

9. Ibid., 76.

10. Ibid.

11. Ibid.

12. Ibid., 78.

13. Colson and Rigdon, *Understanding Your Church's Curriculum*, 45.

14. Ibid.

15. McDonough, *A Church on Mission*, 17.

16. Ibid., 18.

17. Aleshire, 33.

18. Ibid.

19. An excellent reference on many of the concepts dealt with in this chapter is chapter 1 of Orr, *Being God's People.*

CHAPTER FIVE

1. Edward B. Lindaman, *Thinking in the Future Tense* (Nashville: Broadman Press, 1978), 27–28.

2. Ralph W. Neighbour, Jr., compiler, *Future Church* (Nashville: Broadman Press, 1980), 9.

3. Ibid., 11.

4. Ibid., 10.

5. These statements of trends are based on those denominations that provide annual membership reports. They came from the *1991 Yearbook of American and Canadian Churches*, 303, ed. Constant H. Jacquet, Jr., and Alice M. Jones (Nashville: Abingdon Press, 1991), 330.

6. Ibid.

7. Ibid.

8. Ibid., 302.

9. Source: *Emerging Trends*, 2, no. 1 (January 1980), published by the Princeton Research Center, Hopewell, N. J., via *Research Digest*, 2, no. 7 (December 1980), published by the Research Division of the Home Mission Board of the Southern Baptist Convention.

10. For more on this study, see Peter L. Benson, "Educational Effectiveness: The Challenge to Southern Baptists," *Search* (fall 1993): 17–25. *Search* is a professional journal published by the Sunday School Board of the Southern Baptist Convention.

11. Lindaman, *Future Tense*, 44–45.

12. For an enlarged discussion of these challenges and opportunities, and their implications, see McDonough, *Church on Mission*, chap. 3.

CHAPTER SIX

1. Smart, *Teaching Ministry*, 117–18.

2. Harry Piland, *Basic Sunday School Work* (Nashville: Convention Press, 1980), 155.

3. Hobbs, *Baptist Faith and Message*, 75.

4. Colson and Rigdon, *Understanding Your Church's Curriculum*, 104 ff.

5. Ibid., 110–12.

6. McDonough, *Church on Mission*, 46.

7. Ibid., 90.

8. Piland, *Basic Sunday School Work*, 29–30.

9. McDonough, *Church on Mission*, 92.

10. Piland, *Basic Sunday School Work*, 37.

11. See the "Possibilities for Church Organization" chart for total church organization possibilities for five sizes of membership in Bruce P. Powers, ed., *Christian Education Handbook*, Revised (Nashville: Broadman & Holman, 1996), chap. 7.

12. For detailed help regarding the weekly workers meeting, the Sunday school council, and a variety of suggested organization patterns for Sunday school, see Harry Piland and Ernest Adams, *BREAKTHROUGH Sunday School Work* (Nashville: Convention Press, 1990), chaps. 3 and 8.

13. Piland, *Basic Sunday School Work*, 51.

14. For further information about the plans of the Seminary Extension of the Southern Baptist Convention, contact this office at 901 Commerce Street, Nashville, Tennessee, 37203–3631.

15. The Church Study Course will be discussed more fully in chapter 15.

16. Piland, *Basic Sunday School Work*, 156.

CHAPTER SEVEN

1. For any church cooperating with the Southern Baptist Convention, the Baptist Sunday School Board will provide limited quantities of free materials if the church is beginning an organized program of discipleship training. This offer is available for a given church only once, and includes curriculum and administrative materials chosen by the church. The address for information about these materials is 127 Ninth Avenue, North, Nashville, Tennessee 37234.

CHAPTER EIGHT

1. Bobbie Sorrill, *WMU—A Church Missions Organization* (Birmingham: Woman's Missionary Union, 1981), 15.

2. *Woman's Missionary Union Guide* (Birmingham: Woman's Missionary Union, 1995), 1.

3. Ibid., 31.

4. Ibid.

5. Ibid.

6. Ibid.

7. McDonough, *Church on Mission*, 115–16.

8. Carolyn Weatherford, *If I Had Known What Happens When I Study Missions* (Birmingham, Alabama: Woman's Missionary Union, 1985), 3–4.

9. *Guide*, 31–32.

10. Ibid., 32.

11. McDonough, *Church on Mission*, 122.

12. Sorrill, *WMU*, 42.

CHAPTER NINE

1. McDonough, *Church on Mission*, 131.

2. Ibid., 132.

3. Orr, *Being God's People*, 93.

4. Harry Eskew and Hugh T. McElrath, *Sing with Understanding* (Nashville: Broadman Press,

1980), 245.

5. Ibid., 257.

6. McDonough, *Church on Mission*, 134.

7. Ibid., 134–35.

8. Ibid., 135.

9. Ibid., 136.

10. Orr, *Being God's People*, 97–98.

11. Ibid., 98.

12. For detailed help regarding the total church music ministry, see Powers, *Christian Education Handbook,* 168–80.

13. McDonough, *Church on Mission,* 138.

14. Eskew and McElrath, *Sing with Understanding*, 243.

15. Ibid.

16. Ibid., 247.

17. McDonough, *Church on Mission*, 142.

CHAPTER TEN

1. McDonough, *Church on Mission*, 53–56; and Orr, *Being God's People,* 134–37.

2. Orr, *Being God's People*, 135.

3. McDonough, *Church on Mission*, 56

4. These suggestions came from the pamphlet, "Keys to Effective Family Ministry" (revised 1990), produced by the Sunday School Board of the Southern Baptist Convention, Nashville, Tennessee.

5. Ibid., 144.

6. Orr, *Being God's People*, 154.

7. For more information about the Media Library, see Mancil Ezell and Jacquelyn Anderson, *The Media Library in a Church* (Nashville: Convention Press, 1988).

8. McDonough, *Church on Mission*, 148.

9. Orr, *Being God's People*, 156.

10. Ibid.

11. Ibid., 157.

12. Ibid., 158.

13. Ray Conner, *A Guide to Church Recreation* (Nashville: Convention Press, 1977).

14. See current listings on the "Undated Materials Order Form," and in the current "Church Materials Catalog," both from the Material Services Department, 127 Ninth Avenue, North, Nashville, Tennessee 37234.

CHAPTER ELEVEN

1. McDonough, *Church on Mission,* 80.

2. Ibid., 82.

3. Ibid., 83.

4. Ernest E. Mosley, *Priorities in Ministry* (Nashville: Convention Press, 1978), 18.

5. Ibid., 13–18.

6. Seward Hiltner, *Ferment in the Ministry* (New York: Abingdon Press, 1969), 85.

7. Piland, *Basic Sunday School Work*, 50.

8. Bruce Grubbs, *Helping a Small Church Grow* (Nashville: Convention Press, 1980), 3.

9. Will Beal, compiler, *The Work of the Minister of Education* (Nashville: Convention Press, 1976), 30.

CHAPTER TWELVE

1. Lyle E. Schaller and Charles A. Tidwell, *Creative Church Administration* (Nashville: Abingdon Press, 1975), 67.

2. *Master Study Bible* (Nashville: Holman Bible Publishers, 1981), 2021.

3. Ernest E. Mosley, *Called to Joy: A Design for Pastoral Ministry* (Nashville: Convention Press, 1973), 26 ff.

CHAPTER THIRTEEN

1. Truman Brown, Jr., *Church Council Handbook* (Nashville: Convention Press, 1981), 6.
2. Ibid., 10.
3. For additional information about the work of the Church Council (Church Ministry Leadership Team), see the relevant sections in McDonough, *Church on Mission*; Powers, *Christian Education Handbook*; and Orr, *Being God's People, 168–72.*
4. Charles A. Tidwell, *Working Together Through the Church Council* (Nashville: Convention Press, 1968), 51.
5. Powers, *Christian Education Handbook*, 54.
6. Orr, *Being God's People*, 173.

CHAPTER FOURTEEN

1. J. Truman Brown, author-compiler, *Planning for the Next Five Years in a Southern Baptist Church* (notebook) (Nashville: Convention Press, 1989).
2. Kenneth M. Dean, "Building a Sunday School Through Effective Weekly Workers' Meetings" (pamphlet) (Nashville: The Sunday School Board of the Southern Baptist Convention, 1980), n.p.
3. "Growing Southern Baptist Churches" (pamphlet), jointly issued by the Sunday School Board and the Home Mission Board of the Southern Baptist Convention, n.d., 3.
4. Several of these characteristics are discussed in detail in Grubbs, *Helping a Small Church Grow*.
5. Arthur Flake, *Building a Standard Sunday School* (Nashville: The Sunday School Board of the Southern Baptist Convention, 1922), 21ff.
6. Materials for implementing these and other growth strategies are available from Baptist Book Stores.

CHAPTER FIFTEEN

1. Charles A. Tidwell, *Training Potential Sunday School Workers* (Revised) (Nashville: Convention Press, 1985), 13. For additional help on this and many other areas of preservice training for Sunday school workers, see Wayne A. Poling, *Conducting Potential Sunday School Worker Training* (Nashville: Convention Press, 1992); and the accompanying Resource Kit by the same title.
2. See Powers, *Christian Education Handbook*, 255, 258.
3. For a catalog or other information about the Church Study Course, contact the Baptist Sunday School Board, 127 Ninth Avenue, North, Nashville, Tennessee 37234.

CHAPTER SIXTEEN

1. Powers, *Christian Education Handbook*, 205.
2. Ibid., 206–9, for further suggestions such as a literature-handling schedule, a literature requisition form, and other helps regarding securing adequate curriculum materials.
3. See "Supervising Curriculum in the Local Church" in Colson and Rigdon, *Understanding Your Church's Curriculum,* 126ff.
4. For additional help regarding providing space and conserving energy and financial resources, see Gwenn E. McCormick, *Planning and Building Church Facilities* (Nashville: Broadman Press, 1992); and *Designing Educational Buildings*, Robert N. Lowry, compiler (Nashville: Convention Press, 1990).

CHAPTER SEVENTEEN

1. Charles A. Tidwell, *Working Together Through the Church* Council (Nashville: Convention Press, 1968), 64–68.